"I pray this book sells a million copies! My dad used to tell me this too; 'All pastors are interim pastors.' We're stewards, not owners. We're only here for a blip in time, but the church goes on forever."

—**Rick Warren**, founding pastor of Saddleback Church

"Every pastor will face a transition at their church, and it will be one of their best chances at leaving a legacy. *Next* is an invaluable tool for securing a transition that works and a legacy that lasts."

—**Bill Hybels**, senior pastor of Willow Creek Community Church

"Wisdom around pastoral succession is one of the great needs of the church today, so it's about time this book showed up. I have already sent a copy to several of the elders at my church."

—from the foreword by **John Ortberg**, author; former teaching pastor at Willow Creek and pastor of Menlo Park Presbyterian Church, Menlo Park, CA

"Someone said that the moment you succeed, you need to prepare for your successor to succeed. The church has too often failed in this critical mission. I believe this book to be one of the most timely and important of our day. If I could state it more urgently or enthusiastically, I would!"

—**Jim Henry**, former president of the Southern Baptist Convention; pastor emeritus of First Baptist Church, Orlando, FL

"This book is incredibly rich with good advice. Even a simple pastoral handoff like I experienced, from my father-in-law to me, could benefit from the wise insights and great stories my friends William Vanderbloemen and Warren Bird have inked."

—**Wilfredo "Choco" de Jesus**, lead pastor of New Life Covenant Church, Chicago, IL

"Vanderbloemen and Bird are giving leaders permission to ask formerly forbidden questions *now* so that churches can thrive rather than limp through inevitable pastoral transitions."

—**Marnie Crumpler**, executive pastor of Peachtree Presbyterian Church, Atlanta, GA

"In the kingdom of God, success equals succession—looking for a successor all the time. *Next* shows pastors how to do that for themselves, and how to model succession for their staff and volunteer leaders."

Mark Batterson, founding pastor of National Community Church, Washington, DC

"This is a great book. It should have been written years ago."

"Senior pastor succession is the big elephant in the church boardroom, and it is at last coming out of the closet. We will see more senior pastors coming from campus pastors and through church mergers in the next decade. This book describes every imaginable type of succession and encourages everyone how to start preparing *now*."

"Just a few sunrises ago, the church was in someone else's hands. In just a few sunsets, another generation will lead. May we be gracious, skillful, and intentional toward a very good handoff. This outstanding book will help you do just that."

"Too many churches are in crisis—or headed toward it—because we have not learned to think long range. The need is nothing short of a paradigm shift in leadership development. This excellent book rightly helps move these discussions to the front burner."

"This book is an absolute necessity. Far too little has been written on the process of pastoral transitions."

"Change is always hard, especially when you are at the center of it. That's probably one of the reasons that so few pastors think about how they will transition the leadership of their church to the next generation. *Next* will kick-start your thinking and give you some practical steps on how to transition well."

"Every church leader needs to read *Next*. It is a must-read—whether pastor or board member—because every church will need to face this pressing issue. This tremendous work is a 'Who's Who' of the church world, full of real-life facts and lessons learned."

NEXT

PASTORAL SUCCESSION
THAT WORKS

WILLIAM VANDERBLOEMEN
and WARREN BIRD

BakerBooks

a division of Baker Publishing Group
Grand Rapids, Michigan

© 2014 by William Vanderbloemen and Warren Bird

Published by Baker Books
a division of Baker Publishing Group
P.O. Box 6287, Grand Rapids, MI 49516-6287
www.bakerbooks.com

Printed in the United States of America

Library of Congress Cataloging-in-Publication Data
Vanderbloemen, B. William, 1969-
    Next : pastoral succession that works / William Vanderbloemen and Warren Bird.
        pages cm
    Includes bibliographical references and index.
    ISBN 978-0-8010-1647-9 (cloth)
    1. Clergy—Relocation. I. Title.
BV664.V36 2014
254—dc23   2014005619

14   15   16   17   18   19   20   8   7   6   5   4   3

Contents

Part 3 Transition Well, Finish Strong

Foreword

Wisdom around pastoral succession is one of the great needs of the church today.

This is partly because the stress, challenge, and importance of leadership in churches has never been higher (they have become more complex and ever-changing places to lead, in increasingly more challenging contexts). It is also because churches often have fewer resources to help them. In the old days, churches could just call up the denominational pastor store and order a selection of fresh candidates to choose from. Now the pools in which to fish for a pastor have become smaller and harder to find. Should a church look inside its ranks or outside? For someone similar or different than the predecessor?

Churches and pastors often struggle with the issue of "Who comes next?" A spiritual aura can sometimes make open conversation more awkward for a church than for a corporation or a football team.

Sometimes pastors don't choose transition; it chooses them: a forced resignation, a health problem or family crisis, or even death. I have noticed, over the years, that you can pretty accurately diagnose a pastor's personality type by the metaphor he or she uses to describe an untimely death. I know of one pastor who would speak, with a steely courageous glint in his eye, of what might happen "if the plane went down." I know of another who would talk about what the church might do "if I get run over by the ice-cream truck." The ice-cream truck guy had a very different personality type (and body type, for that matter) than the "if the plane goes down" guy.

One of the great leaders and board members I have known, former Herman Miller CEO Max DePree, used to say that a board's single most important contribution was the selection of an organization's leader; in fact he said that this one task was actually more important than all the other tasks of the board put together.

So it's about time this book showed up.

In *Next*, Warren and William walk through what churches and pastors need to know about the hows and whens and whys of who's next. This is a book grounded in immense real-life experience. Scores of church stories are to be found here; the good, the bad, and the ugly. (Apart from its practical helpfulness, students of American church life will be interested in this book partly just for the stories.) It's also grounded in Scripture—the biblical writers dealt with issues of succession in spiritual leadership all the time: Moses to Joshua, Eli to his dysfunctional sons (family succession is always a challenge), Elijah to Elisha, as well as the jockeying of Jesus's disciples ("Can I sit on your right? Your left? Will it help if my mom asks?")

So this is one book that will always need to inform practice. I have already sent a copy to several of the elders at my church. I'm not at the finish line yet, but I can see it from here, and it's never too soon to think about mastering the subtle art of torch-passing.

Besides, you never know when the plane might go down. And hit the ice-cream truck.

John Ortberg

Preface

Every pastor is an interim pastor.

Few ministers consider that truth. Few are eager to admit that their time with their present church will one day end. But ultimately, all pastors are "interim" because the day when a successor takes over will come for everyone in ministry.

Planning for that day of succession may be the biggest leadership task a leader and church will ever face. It may also be the most important.

There's an old saying: "Everyone wants to talk about succession . . . until it's their own." For way too long, the subject of succession has been avoided in the church, in pastors' gatherings, and even in the pastor's home. Those in leadership may not talk about it, but succession happens anyway.

Sadly, the story across thousands of churches is all too common: a wonderful pastor moves to another church or retires. The church takes a long time to find a replacement. The successor doesn't last long. The church is off-kilter for a protracted time. Sometimes it never regains its former momentum and health. This happens in churches of all sizes.

We want this book to be part of a culture change—one that makes the story above less common, one that makes succession planning the norm in churches, and one that creates churches with long legacies of great leadership and service to God's kingdom.

We are already seeing a new day dawn. Today, more than in any other era on record, pastors are anticipating their own succession. And they are not merely beginning to talk openly about it; their awareness of a future transition is also shaping how they do ministry today. We believe their intentionality will increase the likelihood of their successor's success, even in traditions where pastors have little or no voice in what happens after they leave.

Preparing for the sun to rise on that day, we have examined almost two hundred pastoral succession case studies. We have studied where succession has worked, where it has failed, and what might happen to create smooth ministry hand-offs. We believe that what we have learned can help pastors and churches begin difficult but crucial conversations. And if those open discussions become the new standard, the church will be healthier and more effective.

Succession Planning Defined

We like how Dave Travis, CEO of Leadership Network, defines pastoral succession. He says it's *the intentional process of the transfer of leadership, power, and authority from one directional leader to another.* Succession is when one senior leader intentionally transitions and hands over leadership to another. Succession planning is creating a plan for what will happen once you need a new leader, something all organizations face.

Succession planning can (and should) start with pastors early in their tenure at their church. Succession occurs repeatedly, whether it's a first pastorate or a tenth pastorate. The typical pastor will experience several ministry successions over a lifetime. Whether it's the pastor's own decision, the board's, or the bishop's (or equivalent), sooner or later all leaders move on.

In the corporate world, succession planning is now a requirement for nearly all publicly traded companies. Facing a season when no one knows who's in charge is just too risky. You need a plan. The church world needs to ask if its current lack of conversations about succession planning is wise—or whether our silence is instead setting up too many churches for long-term failure.

> Pastoral succession is the intentional process of the transfer of leadership, power, and authority from one directional leader to another.

Scripture, our rule for faith and practice, offers no uniform blueprint, no cookie-cutter template, and no step-by-step approach that outlines a specific path for a seamless succession. As the variety of successions in Scripture illustrate, our universal recommendation about succession is that there is no universal recommendation. Healthy succession is much more art than science. The plan and details must be tailored to each situation. It is also a deeply spiritual process that calls for prayer and recognition of God's leading.

However, we do see a healthy trend growing in more churches where people, whether the lead pastor or others on the staff or board, are openly asking, "How do we transition well?" They want to know what they should do now to lay the foundation for a healthy succession, whether it should occur unexpectedly tomorrow or it's not likely for decades to come.

This book identifies much of the conventional wisdom voiced in various quarters, but it also hopes to challenge every "rule" you've heard. We want to help you discern the pros and cons for each rule and whether your situation warrants being an exception. We tell dozens of actual stories, purposely showing how one pastor went one way and another pastor went a different way. We will map out the options, but you will need to prayerfully sort through them.

The Conversation Is Starting Sooner and Younger

Rex Keener had a dream in his early years as founding pastor of Grace Fellowship Church. He announced the dream to the congregation: "I'd love to be the pastor here for forty years."

The year 2013 marked Rex's twentieth anniversary at the church, which today draws more than three thousand people weekly across four campuses in greater Albany, New York. At age fifty-three, Rex could have followed the path of a successful marketplace CEO who begins creating company-funded perks to make life more comfortable for himself and his family. Or he could have made the church increasingly about him, allowing highway billboards or large portraits inside the church building to depict his image, all as a strategy to build the future on the goodwill that his leadership amassed over the church's first two decades.

Instead, Rex has decided to look way down the road.

"Crossing the halfway mark of forty potential years here, I'm already aware that the single most important thing I'll do is pass the baton well," he says. "I am becoming more diligent to train leaders in a deeper way than ever before."

In West Palm Beach, Florida, thirty-four-year-old Kerwin Santiago recently inherited the senior leadership role for Tabernaculo Internacional Church from his father, who had been the longtime senior pastor. His dad's ministry, done entirely in Spanish, includes an ongoing radio, television, and overseas evangelism ministry. Kerwin, who is very comfortable in both languages, continues to hold worship in Spanish, but the children and youth ministries are in English.

One day Kerwin realized that he was on a collision course with the future. As the church's children become youth and young adults, they want a church that feels Hispanic but continues to speak in English, including in the worship services. Meanwhile, the older core of the church, which is currently the financial base both for the church and the overseas media ministry, is a first-generation demographic that needs ministry in Spanish.

Kerwin began to think of succession as more than going from past to present. It involves more than receiving and continuing to honor the ministry of his father and predecessor. He also needs to anticipate and build for the future.

"I've been focused on trying to keep up all that my dad left me," he said. "But we have to figure out more than how to continue being a church to the Spanish-speaking nations. We have to become a church for this local community as well." And that community is both Hispanic and prefers English. To that end, Kerwin, in dialogue with his father, is building a team of leaders who are his age and younger, aware that one day he will pass the leadership baton to them. He wants to be able to bless them so that they too can transition the church as needed to a new generation and an ever-changing neighborhood.[1]

Don't Confuse Succession with Retirement

In 2013, the world watched as Pope Benedict XVI made the unprecedented decision to transition to pope emeritus. *Christianity Today* used the event to ask Protestants a pointed question in a headline: "The Pope Retired. Should Your Pastor?"[2]

According to the article, most pastors are not facing the reality that one day they will need to step down and retire. A study of one denomination, for example, found that only 1 out of every 4 pastors (25%) has plans for full retirement[3] and another 1 in 4 (27%) said they didn't plan to retire at all.[4] Even when pastors do want to retire—let alone those who are forced to retire because of health issues—too many lack a financial plan to make retirement economically viable.

> Pastoral succession is not primarily about retirement. Retirement is often only a final step in a series of pastoral successions.

So if pastors facing retirement have a hard enough time addressing retirement issues, it is easy to understand why succession planning gets even less attention. But equating succession planning with retirement planning is a major error in perception. Pastoral succession is not primarily about retirement. Retirement is often only a final step in a series of pastoral successions. And in a few cases, if no one has planned for the unexpected, a leader's abrupt or untimely death leaves a congregation in unnecessary pain, entering an era of chaos.

Our Research and Experience

We wrote *Next: Pastoral Succession That Works* to offer a unique, hope-filled tool for pastors and church boards as they face crucial decisions regarding succession. As our "Research for This Book" section explains in more detail, we examined almost two hundred case studies of high-visibility successions, including some of the best and worst. We conducted more than fifty extended interviews—many onsite in the pastor's office. We read numerous books, research reports, and doctoral dissertations on the subject, and we tracked dozens of newspaper stories and articles that chronicled a senior pastor transition.

Through Vanderbloemen Search Group, William and his team actively oversee succession planning for hundreds of churches (see "What Our Organizations Can Do for You" on page 182). Through his firm's work in helping churches find their key leaders, William has a breadth of experience with succession planning and has witnessed firsthand some of the best practices being used today.

> We want to help you shape the culture of your church now so that your eventual succession will be as seamless as possible.

Through Leadership Network, Warren has conducted dozens of lengthy interviews with outgoing and succeeding pastors. He has been part of several focus groups with pastors at various points in the succession process, consulting with several church leadership teams before, during, and after their pastoral transition. He has participated in three online video conferences in which some or all of the sessions were on pastoral succession, many of which he moderated.

These rich contexts allow us to recount many real-life stories from successions, some that went well and some that went awry.

Who Is This Book For?

We're writing primarily to pastors. We suspect the most eager readers will be those who know they will be leaving their churches in the near future and want to do everything possible to be part of a healthy transition.

But we hope a much wider audience hears our message. We are intentionally writing to the far larger group of pastors not actively in a succession countdown, who are happily serving their church. In fact, perhaps you and the church you serve couldn't be in a better season. We want to help you shape the culture of your church now so that your eventual succession will be as seamless as possible for the ongoing momentum and future health of your congregation.

We're also writing to church boards and other key leaders as you look over the shoulder of your pastor. We're aware that you too not only think about your pastor's eventual succession, but you will likely be part of the process. We want to give you ideas, examples, case studies, and other wisdom in how to prepare.

We're writing as well to future pastors in training and to the seminary professors who train them. Succession planning is an essential part of leadership development, and our hope is that you'll represent a new generation that talks openly about forming the kind of leadership culture designed to create an optimal succession.

This book, therefore, addresses the important issues up until the time the church is actually without a pastor. As a result, we are not primarily writing on how to establish a pulpit search committee. Many excellent books exist with that focus, including *The*

> Most of the patterns and lessons we have gleaned from the churches profiled in this book will transfer well to churches of any size.

Alban Guide to Managing the Pastoral Search Process and *So You're Looking for a New Preacher* (see "For Further Reading" on page 207).

Does the size or setting of your church matter for how helpful this book will be? We have studied churches of all sizes. Most of the patterns and lessons we have gleaned from the churches profiled in this book will transfer well to churches of any size.

Overview of the Book

Upon reading *Next*, senior leaders will have the tools needed to anticipate succession and begin preparing their churches for the next generation of leadership. The book is framed in three parts.

The first part, "Why Succession Planning Can't Wait," vividly depicts present reality. It argues that every pastor and church should develop a succession plan now.

The second part, "Be the Exception," walks you through each of the issues pastors and leadership boards need to address in mapping out a succession plan.

The third part, "Transition Well, Finish Strong," walks pastors and churches through the actual transition, offering hope and guidance toward success. Almost every chapter tells actual stories from start to finish, as does this preface. Whenever possible, we sought permission and editorial help from the people being featured.

Rather than offer you a one-size-fits-all approach with a singular answer for how to achieve success, we've put forth a study of key issues and have tried to raise the questions to ask and steps to take as you face the issue of succession. Each chapter ends with *Next* Steps—one set of discussion questions and/or suggested action steps for the senior pastor and one set for a church board or equivalent. Our goal is to touch on the right dynamics and help you raise the right questions as a result.

Our Hope and Prayer

An honest and productive conversation by pastors and leaders about what will happen in their church's future has been missing for too long. We believe the day will come when pastors can readily and confidently say, "No matter how long I stay at this church, I am just an interim pastor. So I have done everything possible to lay a solid foundation for what will happen once my time here is done."

We hope you'll make that statement no matter how long you've been at the church and whether you're anticipating a move just around the corner or not for years to come. The key is that you realize that what you do now is important to that succession day.

To plan is wise, even in cases where succession seems far away or unnecessary. Mark Driscoll founded Mars Hill Church in Seattle at age twenty-five, and he says he'd love to remain pastor there until age seventy-five. "If that's the case, then I get to think really long term about what I'm doing," he says. "When you plan on staying in one place for a long time, you tend to view the job differently."[5] But while Mark is preparing for a transition far down the road, he's also planned for a sudden change of circumstance (an emergency succession) should an unforeseen situation arise.

We also hope people will think of the term *interim* as relating to *all* pastors. If they do, it will be a shift that will make a lasting difference.

So turn the page and get started developing your own and your church's succession plans. By starting now, you can set up yourself, your church, and your community for long-term success. Join us and others in reversing the unhealthy pattern of failed successions in the church and revolutionizing the way we model the kingdom of God inside our own church staff.

Part 1

Why Succession Planning Can't Wait

1

Why Every Pastor Needs This Book

Top Reasons You and Your Church Should Start Planning for Succession Right Now

Wisdom consists of the anticipation of consequences.

Norman Cousins

Thinking about what's next before they have to—that's what marks the greatest leaders, business people, athletes, and politicians of the world. It's also a common trait of exceptionally wise pastors. What's next for you? Sooner or later, unless Jesus returns during your lifetime, there will be a pastoral transition. Thinking about that transition ahead of time might make all the difference in your and your church's legacy.

There's an old saying the US Marine Corps used during battle: "If you're early, you're on time. If you're on time, you're late. If you're late, you're dead."

The same can be said for succession planning. The earlier you start planning, the better. In fact, we believe no date is too early to begin planning. Wait too long, and you may find that you're late—or metaphorically dead.

In that spirit, you should *avoid* this book if

- You are confident you can remain as pastor of your church until Jesus returns.
- You can avoid bodily death.
- You can stay relevant to a changing culture for the next several hundred years.

- You are planning on shutting down your church.
- You already have an outstanding, bulletproof succession plan and don't need to learn anything from hundreds of case studies.

The sobering reality is that the majority of pastors do not have a plan for the inevitable moment when they leave their current church. We believe they should. Likewise, the majority of churches do not have a plan for the inevitable moment when their current pastor leaves. We believe they should as well.

This book argues that the best time to begin thinking about pastoral succession is *now*. Every pastor—young and old, new or long tenured—will end up better by starting *today* with succession preparations.

The purpose of this book is for pastors and boards to have a resource that enables them to ask the questions necessary to create a succession plan. We are also convinced this is something any pastor and leadership team in any church can do at some level—regardless of age, church size, or denomination/tradition. Some pastors actually select their successor, but most everyone can build the kind of environment that will lead to the smoothest possible succession when the time comes.

That's a different perspective from much of the advice you'll hear out there. It may be different than what you want to believe, and perhaps you feel you can put off the task for tomorrow. In reality, succession is more urgent than you think and probably more important than you have imagined.

Current Models Are All Over the Map

While succession is uniformly important and urgent, there is no uniform approach that works for all churches. Consider the breadth of the spectrum among some of these pace-setting churches.

- Charles "Chuck" Swindoll, senior pastor at Stonebriar Community Church and popular author, has said publicly that "pastors don't retire" and he hopes to preach until he dies.[1] Many other high-visibility pastors have made similar statements, shaping today's culture of succession.
- Leith Anderson, president of the National Association of Evangelicals, and for thirty-two years senior pastor at Wooddale Church in greater Minneapolis, started planning his succession early in his ministry. When he stepped down, he also stepped away from having anything to do with the succession process, other than affirming the idea of an intentional interim of up to two years before his successor was named.[2] "I've always encouraged long-term pastors to step away from influence in their congregations with trust in God and confidence in the church leadership and new pastor to effectively minister

to the next generation," he said.[3] Indeed, his successor was announced at the sixteen-month mark and installed at the twenty-month mark.

- When the church with the world's largest attendance announced the name of its new senior pastor, one of the most surprised people to learn about it was the new pastor himself. Yoido Full Gospel Church in Seoul, Korea, was founded in 1958 by David Yonggi Cho. As he announced his retirement, an extensive search was begun for a successor. Young Hoon Lee and his family had joined Yoido in 1964 when Lee was still in elementary school. He then became a member of the church staff after graduating from college and seminary, and in 1982 became one of Yoido's five-hundred-plus pastors. Then he moved on to pastor other churches. He was in Los Angeles pastoring a Yoido-affiliated church when he received a phone call to announce that he had been selected. "I didn't even know I was being considered," he said.[4]

> Succession is more urgent than you think and probably more important than you have imagined.

Likewise, smaller churches lack a consistent model for dealing with succession, as these emails or conversations represent.

- "I recently joined a church as an associate vicar (pastor) with the understanding that I will succeed the vicar (senior pastor) when he retires next year. What should I do to help make it a good transition?"
- "Our pastor has served here faithfully for twenty-seven years. Her first decade was rough, but her second decade became our church's greatest growth era. Now in the last seven to eight years we've been declining in attendance, the congregation is aging, facility repairs are demanding a bigger slice of our dwindling finances, and the neighborhood is changing. She doesn't give any hint of transitioning. How do we honor her but also begin this important conversation?"
- "I was brought into the church as a potential successor to the senior pastor. After spending years on a leadership development track, I was told that the senior pastor has decided not to move on. Now what do I do? Is this normal in churches?"
- "We're in shock. A few months ago our pastor abruptly resigned and moved away, citing vague 'personal reasons.' Every week seems to turn up new evidence of a mess, including likely misuse of church funds. Trust and morale in the church have plummeted. Our denomination is helping, but can you help us as well?"
- "Our long-term pastor recently asked the board what it might look like if he resigned from the church and we sent him as an overseas missionary through

an organization our church has long supported. Both he and we want to do a smooth hand-off, but we don't know where to begin."

For all the talk in churches about vision, there is an unmistakable blind spot in churches large and small: succession isn't being discussed enough, and when it is, church leaders often lack wisdom in identifying the questions to ask or in what order to tackle them. This book seeks to be a part of the solution to that blind spot. While we agree that no two successions are identical, we have identified several common topics that must be worked through in most successions, backed by data we've uncovered.

Succession Is Inevitable

Consider these numbers about pastoral succession among US Protestants:

- The average senior pastor tenure per church is 8 years, a number that has inched upward over the years.[5]
- The average senior pastor career is 18 years,[6] which suggests the typical pastor faces succession two or more times.
- Senior pastors state a wide variety of reasons for moving to another church, such as wanting to serve in a different community (27%) and moving to a higher position (20%).[7] Long gone is the standard practice of pastoring one church for life until retirement.
- The average senior pastor plans to retire from full-time active ministry at age 65.[8]
- Among senior pastors of megachurches (weekly worship attendance of 2,000 or more adults, youth, and children) according to Leadership Network research, 1 in 5 (22%) are founders and 4 in 5 (78%) are successors. Founders have served on average 19 years and are age 53; successors have served 14 years and are age 52.

The message behind these facts is clear: succession is an inevitable issue for pastors and churches. The time to face that reality and to plan for it is now.

God Is Interested in Succession

The most important news about succession is that God knows how to make leadership transfers go well. God seems to be very active in preparing leaders and churches for the inevitabilities of pastoral transition, even before successors realize they are being prepared for a transition. Again, successions are inevitable; when we read "Moses my servant is dead" (Josh. 1:2), we also see the reality that the transition had started years before as God prepared Joshua. The church is God's bride. Perfecting her is God's primary goal, and a big part of that perfection is ensuring seamless, fruitful leadership transitions.

In fact, Moses had a direct hand in those preparations. As his tenure was drawing to a close, Moses cried out to God, "May the LORD, the God who gives breath to all living things, appoint someone over this community to go out and come in before them, one who will lead them out and bring them in, so the LORD's people will not be like sheep without a shepherd" (Num. 27:16–17).

> The church is God's bride. Perfecting her is God's primary goal, and a big part of that perfection is ensuring seamless, fruitful leadership transitions.

Luke Barnett started his first pastorate at age twenty-six. It was a rough but wild and wonderful ride. After three years, he accepted a call at another church. That pastorate too was full of both challenges and growth. Then the church he grew up in called him to eventually succeed his father, Tommy Barnett. The formal transition was in 2012 when Tommy Barnett was seventy-four and Luke was forty-two.

Now, several years into leading Phoenix First Assembly of God (worship attendance of seven thousand), Luke realizes that God's hand was preparing him. "The first pastor I followed had been there forty-seven years and the second pastor, thirty-seven years," he said. "Looking back, I see how God prepared me through following pastors of long-tenured churches. Those were great days when God was forming me, preparing my wife and me for the ultimate transition here."

The elder board affirms similar evidences of God's hand in their own spiritual preparation. The specific date for Tommy Barnett to be succeeded had been triggered by a health issue. He needed surgery to repair a heart valve, with an anticipated recovery time of eight months. Before taking this leave of absence, Tommy told the elder board that he wanted Luke to be in charge of the overall ministry, which both the board and the Assemblies of God district leadership affirmed.

They also developed a transition plan. As Luke described it, "There's a critical moment for relay races when both runners are holding onto the baton. There was an eight-month period when we both held it, before he fully let go. We wanted people to look back and say, 'We didn't know there was a transition.' We wanted it to be seamless."

About four months into the transition, one of the elder board meetings became very emotional as the elders voiced their earlier fears when they wondered how anyone could follow Tommy's thirty-three years as senior pastor of Phoenix First. "Only God could give us a glimpse of what could happen if you were not at the helm here," one of the elders said to Tommy with gratitude. A year later, Luke and his teaching team began to preach all four services each weekend. Tommy, busy preaching all over, began preaching at the church around three times a year.

The right person to succeed is often the one who has been prepared elsewhere.

"Whenever he comes, it's a big celebration," Luke said. "We all see God's hand at work."[9]

One trend we've noticed is that the right person to succeed is often the one who has been prepared elsewhere. In other words, the best job you could possibly undertake is a job you never could have undertaken had you not done everything leading up to now.

God Is Never Caught by Surprise (Even If We Are)

While this book gives you a glimpse into the wide variety of succession styles across scores of churches of all sizes and equips you with a myriad of good ideas and tools, the foundational theology of this book is that God is never caught by surprise. If you're the pastor, God is preparing you—for your arrival at a church, for your departure, and for your successor. After all, every pastor is an interim pastor of some sort.

If you are a church board member, on a church search team, or in a denominational role of finding and/or appointing pastors, the message applies as well: you are not alone. You have

The most foundational theology of this book is that God is never caught by surprise. . . . After all, every pastor is an interim pastor of some sort.

invitations throughout Scripture to call upon God for your every need. You also have the reminder of God's special love for his church and of his promised provision for it. "Christ loved the church and gave himself up for her" (Eph. 5:25). God has also affirmed that he will be glorified through the church. "Now to him who is able to do immeasurably more than all we ask or imagine, according to his power that is at work within

us, to him be glory *in the church* and in Christ Jesus" (Eph. 3:20–21, emphasis added).

If your pastoral search comes at a time when things have fallen apart and you don't know what to do, remember that "He who began a good work in you will carry it on to completion until the day of Christ Jesus" (Phil. 1:6). God's church depends far more on the Great Shepherd than the human undershepherd (1 Pet. 5:1–4). Any church's future depends ultimately on God far more than the coming and going of human leadership.

The Bible Is Full of Succession Stories

Succession isn't just an organizational issue; it's also a spiritual one. It's not just a topic found on church board meeting agendas. Scripture contains a wealth of guidance and insight, all affirming the importance of leadership development, especially for the next generation.

Just as we have found in our case studies, Scripture illustrates that there is no singular model or plan to create a smooth succession. Even in the great transitions in the Bible, hand-offs take place in a variety of ways.

- Moses, mentioned earlier in this chapter, leads until his death, but before then he spends many years training and grooming Joshua—who is not one of his sons or nephews.
- Aaron's third-born son Eleazar, rather than his firstborn son, becomes Aaron's successor (Num. 20:25–29).
- Saul wants his son Jonathan to succeed him but has to learn that God wants David, an outsider (1 Sam. 23:16–17).
- Elijah apprentices Elisha, but before their leadership transition, God has made it clear that Elisha is to be the successor—and in the transition, Elisha asks for and receives a double portion of the anointing that was on his mentor (2 Kings 2:9).
- Barnabas disciples Paul (Acts 9:27; 11:22–30), but over time the roles reverse and Paul becomes the lead player (e.g., Acts 12:25–13:7; 13:42–14:3; 14:14; 14:23; 15:2).
- Jesus spends his final days on earth preparing others to carry on the mission he has begun (John 21). Jesus hands off the church to his disciples, a hand-off he's openly spoken about, prepared for, trained them for, and empowered them to do. By both word and by deed, Jesus demonstrates that success in ministry is defined by successors.

Preparing Successors Is Key—and Biblical

Throughout the Bible the message about succession is consistent: effective leaders plan ahead for the time when they can no longer lead, and they prayerfully prepare for that day.

The Bible also provides many examples of leaders training their successors, including our Lord himself. The approach of Jesus was to call the apostles first and foremost *to be with him* (Mark 3:13–14), as Robert Coleman points out in his marvelous book, *The Master Plan of Evangelism*.[10] Over time Jesus gave them jobs and supervised their work (e.g., Mark 3:9; 6:35–44; John 4:1–2); later, he sent them out on preaching missions

> Effective leaders plan ahead for the time when they can no longer lead, and they prayerfully prepare for that day.

and then debriefed them (e.g., Luke 9:1–6, 10). It was clearly an apprenticeship role with increasing responsibilities over time.

The apostles also followed that model by preparing their successors. Paul discipled a number of important leaders for the early church, but his relationship with Timothy is a particularly clear example of leadership development principles. He identified Timothy as a potential leader, an identification confirmed by the Holy Spirit (1 Tim. 1:18); he traveled with Timothy, taught him, and modeled good leadership; he sent Timothy out on a variety of assignments, and eventually entrusted to his leadership the very important church in Ephesus.

Leaders understand that there is no success without a successor.

Timothy seemed to have been apprehensive about his job (e.g., 2 Tim. 1:7). But Paul encouraged him in his work and laid out the pattern for developing future leaders: "You then, my child, be strengthened by the grace that is in Christ Jesus, and what you have heard from me in the presence of many witnesses entrust to faithful men who will be able to teach others also" (2 Tim. 2:1–2 ESV). Four generations of passing the leadership baton are evident in that verse—as Paul has equipped Timothy, so now Timothy should train others, who in turn will train others.[11]

Leaders understand that there is no success without a successor. No one wins when transitions don't go well.

Human Planning Does Not Remove God's Role in Succession Planning

People sometimes ask if creating a succession plan takes God out of the equation. Does the use of intentional succession plans, search firms, or even books like this put too much emphasis on human mechanism and not enough on the Holy Spirit?

Our sense is that God does use people and systems in conjunction with the Holy Spirit to help build leadership teams in the church.

Consider Jesse. He lined up all his grown sons for the prophet Samuel to choose a new king, but Samuel asked for the boy David, who was still out in the fields. In other words, Jesse planned well, doing everything that made the best sense to him. He brought in all his strong sons, and knowing that someone needed to watch the sheep that day, left the runt of the litter to watch the sheep. Most of us also overlook potential options, but God used Samuel to see what Jesse couldn't see on his own. Granted, Samuel was a prophet of God (and we are not). But one of the key dynamics in using a plan, a denominational process, a search firm, or even this book is that you gain a "third set of eyes" looking at your situation with objectivity, experience, and data to help you.

Most of us know how to line up succession candidates, but we're not as skilled at predicting whom the Holy Spirit will select. This is where prayer and godly counsel are essential. If we miss someone despite our best efforts to identify the right choice, the Spirit will still show us, just as the Spirit worked through the prophet Samuel to select David (1 Sam. 16:11–13).

The selection of David was not the only way God worked through the prophet Samuel in modeling succession. In his role as a prophet, Samuel provided for succession, but not through his sons. Rather, he apparently developed a school of prophets (1 Sam. 10:5–13; 19:18–24), which established a group known as "the sons of the prophets" that lasted until Israel's Northern and Southern Kingdoms were destroyed. This helped build a succession pattern into the culture of Israel.

Pastors Are Reluctant to Plan (but Can't Afford to Make Excuses)

It seems odd that so many pastors give strong leadership in many strategic areas but stop leading when it comes to succession issues. Why? We think it's because there are so few models. It's just not the norm—yet! Pastors and church leadership teams simply don't think that way, although a few are beginning to.

The authors of *The Elephant in the Boardroom*, an excellent book with the intriguing subtitle of *Speaking the Unspoken about Pastoral Transitions*, suggest additional reasons: fear and low self-confidence. They reason:

- If I talk about pastoral transition, I might put the idea in someone's head and make it more likely to happen sooner than I'm ready.
- I will create a lame-duck situation in which effective ministry becomes impossible.
- My peers and colleagues won't support me in doing it a different way, and I am not sure I want to be a pioneer on the road of better pastoral transition if this means going it alone.
- A discussion about pastoral transition might have unintended consequences that I (and others at this church) do not know how to manage.
- I (and we) don't have the resources to deal with transition planning and be successful.[12]

The list could go on. The more we have examined case studies of succession, the more we see a myriad of rational excuses to skip or delay succession planning. Such reasoning is as fatal as the old saying, "The road to hell is paved with good intentions." Whatever the excuses or reasons, succession conversations haven't happened frequently or early enough. For the church to reach a new level of health, that reality has to change.

You Shape Your Future More Than You Realize

This biblical pattern is not what typically happens in churches today as a pastor's era reaches an end. Instead the process is more jagged. Here are a number of more usual approaches and situations, many with unintended consequences:

- There is no succession discussion. Then one day the leader dies, retires, burns out, resigns to take another church, or sadly, has a moral failure. The church is then left in a leadership tailspin. Momentum is lost. Members are lost. Offerings dip.
- The leader announces an upcoming retirement date, but doesn't allow significant planning time or release of pastoral control.
- Sometimes a relative (most often the pastor's child) is announced as the successor, but with little or no training or examination of whether or not that offspring is the best successor for the church.
- An intentional interim pastor is appointed, during which time the church loses momentum, people, and focus as all long-term or strategic decisions are put on hold. (This is, however, sometimes a good option if the context dictates it, as chapter 12 will discuss later.)
- An untrained search committee made up of volunteers who have never hired a church staff person or a pastor who works more or less in secret, with minimal church-wide communication.
- A committee hires a pastor who "seems" right, but who spends a one- to three-year tenure as a "sacrificial lamb." The church becomes smaller and finances become tighter, the vision is downsized, and the congregation becomes discouraged and inwardly focused.
- Denominational leadership finds a candidate but proceeds with little consultation with the church's remaining leadership. The new pastor arrives but starts at a point of low or eroded congregational confidence due to the aloof denominational appointment.
- The church is displeased with the last pastor and hires someone who seems to be the direct opposite. This approach, over time, creates a whole new set of issues and points of conflict in the church.
- Another new pastor comes, but much hope of building on the great heritage and momentum of the long-term pastor has been lost. This new pastor, in many ways, must start over.
- The search committee hires a great person to "grow the church," but that assignment is a false picture of what the church really wants and/or needs. The congregation isn't aware of the pain that will come with growth and change. Likewise, the new pastor discovers the next pastorate to be something like marrying Rachel, but instead waking up next to Leah (Gen. 29:25). This form

of bait and switch can lead, in the worst case, to conflict throughout the church. In the best case, the frustrated and disillusioned pastor graciously moves elsewhere at the first opportunity.

The Time to Start Talking about Succession Is Now

Our present models of succession create lots of problems. Too many high-capacity leaders are waiting, perhaps even already named as the potential successor, but with no date given and no clarity on how succession might unfold. Too many older pastors are being forced out or thrown out without proper care and honor. Most importantly, too many churches flounder and lose momentum simply because a church's leadership failed to anticipate and begin planning for one of their most important responsibilities.

> Succession is a process, not an event.

It's time for a new model. It's time to go far beyond putting a name in an envelope in case of the leader's untimely death.

In many denominations, the current processes, policies, and polities discourage and even preclude any proactive planning or preparation by pastors and congregations for changes in pastoral leadership. Even so, we believe there is much a church in those situations can still do to plan for its future.

Succession is a process, not an event. It's a leadership value and practice. It is a big deal. We are frequently asked, "What's the right way to do succession?" The right way depends entirely on your situation. There are very few cardinal rules in succession. It's much more art than science.

While every church is unique and no two pastoral successions follow an identical pattern, a few common denominators emerge.

- The process will be messy.
- Your process will be unpredictable in ways that predecessors, successors, leadership boards, and congregations do not fully anticipate.
- It won't take the amount of time you think. Some successions take longer than planned (more common), while some move more quickly (less common).
- The process will almost always be healthier and more effective if an objective third party speaks into the process. This could include a denomination, judicatory, or district; a search firm; or an objective trained consultant.
- Pastoral transition is not over when a new pastor's tenure officially begins. There is still transition work to be done during the first leg of any new pastor's appointment. The complete process typically takes two to three years from that point.

To date, very few full books are available on pastoral succession (our bibliography lists several of them), but one of the best is the above-mentioned book *The Elephant in the Boardroom*. The unusual title refers to the idea that too often a giant, unmissable issue is in our presence, but no one wants to name it or deal with it. As the dust jacket to that book aptly says, "One way or another, every church will eventually lose its pastor—yet few churches plan ahead for this dramatic event."[13]

Published ten years ago, the book rightly identified the elephant and significantly helped begin the conversation. Now it's time to go to a whole new level: creating church cultures where the conversation is normal and natural and supported by structures that develop leaders at every level, including potential successors for the senior pastor.

What would happen if a new story emerged? We believe the new norm can be one of seamless pastoral successions—sadness in saying farewell, but continuity of momentum, vision, direction, and ministry support.

Now is the time to start talking about succession, whatever the size of your church, your age, or how long you've been there.

Key Lessons Learned

The Bible teaches and models succession planning. In the Bible, leaders plan ahead. Scripture contains a wealth of guidance and insight, all affirming the importance of leadership development, especially for the next generation. Smart pastors will follow the biblical lead.

Conversations are starting. Despite a history of avoiding personal discussions about succession, the culture is starting to change. More people than ever are thinking, talking, and beginning to enact succession planning.

Every pastor is an interim pastor. The sooner pastors recognize that all leaders are "interims," the more likely they are to build a church-wide culture of leadership development.

Constant succession planning builds long-term health. Succession planning motivates top tier leaders and board members to think long term, both for the church and personally.

Early planning produces higher-quality planning. Succession planning becomes better when done as a team, validating the Scripture that says there is wisdom in a multitude of counselors (Prov. 11:14; 15:22).

Succession clarity requires time to develop. Succession planning is oftentimes like old Polaroid film. It develops before your eyes over time. Give succession planning additional time, and you will have a clearer picture of what's needed as the time for transition draws near.

The earlier you plan, the more likely you are to succeed. Advance planning leads to better outcomes. Those churches that periodically review their succession plan tend to do a better job with succession once the actual day comes.

N E X T Steps

For Pastors: Name three people (e.g., colleagues, mentors, board members) with whom you can privately discuss succession, and determine the date you will call them to discuss it.

For Boards: When was the last conversation you had about succession? If it is unlikely to be at the top of your next board meeting agenda, can you identify what is preventing it from being there?

2

The "Ten Commandments" of Succession Planning

Practical Actions Whatever Your Age or Tenure

This book repeatedly affirms that no succession is the same. We stated earlier that there is no singular pattern or set of rules for succession planning. But throughout our studies, we've seen a few cardinal rules pop up. They're stunningly clear and universally applicable, no matter your situation.

We think you'll be surprised at how many actions from this chapter you can begin taking right now. The ideas can apply whether you're thirty-two or sixty-two, whether it's your second year at your current church or your twenty-second, and whether or not you're in a denominational appointment system.

As we said in the previous chapter, you shape your future more than you realize. Too many pastors push away ideas of succession planning, initially thinking of it as an unrealistic task. Indeed the unknown variables abound. They include not knowing the future burdens and dreams God might develop in your heart, the health and growth momentum of your present church, the ongoing "fit" between you and your present church, what your church board or district superintendent might do, or how your health or family circumstances might change.

However, in reality you can do much to plan your future, beginning with the immediate present.

The "Ten Commandments" of Preparing for Succession

How many of the following steps can you take now that will prepare you for the inevitable day when you are no longer pastor of your church? Here are "ten commandments"—a checklist—that will help you well as you travel down the road of becoming ready for transition. The rest of the book explores these issues and their many variations in greater detail.

1. **Read this book with others.** First, ask your board to read it. If you're a young pastor processing this book, you are already headed in the right direction. Whatever your age and no matter how long you've been at your church, your board will appreciate knowing that you want to plan for your church's future as well as your own.

Additionally, find a trusted friend or colleague to read the book with you. You may think that few if any of your colleagues are seriously contemplating succession, especially if you're younger. But you're wrong. An increasing number welcome the conversation if they can know how to do it in a safe context and with a practical resource.

2. **Set a healthy pace for the long run.** If you don't have one, establish a sabbatical policy in conjunction with your church board. The most common practice is a paid three-month break every seven years. If you're a multi-staff church, include them in the policy.[1]

Additionally, consider mandating a policy that requires you and your pastoral staff to actually take your days off and vacation time. Also, if you're not in one, find an accountability group that can be your safety net. Too many successions are on the heels of a moral or financial failure. And nearly every one of those failures happened because the pastors were (a) tired and (b) didn't have anyone to talk to about their personal fatigue.

3. **Prepare an "emergency envelope."** It's important to formulate an emergency succession plan and communicate various pieces to the proper parties. This isn't as daunting as you might think. Ask yourself this question: "What would happen next if I were hit by a bus today?" Answer it on two levels: personal and church. On the personal side, is your family provided for? Do you have adequate life insurance? Disability insurance? (You're seven times more likely to be disabled than to die during your working years.) A will? If you have children, have you named a guardian for them if their other parent dies as well? In your personal finances, if you have debt, are you on a path toward financial freedom and a life of ever-increasing generosity toward others?

On the church side, how prepared is your congregation if that bus should take your life or incapacitate you for an extended season? Is the church prepared by knowing who would be in charge in the first hours of your absence? Who would preach on the initial Sundays? Who would carry out your key duties? Form a plan, write it down, and have your board collaborate with and/or approve the plan.

Now ask each staff or key volunteer to create their own "hit by a bus" plan for their own succession. Affirm that they should all include the idea of actively developing one or more apprentices (more on this in #6 below).

Finally, add a line item in your church budget for emergency/interim hires. Or create a financial reserve buffer that could be used for this purpose. To determine the amount, imagine, if you as the pastor were sick for a three-month period, how much funding would be needed to bring in and pay guest preachers?

4. **Develop a plan for a nonemergency but unforeseen departure.** Succession is not a synonym for retirement. It's also not just about emergency planning. Many other reasons for departure can come up. You might sense God's leading to leave your current church for another one. You might decide to leave ministry for another profession. Trends are showing this to be more and more common.

Does your church have a plan for how to handle a vacancy outside of your emergency plan? Who would determine how a search team would be created? Have you developed internal candidates from your current staff or perhaps from a key volunteer? Do you have a short list of people who might be candidates to replace you, such as one of your teaching team, a favorite guest speaker, sons/daughters of the church now serving elsewhere, or previous associate pastors? Are there rules or bylaws you need to establish now, such as whether you would allow current staff to be considered? Do any other board policies or church bylaws need to be created now to preclude a future crisis or conflict? Would you hire a search firm? Write out your process. Have it board approved and communicated to the appropriate people and accessible by more than one person.

5. **Anticipate your (eventual) retirement.** Some succession is linked to retirement. Is part of your compensation set aside for retirement? The primary reason many pastors hang on to their job too long is a lack of finances for retirement. Boards should have a compensation committee that meets to help you plan now for your eventual sunset years. Request funds for the use of an outside CFA or CFP. If the church has one who offers to work pro bono, request the financial equivalent of CFA fees be deposited into your retirement account.

6. **Annually evaluate the state of your succession plan.** Place "succession planning" both as the first item of your own annual performance review and also schedule a full board meeting once a year to discuss the state of your succession plan. Succession planning is an ongoing process, not a single event. The discussion can include many of the elements in these "ten commandments."

Suppose you're developing your son as your successor. What experiences does he need in the coming year in the next step of his development? What kind of staff, volunteer or paid, does he need to be developing? Or if your plan is not yet that specific, what do you need to do in the coming year to develop, strengthen, and "test" the pool of potential candidates in your leadership pipeline?

7. **Create a broad culture of leadership development.** Intentionally build a leadership pipeline by making relationship-based leadership development a regular part of your planning, programming, and budgeting. Develop a system in which many people at many levels are offered next steps in their own leadership development. Could you use the small groups and other ministries in your church to create a pathway through which someone, if called by God and suitably gifted, can receive training to travel the journey from new Christian to pastor or missionary? In the spirit of 2 Timothy 2:2, what if you create an environment of apprentices, interns, and assistants in which every leader, both paid and volunteer, sees it as their number one job to develop one or more other leaders? A church-wide culture of leadership development will not only help your church in its current mission but will also help develop potential future successors.

> A church-wide culture of leadership development will not only help your church in its current mission but will also help develop potential future successors.

8. **Share the teaching.** If you haven't done so already, now is the time to be proactive in building a well-rounded teaching team. This involves far more than making a preaching roster or giving visibility to certain politically important people in your church or denomination. Creating a culture where the church isn't dependent on one communicator will mitigate the damage of a sudden departure of the pastor. If you're a smaller church or cannot afford a second teaching pastor, or do not have ready access to capable communicators (such as through a nearby parachurch ministry or seminary), consider having a "preaching contest" among the laity, allowing the winner or top finishers a chance to deliver the weekend message. Our friends at Austin Stone Community Church, Austin, Texas, have done this with amazing success.

9. **Share the leading.** This is a very different function from a preaching team. The senior pastor should identify key staff with potential for higher levels of leadership and be intentional about mentoring them to participate regularly in senior-level decisions. The goal would be to make sure each of the senior pastor's responsibilities has one or more people who have participated in it enough that they could take it over. Another way to approach this is to make a list of what presently "only" the senior pastor knows in terms of information about the church and how it is run, and then train others by enlarging the circle of senior-level decision making. Doing so will also preclude the idea of a personality driven church culture or environment.

10. **Look beyond the baton pass.** If your succession is a retirement scenario, what will you do with your time once you've stepped down? Having a clear identity and role will make the transition out of the pulpit much easier (as the next chapter will explore). Could you begin building a nonprofit around an area of passion? Could you become certified as an interim pastor? What else has God blessed in your ministry

and given you passion for that you might do part-time as you transition from full-time pastoral ministry? Is there something you and your spouse have dreamed about doing together at this stage in your life and marriage?

While every succession is different, carrying its own complexities, these steps seem to be applicable to the majority of the case studies we've encountered. If you take nothing else from this book, begin applying these "ten commandments" to your setting, and you will be well on the road to a successful succession.

A Role Model for All "Ten Commandments"

Larry Osborne of North Coast Church, Vista, California, models well someone who has lived out the intent behind each of these "ten commandments." At age twenty-eight he became pastor of a church plant in northern San Diego County, part of the Evangelical Free Church denomination. The previous pastor was a good friend; he had been an usher in Larry's wedding. The congregation was small, and Larry figured it would be a rather seamless transition.

Unfortunately, it didn't unfold that way. As Larry tells in his excellent book *Sticky Teams: Keeping Your Leadership Team and Staff on the Same Page*,[2] the chair of the elder board had been in Europe for an extended vacation when Larry candidated and was called as pastor. "While that seemed a little odd, everyone told me not to worry, that we'd get along great," Larry said. Sadly, at their first meeting, after Larry shared his dreams and vision with this elder who was the former mayor of a large suburban city, the elder leaned across the table. "Son," he said, "don't you get too many fancy ideas. You just preach and pray. We'll run the church. And don't dig your roots too deep either, because it's a good idea for a pastor to move on every three or four years."[3] Ouch. Larry was stunned.

But things got worse. Six months in, Larry was embroiled in controversy. Attendance was steadily shrinking. "The board and I were having a hard time seeing eye to eye on anything," Larry said. "I literally lay awake at night wondering what I'd do when they finally asked me to leave, or when the church split, or when a congregational meeting turned raucous."[4]

Fortunately, none of that happened. Larry has had the privilege of staying at the church for over thirty years. As he recounts in several different books,[5] he and his board have learned to work together with remarkable unity. Along the way, Larry shifted to the role of an initiating and directional leader. The journey has had bumps, including an attempted coup by two staff to remove him as leader ("I never saw it coming," Larry admitted),[6] but the church has developed a powerful track record of making disciples of Jesus Christ—at first dozens, then hundreds, and now thousands.

This includes pioneering the way through ministry innovations, such as one in 1998: on-campus video venues where the music and atmosphere target a certain attitude more than age range but with teaching that's the same across all the venues. For many years, more people have attended one of the venues than have chosen to go to the sanctuary where the teacher is based. This approach requires a wide array of lay leaders. The church has also developed a strong system of small groups, with more than 80 to 90 percent of the adult attendance involved at any given point. According to Larry, "our small groups are the hub of our ministry and the primary vehicle for relationships, discipleship, and church health."[7]

These ministry teams, small groups, and other structures have emerged as the church has developed a robust culture of leadership development. The church offers strong pathways for leadership development from lay volunteer to staff pastor. This means staff are less "doers" and more "empowerers." For example, initially the worship pastor was hired to personally lead worship.

As a culture of leadership development has emerged, that role has changed to someone who raises up other worship leaders. "Because of this," Larry explained, "we've always been able to add services quickly and cheaply when needed. We aren't limited by the physical capacity of our worship leader to be present or by our budget's ability to hire additional leaders."[8] The same approach holds true in almost every other area of ministry, from youth pastors to administrators, from office support staff to children's workers. "Specialists who can't become trainers or who aren't willing to become trainers will eventually put a ceiling on the growth of your church or bust your budget," Larry said.[9]

Then after the first five years of preaching almost every Sunday, Larry began sharing the pulpit on a regular basis. Not only did he develop a preaching team, but more than that, a true leadership team made up of multiple senior pastors (think of a law firm with "partners" rather than the model most churches follow of a sole proprietorship with valued employees). Under this model decisions are shared among the senior pastors.

In 2004, Chris Brown, seventeen years younger than Larry, became one of the senior pastors and a teaching pastor along with Larry. For years they've shared the preaching load (trading off on Easter), with each preaching twenty-three to twenty-four weekends a year. Both would like to preach more! But for the health of the church and to model the necessity of raising up a team, they sublimate their desire for the sake of the mission.

The congregation, spread across three campuses for this multisite church, recognizes both men as directional leaders. One could face illness or other changes, and the other would continue in every area of leadership without missing a beat.

Frankly, if both were hit by a bus at the same time (God forbid), the board and other leaders would still know what to do. The loss would certainly be sad and painful, but the church would have the strong potential of making it through the crisis because Larry and the team have planned well for replication of leadership at every level.

Finishing Strong Even When Coming from Behind

Not everyone gets to go to a church at age twenty-eight and then stay as long as Larry Osborne has. In Colorado Springs, Colorado, forty-seven-year-old Brady Boyd started from behind but is today looking ahead. Arriving in 2007 as pastor of New Life Church, founded twenty-two years previously, he followed the sudden departure of founding pastor Ted Haggard because of moral failure—a transition that was widely publicized because Ted was also president of the National Association of Evangelicals and a spiritual advisor to the US president.

Predictably, Brady had much rebuilding to do. He started by pastoring the staff. "My first mission and priority was to gain their trust because if we don't have trust and unity on the inside, I can't expect trust and unity on the outside or among the congregation," he said.[10] One way of caring for them was to note that many of the staff were exhausted. The scandal, all of the accusations, and the search for a new pastor had taken a deep physical, emotional, and spiritual toll. "As the fresh new guy, my temptation was to jump in saying, 'Let's start doing some new programs and other new things.'" Instead Brady developed a staggered schedule to allow many of the staff to take their first-ever sabbatical. He also launched other initiatives to care for the staff and their families, both paid staff and key volunteers. As the church began to rebound, he also authorized pay raises for many who had worked for years without any upward financial adjustment.

On Brady's one hundredth day as pastor, yet another tragedy happened. A murder was committed on the campus. Just after Sunday services, two girls were slain by a man with an assault rifle. Then, cornered by a campus security volunteer, the man killed himself. "It was awful. It was the darkest day of my life, but that tragedy probably drew us closer," Brady shared.

Ironically, God used that event to bring the church together. "In a strange way, it gave a chance to bond with the church and staff on a level that otherwise would have taken years," Brady continued. "I don't know of any church that has experienced a scandal on as national a level as ours followed by something as traumatic as these on-campus murders."

Brady also traces a direct link between anything good that happened and prayer. "Our story is a miracle story. I know that. It is a miracle of God that we still exist as a church, and an even greater miracle that we are able to look forward, grow, and continue to reach out. Much of that is because I inherited a praying church."

Even with all these developments, Brady—who is still in his first chapters as leader of New Life—is already thinking about what happens after he leaves. "If you don't plan your succession, you are planning to fail," he said.

For Brady, this means that on more than one occasion he has talked with the church's elders specifically about what will happen when he's no longer the senior pastor of

New Life—whether that's one, ten, or even twenty years from now. They have a plan that they revisit from time to time.

Brady is also troubled by some of his friends, such as a sixty-year-old pastor friend whom he asked, "What's your plan for when you leave your church?" The friend replied, "I haven't ever thought about that."

One of Brady's favorite word pictures about succession comes from a popular track event in the Summer Olympics—the 4 x 100 relay. It typically involves four world-class sprinters, each running at top performance, passing a baton from one to another. "To me, that's what succession should look like in the local church—but very rarely does," he said.

> "If you don't plan your succession, you are planning to fail."
> —Brady Boyd

In this metaphor, a pastor who is strong and capable but has never been intentional about raising up others is like someone standing in the middle of a track with a baton in hand—standing still with nobody in front to hand it to. "I've told my elders that I don't want to wait to hand off the baton until I can't run anymore. I want to be running full steam, full stride, handing off the baton to someone else who is likewise able to run in full stride," he said.

Brady has not been secret about his present work to set his successor up for success. "Even if I had to leave earlier than I had hoped," he said, "I would rather leave New Life as a senior pastor earlier so that someone could run fast in front of me than hold on a few more years and then look up one day and have nobody to hand the baton to."

As Brady well illustrates, conventional wisdom may say to hang on to a great church as long as possible. A longer, wiser view of succession is always asking the bigger question of what's the next chapter for the church. Early in this chapter, we said that there are no cardinal rules for succession. But this rule gets close: leaders who continually plan and pray for the next chapter for their church will almost always have a better ending and a brighter future than those who do not.

N E X T Steps

For Pastors: Which of the "Ten Commandments of Succession Planning" do you think you are doing the best job with, and which one needs the most improvement?

For Boards: What steps have you taken and what next three steps can you take to help your pastor manage a healthy pace of life in ministry?

3

Three Essential Questions

What Is Succession Success? What Captures My Passion?
How Are My Finances?

As chapter 1 affirmed, all pastors, even those serving very happily and fruitfully, need to begin thinking *now* about their succession. But long before they look to relocate or retire, they need to deal with three issues. The starting point for most pastors will be the discussion of this chapter.

It has been said, "A boy becomes a man when he begins to consider how he will be remembered." Pastors pass a similar milestone in their career. Somewhere along the way, they begin to consider their legacy. While attendance, membership, and other metrics dominate many young pastors' minds, legacy is usually in the forefront of the minds of wise pacesetters who take a big-picture perspective.

Unfortunately, even "legacy thinkers" rarely represent a succession mind-set. Far too often, their big-picture thinking strives for a new record of conversions or baptisms, a new partnership or impact on the community, a new wave of sons and daughters of the church that go out into ministry, one more building, one more new worship service, or one more best-effort attempt to voice the unchanging gospel in a way that stays relevant to the next generation.

What would happen if pastors would focus some of their thinking on what happens *after* they are no longer pastor? In corporate settings, it is not uncommon for a CEO's first board meeting to be one that focuses on succession. What would happen if a new pastor at his or her first board meeting asked, "Let's talk about my last months or years here. What needs to be in place at that point, and what should happen to both the church and to me after my time is over?" That question may not be decided at the first meeting, but a team can be commissioned at that meeting to begin working on it, with the goal of having a plan in place within one year, to then be reviewed at the pastor's first anniversary.

To address that question of legacy thinking, three key issues must be sorted through. Developing sound answers can free pastors to go to new levels as they deal with the big picture of legacy.

1. **Define succession success.** What would a successful hand-off look like and how do I achieve it? What do I need to do now to prepare for passing the leadership baton?[1]

2. **Identify life passion.** What should I do next? Is my next stop a similar role in another church? If not, in light of how God has made me and the opportunities before me, what area would I love to pour my energy into after my time at this church is over?

> So much of a good succession rises and falls on setting expectations before the process ever begins.

3. **Determine financial need.** Stated positively, are my household finances in order so I'm free to go when and where God calls me? Stated negatively, how can I make sure finances don't keep me hanging on to my present role (and its salary) longer than I should?

All three questions help set the tone for a pastoral succession because they help all parties set expectations. They help clear the air of any premature assumptions about what kind of outcome is best. So much of a good succession rises and falls on setting expectations before the process ever begins. These three questions will help set expectations for your church and for the outgoing pastor as well as for the incoming pastor.

Once those expectations are set, a distinct style will emerge for your succession plan.

Blocks to Your Future

What keeps pastors from thinking about these questions?

Perhaps no career ties identity to job more than the pastorate. What other job coincides with more key parts of life? Who else performs their daughter's wedding at work? Who else buries longtime friends as part of their job? What other career ties personal spiritual formation to career performance?

The same things that make the pastorate the best job on the planet can also make it the hardest type of work to leave. That's why focusing on legacy questions from day one matters so much. What would happen if part of a board's annual review of their pastor included a progress report on these three areas? It's not uncommon in the corporate world. If it's an increasingly standard practice for business, why wouldn't the church deserve the same level of planning and care?

Defining Success Three Years after You're Gone

What does success look like three years after the hand-off from the retiring pastor to the successor pastor? Even if you're part of an appointment system where you have no say in the person who will follow you, you still can have a huge influence in how you end, how well the church is prepared for a successor, and what path and direction the church's momentum will be moving toward when the successor arrives.

One pastor who tried hard to define what succession success would look like is Dennis Gingerich, founding pastor of Cape Christian Fellowship, Cape Coral, Florida. In 2004, at age fifty, he purchased the newly released book *The Elephant in the Boardroom* from the Leadership Network website. "I was hooked," he said. "I read the entire book and bought a copy for each of our church board members."

Through some frank and honest discussions between pastor and board, their view of succession changed. "Gradually, my new framework for success was no longer about graphs and charts going up and to the right now, during my tenure," Dennis said. "Instead, I began to verbalize that my measure of success in ministry was going to be based on whether the congregation was continuing to grow and thrive five years after I was out of the pilot's seat." He also explored these new ideas of ministry success with the pastor's group he had been doing life with every Monday morning for over ten years.

Dennis and his board tried to envision together what succession might look like three to five years down the road. One aspect was that the church's next pastor might be considerably younger and come from the staff of the church. One person seemed to qualify well; Wes Furlong was from the area, was doing a great job with the young adults and in occasional teaching, and was twenty-three years junior to Dennis. "By 2006 I shared with Wes the vision I had of raising up the future lead pastor of the church from within so that we could see continual growth and fruitfulness for the long haul. He was interested," Dennis said.

Dennis also sensed a call to stay at the church after the succession, remaining a vital member of the lead team. He and the board, and now also with Wes, imagined together what that might look like. This would include Dennis's dreams of being able to travel and train church planting movement leaders overseas, serve as mentor to local government and business leaders, and influence successful business leaders toward living with significance.

To launch the transition, Dennis began to share a greater percentage of the preaching. "We actually made a really good team," Dennis said. "I also gave Wes more responsibility in leading various staff meetings."

In 2007 the local construction-driven economy collapsed. That area of Florida became the foreclosure capital of the world. The church had to lay off several staff members. Dennis volunteered to take a 30 percent cut in pay. Other transition issues came to the forefront. Rumblings among the staff, church board, and some in the congregation led to the departure of almost 20 percent of those in weekly attendance, some of whom established a new church nearby. Dennis and Wes worked well together through that tough season.

Dennis included his wife, Linda, fully in the discernment and planning process. "She fully supported me and Wes in this planned transition," he said, "but I wasn't anticipating her response the day I came home from the office and told her I had set a specific date for the transition."

"I started crying," Linda shared. "The church was like one of our children, so dear to us. But as we talked it through, I realized that all children grow up. That's what they're supposed to do, and we can have ongoing relationship with them just like we do with our now-grown children."

In 2009 the final step of the plan involved a church-wide celebration. At that point Dennis's title changed from senior pastor to founding pastor, and Wes moved from teaching pastor to lead pastor.

Now several years later, they view the developments with great joy. "It's been astonishing and amazing," Linda said. "We've grown significantly. We've launched a new campus. And the church is full of the kind of people we originally came to reach—the twenty- to thirtysomething generation we drew when our kids were three, seven, and ten years old. And now our new pastor, Wes, is doing just that again."[2]

Looking Forward to a New Identity

A second issue to explore involves the question of "What's next?" for the outgoing pastor. Having a plan for where outgoing pastors will spend their energy is crucial to a healthy succession. Chapter 4 will help you frame when it's time to move on from your present place of service. More fundamental is the issue of what you should do next in God's big picture for your life. To put it bluntly, too often pastors stay at a church not because they're thriving there, but because their identity is tied too much to their present role and they don't have anything else to put their passion into.

> Too often pastors stay at a church not because they're thriving but because they don't have anything else to put their passion into.

Frank Thomas gives a powerful window into his journey toward a new identity as he prayed over his future transition out of Mississippi Boulevard Christian Church. "It dawned on me that some of my grief about the loss of preaching in the pastoral role is the concept of 'loss aversion,'" he wrote in his excellent chronicle *The Choice*, which he aptly subtitled *Living Your Passion from the Inside Out*. But he also discovered "my lament about no longer preaching from the pastoral role was more a focus on what I was losing rather than what I was gaining in my new assignment."[3]

Bill Ritchie is a great example of finding a new passion and pouring himself into it. On Easter Sunday 2012, he was the clean-cut, energetic, sixty-seven-year-old minister who was delivering the sermon just as he had for nearly forty years as founder of Crossroads Community Church, Vancouver, Washington.

But halfway through the message, something different happened. His soon-to-be successor, Daniel Fusco, a thirty-six-year-old jazz musician with a beard, dreadlocks, and an uncanny resemblance to Counting Crows lead singer Adam Duritz, joined the pastor on stage and took over the second half of the sermon.

The contrast between the two men was striking, an image of two distinct generations and a signal that things were changing. Daniel had been hired six months previously to usher in a period of transition that would enable Bill to shift over to a ministry he had started at the church, designed for baby boomers. Called nxtSTP (text jargon for "Next Step"), the ministry is designed to motivate those in the second half of life, boomers and beyond, to use their expertise and vitality to give back to the community.

"I had been feeling for some years that we needed to transition if we were going to meet the needs of the next generation," Bill told a local newspaper. "I had pretty clear criteria to follow."

Bill wanted someone with experience planting a church, a strong educational background, a hunger to learn, good communication skills, and a love of people, he said. He and Daniel first met at a pastors' conference. After further conversations, Daniel came to the church to meet with the church's board of directors and to give a sermon. Further explorations led to a formal call and the transfer of leadership.[4]

Today both men have offices in the building—each in a very different décor—and both couldn't be happier. "I have been growing in excitement for years about developing this ministry to older baby boomers," Bill reported. "I wake up each morning with the same anticipation as years ago when I started the church."

Amy Hanson, author of *Baby Boomers and Beyond: Tapping the Ministry Talents and Passions of Adults over Fifty*,[5] affirms the importance of older pastors being encouraged to start another chapter. "Pastors need to be encouraged and given the opportunity to explore other interests that may lead to future ministry endeavors, even while they are still in their current role. They should have permission to wrestle with questions such as 'What's a ministry I've always wanted to start?' or 'Where is a place I've wanted to serve, but I've never had the time or opportunity?' And then, simply granting them extended time off to take a class, go on a mission trip, or volunteer with an agency might be all that is needed for them to find a new place to invest themselves and make an impact."[6]

Getting Your House in Financial Order

It may sound crass and worldly, and it's not a subject many want to explore. Far too many pastors face retirement with no way to fund it. This reality can wreck a succession before it even begins. Most pastors believe that if they focus on ministry, the money part will work itself out. Most also have little to no training about preparing for the day when the church isn't there to support them or in the eventual day of retirement.

Headline stories about pastoral salaries and lifestyles tend to highlight the extravagant, flamboyant, and hypocritical. So do television shows like *The Preachers of LA* or the occasional minister featured on *American Greed*.

Most pastors know the reality to be quite different, aware that these media examples are the exceptions by far. According to many studies, the most prominent coming from Leadership Network and *Christianity Today*,[7] the vast majority of pastors receive a modest income from their church. Church size measured by budget and attendance is the strongest variable in predicting a pastor's income, but even as size increases, the vast majority of pastor salaries could not underwrite the level of luxury that invites news coverage.

> Far too many pastors face retirement with no way to fund it. This reality can wreck a succession before it even begins.

Some pastors have the ability to plan for their family's financial future but simply haven't. Others can't begin to think about preparing for the future because they can barely make ends meet today. As our friend Thom Rainer observed, "Many pastors are under extreme stress because they do not have adequate income to meet their financial obligations. . . . The reality is that, for a number of pastors, the issue of compensation is a major push from one church to another, or from the church to a secular vocation."[8]

As well, pastors who ought to explore other lines of work or perhaps retire because of reduced effectiveness are frequently tempted to hang on to their present position because they don't have any other means to support themselves or their families. Sadly, some baby boomer pastors approaching retirement saw a hit to their meager savings during the economic recession of 2008–2010. Needing to play catch-up will prolong their ministry tenures beyond what they had originally intended.

The lesson for younger pastors is that personal finances cannot be overlooked as an important and ongoing foundation to a future succession decision. The challenge for pastors of all ages is to live on less than you earn so that you can give generously and save diligently. Older pastors approaching retirement with minimal savings might consider the following options:

- **Pray diligently.** Numerous Scriptures remind us that God not only cares for our every need but promises to provide for us. If your financial future is not a matter of regular prayer for you, your spouse, and your prayer partners, you must realize that it needs to be.
- **Talk frankly.** Speak with your church board and with those in authority over you if you're part of a denomination or movement. They may be able to help in unexpected ways. If you ask, the worst that can happen is that they say, "Sorry, we love you, but we just cannot help."
- **Set goals.** It is never too late to set goals. People who aim at specific targets are always the group more likely to achieve or come close to their objectives.
- **Exercise faith.** If you find yourself staying in the pastorate primarily for financial reasons, try to find competent business persons or career counselors whom you trust to confide in. Seek their advice about other possible vocations.

Tough Self-Management Issues

Management expert Peter Drucker offers a strong word about the changes of this era that provides a helpful framework for why the questions voiced in this chapter are essential for pastors of all ages, church sizes, and tenures to seriously wrestle through.

> In a few years, when the history of our time is written from a long-term perspective, I think it very probable that the most important event those historians will remember is not technology, not the internet, not e-commerce—but the unprecedented change in the human condition. For the first time—and I mean that literally—substantially and rapidly growing numbers of people have choices. For the first time, people have had to *manage themselves.* And we are totally unprepared for it.[9]

The days of fixed-income pensions are waning, if not gone. The days of the church "taking care of everything" are either gone or are in short supply. Now more than ever, pastors must focus on self-management, taking a long view of their future and planning accordingly. How will you fund your life after retirement? Where will you spend your energy after retirement? How will you plan for your succession in a way that history will judge as successful? Answering these three questions will pave the way for a bright future with a great finish. It may be your chance to leave the greatest legacy of your ministry.

——————————— N E X T Steps ———————

For Pastors: Rank the three questions in this chapter in order of urgency in your life and identify an actionable step you can take in the next three months to move toward solutions.

For Boards: Rank the three questions in this chapter and name one actionable step you can take in the next three months to help your pastor face these issues. Also, if you are not providing a retirement benefit program for every new pastor to remove the tendency for them to stay too long for lack of financial security, ask yourselves why not.

4

Deciding When It's Time to Leave

Finding Space and Permission to Explore the Options

Brett Favre is one of the most decorated quarterbacks in NFL history. His legacy is largely defined by gritty, gutsy play. That kind of courage and the confidence that comes with it are a big part of what made Brett Favre one of the best.

But his legacy is now also defined by his inability to recognize when it was time to move on. When it came time to find a new future, Brett didn't end well. He retired, then un-retired several times. He kept believing that he had one more year in him, even when his body and performance clearly told him otherwise. His series of transitions was so tragic that it even became the butt of late-night television jokes.

What does Brett Favre have to do with pastoral succession, including those who are still far from actual retirement?

A person's greatest strength, when unguarded, can become that same person's greatest weakness. And Favre's story, like that of so many other aging athletes who stay one too many seasons, is played out in churches by highly competent pastors far too often. In ministry, a pastor's confidence—one of the qualities God uses to build a church—can become one of the biggest obstacles to pastoral succession. The very voice of confidence that overcomes a fear of public speaking and enables a pastor for years to get up in front of the congregation and boldly proclaim God's Word—that voice, if unchecked, can also whisper in the pastor's ear, "You've got another good year or two in you."

The voice may have many different translations: "Stay, because this church still needs you," or "You've been here so long that you can do things a newcomer couldn't," or even "This church owes a great debt to you that you need to receive and cherish here."

And so begins the far-too-often-played story of the pastor who keeps hanging on, long after the vision and energy for the current ministry are gone, long after the community around the church has changed, or long after the congregation has stagnated.

No pastor wants that for a legacy. No pastor wants to be the leader who walks out of a meeting, only to be the subject of the next conversation that centers around, "How do we tell Pastor that we think it's time to consider a change?"

So how do *you* know when your time has come to let go? What questions can pastors and their trusted advisors ask and discuss that would help them decide whether or not they really have one more year?

Below we list four different types of succession along with examples of pastors who have made the tough call to either begin the conversation or actually make the transition. We're hopeful that stories of hanging on too long will be relegated to professional sports and that the church will be known as a place that operates on a higher, healthier level.

Different Types of Succession

While no succession is identical to another, and all have complexities unlike any other, it is still helpful to identify categories or types of succession. Much like unique animals can still be grouped by genus and species, so you can gain a head start on understanding your particular situation by understanding what type of succession you are facing.

The simplest dividing point is to ask whether the transition was unexpected (first three categories below) or expected (final category).

Emergency. Unforeseen, sudden, often crisis-laden successions that can include death or other tragic events are one of the following:

- *Short-term:* A temporary, unplanned absence that arises unexpectedly and is projected to last for three months or less.
- *Long-term:* A temporary, unplanned absence that arises unexpectedly and is projected to last more than three months.
- *Permanent:* A permanent absence is when the pastor will not be returning to the position.

Disqualified. Sometimes a pastor is no longer qualified to be pastor of a church. Reasons can include:

- *Moral failure:* Most disqualifications stem from moral failure. The majority involve abuse of sex, money, and/or power. Some involve serious breaking of the law or other major improprieties.

- *Doctrinal heresy or deviation from accepted biblical standards:* This includes pastors whose approach to ministry shifts drastically enough that they are no longer a fit for their church.

- *Loss of physical core competencies:* Sometimes disqualification relates to loss of energy, vision, preaching ability, or other physical core competencies required for the role of pastor.

Forced. Whether or not the term is used, the pastor has been fired. (A significant portion of chapter 13 addresses forced terminations.)

Expected. Expected successions are largely the focus of this book. They include:

- *Ministry transition:* Sometimes church and pastor partner together on a new ministry venture. It can involve any number of roles the pastor might shift to, e.g., church planter, missionary, seminary professor, chaplain, interim pastor (at other churches), mentor to other pastors, or author.

- *Church rotation:* The bishop reappoints the pastor to another church or the pastor accepts a call to a "next step" church.

- *Retirement:* In many cases, retirement is long planned, but sometimes circumstances prompt a short countdown to retirement, whether partial or full. Partial retirement may involve shifting to a new role in the existing church, such as visitation pastor, mission pastor, or senior adult pastor.

Ways God Might Show You It's Time to Move

If your succession is one you can plan and have some control over, these ten indicators might help you know when it is the right time to leave. They can also help you discern if you should stay longer but not too long.

God gives you a clear sign. This may range from Scripture that comes alive to a vision or dream—or even to contemporaries who begin to hint at their own transition and/or retirement. Sometimes compelling circumstances serve as a divine sign, such as a financial situation becoming unworkable or unsustainable personally for you or your family.

Your leadership speaks. Your spiritual authority may be a denominational superintendent or bishop or the governance board at your church.

Your part of the mission is complete. You have fulfilled what God originally called you to do, and God has not extended or enlarged the challenge.

You lose heart. The passion or other spiritual fire you once knew for this church and situation has clearly departed (and hopefully you are now sensing in its place a big heart for another location or ministry).

Others confirm it. Your close friends or other trusted advisors affirm that your time at this church is finished.

You receive a new call. This may start in your heart or in an actual invitation from another church or ministry.

A mismatch develops. You can no longer reach those your church needs to reach, such as a certain age group, economic level, lifestyle, or racial demographic. Perhaps the church's vision has shifted and you can no longer align with it.

Collaboration ends. The place you serve becomes more of an enemy than your ally. Or perhaps your family is experiencing deep pain because of your present environment.

The church begins to show a lack of confidence in your vision and/or leadership. Attendance may decline or plateau. Perhaps it has potential to go forward in its mission, but you don't seem to be the right one to provide the leadership training and outreach the church needs for its next chapter.

You reach physical or emotional limits. You no longer have the physical strength, mental quickness, or physical agility to do the job needed.

Typical Ages When Pastors and Others Retire

If your life stage is not one of moving to another church or ministry but retirement, then consider how the table in appendix 1 (page 185) highlights the ages of prominent pastors at the time of succession. It might be interesting to look at how many retired and at what age.

For other church size and general population data, here are some retirement statistics:

Church World

- 61, retirement age of the most recent Archbishop of Canterbury, Rowan Williams[1]
- 65, average retirement age for Presbyterian clergy (PCUSA)[2]
- 72, required retirement age for United Methodist clergy[3]
- 85, retirement age of the most recent pope, Benedict XVI (who was elected at age 78)[4]

General Marketplace

- 58, average age of outgoing CEOs at S&P 500 companies in 2012[5]
- 64 (men) and 62 (women), average retirement age in United States for *all* workers (any profession)[6]

Turnover Rates

- 7%, the number of S&P 500 companies that experienced CEO transition in 2012. Of the newly appointed successor CEOs, 78% were internal placements.[7]

Starting the Conversation Can Be the Hardest Step

Many (and perhaps most) pastors need the help of others to begin developing a succession plan. It may require a spouse, a close friend in or out of the church, an independent advisor such as a denominational leader—or a combination of all three.

For some people, the hardest step is to begin the discussion. Sometimes someone other than the pastor, such as a caring elder or board member, needs to broach the topic.

Such is the case with Bill Hybels at Willow Creek Community Church. His leadership skills are stellar. He has significantly influenced tens of thousands of other leaders and congregations through his speaking and writing. Willow Creek has arguably sponsored more conferences than any church in the country. The church's growth trajectory has consistently placed it in "Top 100" lists as one of the nation's largest churches year after year.

Outreach magazine's "Top 100" tally for 2013 observes that Bill is the longest-tenured megachurch pastor on that list. He founded the church in 1975 at age twenty-four. The church has always shown the kind of strong management that would keep a name in an envelope should an accident take Bill's life.

Yet Bill turned forty and then fifty without a board-developed succession plan. As Bill approached sixty, the board commissioned one of its elders to initiate a conversation.

"It really starts with a trusted relationship, one of absolute trust," said Mike LaMonica, longtime elder and friend of Bill's.[8] "Talking about succession is an emotional process for a pastor. You have to convey both your care for the pastor as a person and also about the future of the church." Mike didn't try to lecture or impose any decisions. Rather, he simply tried to lead the discussion.

Mike and Bill spoke many times over an eighteen-month period. Some talks lasted only five minutes, others for much longer. "I didn't want to force him past a point he wasn't ready for. He had to take it at his own pace," Mike explains.

Mike sometimes began his conversations by quoting things Bill had said. "I heard a great sermon where the preacher said the death rate is still 100 percent," Mike once said, quoting a line Bill had used several times in recent talks. Predictably, Bill started laughing. Then Mike became more serious: "If you're not the exception, at some point, someone else will lead this church. We want to partner with you for success—not just for the church, but for your life as well."

> "Board members have to understand how deep feelings run in the hearts of long-time or founding pastors. These will be delicate conversations."
> —Bill Hybels

Bill appreciated Mike's approach. "If Mike had tried to rush these conversations, it would have been very hard on me," Bill said. "Board members have to understand how deep feelings run in the hearts of longtime or founding pastors. These will be delicate conversations. I am extremely proud of our board and how they did the process."9

Mike and Bill talked through the three questions outlined in the previous chapter. They also addressed other issues, such as the phases of the succession plan: what will happen next, when, and how that will be communicated.

As soon as Bill got to the point of saying "Yes, I own this," he was ready to have conversations with his key leadership team, those who will be impacted most by any transition he makes. Bill even went public with the process to date in his 2012 Global Leadership Summit talk, explaining that the next steps would involve defining the DNA the successor will need to embody and a process of exploring specific individual candidates.

"Our overall goals of success in the succession are that the DNA of Willow will continue and that Bill will use his giftedness in an effective way," Mike said. "Bill's fundamental gifts won't change. It will be a new pace and new setting."

When should your succession planning begin? Now. As seen in Willow's story, if you plan before succession is imminent, you afford your board both time and flexibility. Bill and the Willow Creek board have given the church opportunity to extend its DNA and to continue to employ Bill's giftedness in a new way. This strategy marks a model that many of the best churches we have studied are using and that many smart churches will employ going forward.

No Longer the Best Fit

"Everyone set me up to win," said Tim Lundy of his time as pastor of Fellowship Bible Church, Little Rock, Arkansas. Since its founding in 1977, the church received leadership from both its elder team and a pastoral team. Tim was called in 2003 to become the directional leader, following Robert Lewis, who had served in a lead role since 1980. The board, the two other teaching pastors on the leadership team, and Robert all worked hard to make the transition a success. "Robert was my greatest cheerleader and sounding board," Tim said.

During his ten years at Fellowship Bible Church, Tim proved not only to be a capable preacher, but he led the church to buy, build, and relocate to new facilities four miles away, and in the process to modify its multi-venue and multi-campus approach. He also helped to honor the two other long-term teaching pastors as they transitioned into new roles, and then he helped find their successors.

"I have a clear sense that God definitely used me during a time of transition in the history of Fellowship," Tim said. But as the church moved forward out of that season of change, Tim wondered if he fully matched Fellowship's leadership model for the future.

Each pastor, including Tim, had worked closely with the church's elder team. The elders had played a strong role in launching the church, and as part of the transition between Robert and Tim, they began to move into a more active role in setting the vision and direction. They desired to move away from having one pastor as the directional leader and to share that role among the three teaching pastors. This would flatten out the team model that Tim came into, returning to what the elders believed to be the original model of the church's leadership.

As Tim prayed and talked with his wife and other mentors, he became convinced that the shift of model might mean his greatest strengths would not be as well used. Then he received a totally unexpected phone call from a pastor he knew, asking if Tim would consider coming to his church to partner with him as teaching pastor and to lead in the rebuilding of the church's executive team. The church is located in the San Francisco Bay area, and the Lundys were drawn to the potential of reaching this largely unchurched community.

In the next months, Tim accepted the invitation and said farewell to Fellowship Bible Church. "Sometimes God says, 'You've done what you need to do there, and I've got something else for you.' It's not an issue of right or wrong," Tim said. "It was a great experience at Fellowship Bible, and I will always be thankful for the people there. But as I read through the New Testament, I am struck by how many times God moves leaders for the sake of the kingdom. It is not always comfortable or easy, but we must be willing to follow."

Tim's self-awareness is rare. Few people would leave a prestigious pulpit like Fellowship. But his reliance on his own spiritual prompting, coupled with a confirmation of that prompting by a phone call and search, led him to make an uncommon move that has proven to be fruitful for Tim, his new church, and for Fellowship Bible.

Going Out on Top Can Open Doors to a New Future

Jeff Bigelow was forty when he started Rolling Hills Christian Church in El Dorado Hills, California.

With no contacts there, he and his family moved to the affluent Sacramento suburb in 1995 and built the church from the ground up. After successfully setting up a launch team, Jeff delivered his first sermon to about one hundred people in a high school wrestling room.

From there, the church grew rapidly and steadily in both number and reputation. Eventually, it found property on eighteen acres and built a lovely facility. Jeff had a great ride there for seventeen years. "Those were the best years of my life but also the hardest," he reflected. With a focus on reaching the unchurched, the congregation grew year after year—heavily through conversion growth. The church recorded over 1,900 baptisms during Jeff's time there. "I didn't want to just swap fish in the aquarium," he said. Rolling Hills became a well-known church among independent Christian Church/Churches of Christ that are part of the Restoration movement.

During Jeff's seventeenth year there, he took his usual five-week summer vacation and sabbatical leave. As he prepared to jump back into the flow of church life, Jeff's wife, Jerri, observed that he lacked his usual energy. A sense of foreboding seemed to be validated in other ways.

Seven years previously, Jeff's leadership team had suggested that they start thinking well in advance about a succession plan for the day he would eventually step down or if a health issue should force it. "Succession hadn't even entered my mind yet," Jeff admitted. "These were simply forward-thinking leaders."

Three years earlier, when Jeff and the church's leaders added an associate teaching pastor, they raised the question of whether this might be the heir apparent. Over time, Jeff and the board gained clarity that the associate was not the right successor and communicated that to him. That staff pastor resigned and moved on. No other succession plans were developed beyond the seed planted by that initial discussion.

But after the vacation in his seventeenth year, Jeff's unease moved him to action. After much prayer, he wrote a letter to his lay leadership team, saying in essence, "I think it's time," and he invited them to help him map out a succession strategy.

The board pushed back, asking, "Are you sure?" They urged him to stay. "No one came to me to ask me to resign," he said, "but pastoral fatigue, weariness, and a desire to finish at the top of my game all confirmed that I needed a change. My goal was to pass the baton to the next leader while I was still running with full vigor and enthusiasm. I wanted to be running hard, pulling my full weight."

The church wasn't in decline. There wasn't a "story behind the story." Jeff simply felt a call to go out on top and leave the church in great shape for a successor. Jeff insisted it was time, and he and the board began the hunt for a successor pastor.

At first, Jeff tried to oversee a pastoral search team, but to no avail. "I couldn't give it the attention it deserved, and I didn't know how to do it well," he admits. So they chose Vanderbloemen Search Group to conduct a full-scale search for a new pastor. The firm walked him through the process, and within four months, a successor was found. When Jeff departed at age fifty-seven, roughly ten months after those summertime forebodings, the church was averaging just over two thousand in weekly attendance and had a healthy momentum, including the best general-fund giving in the church's history.

Jeff's last Sunday in May 2012 was followed immediately by the new pastor's first Sunday, where the two of them had a public baton passing ceremony. After the inevitable adjustments of grieving the loss and welcoming the new leader, the church has been enjoying a new chapter of energy and life.

The best succession typically occurs when the outgoing pastor has lined up a new challenge and is excited about what's ahead. But Jeff wanted to do what was best for the congregation, and to end his part well, even without knowing at the time what his next step would be. "The church had not yet reached its full redemptive potential. I love the people and I knew I would miss them. I could have coasted, but I knew that with each passing year I'd lose my window of effectiveness with young couples."

> The best succession typically occurs when the outgoing pastor has lined up a new challenge and is excited about what's ahead.

As an introverted person who never had the craving to be on stage, Jeff began to search for new ways to use his desire to help churches grow. He decided that the best way was to become a consultant who helped other pastors like him in transition. Jeff is now experiencing his own "halftime" (an idea introduced further in chapter 5), successfully beginning a new career consulting with churches. He now is on staff with Vanderbloemen Search Group and flourishing in his work helping churches navigate pastoral transitions and searches.

Parish Poker

Leith Anderson, introduced in chapter 1, suggests that Jesus's counsel to "count the cost" (Luke 14:28–32) can be applied to pastoral risks related to succession. To illustrate, Leith uses a metaphor he calls parish poker, likening ministry credibility to available poker chips. "Like poker, pastoring is an exercise that combines skill and providence to sort out winners and losers, often with frighteningly high stakes," he says.[10] The object is to help pastors discern whether they have enough credibility to continue forward with the same church.

Leith says most pastors start with a positive balance of chips. "When a new pastor is called to a church, a pile of chips is normally stacked up for use as the pastor chooses. They represent the good favor and support of the church people. They may be saved for a rainy day or risked in the first hand of play," he explains.

Every good sermon is worth at least one good chip. Individual ministry is a slow but sure chip builder. But chips can also be lost for yawner sermons, botched personal ministry (like forgetting a funeral you promised to preach), or leading the church on a big risk that doesn't pay off.

Pastoral succession issues, for both incoming and outgoing pastors, Leith says, affect the number of available chips:

> Long-term pastors are hard to follow; they often seem to take most of the chips with them. Long-term pastors who died in the church are particularly unfollowable. . . .
>
> In contrast are those marvelous predecessors who prepare the way. They teach the congregation to love and support the next pastor "no matter who." They even make a special point to endorse their successors and thereby confer hundreds (maybe thousands) of their own chips.

(While affirming Leith's cautions, we found several successful successions after a pastor died in office, one of which we profile in chapter 16.)

Church size strongly affects chip accumulation. Citing Lyle Schaller's *The Small Church Is Different*,[11] Leith summarizes the differences in expectations:

> While some professional competence and personal relationships are necessary in both, the smaller the church, the greater the expectation of relationship, and the larger the church, the greater the expectation of function. Churches of fifty are more interested in a pastor who relates well to every member, even if the sermons are marginal. Churches of five thousand expect super sermons whether everyone knows the pastor or not.

Introducing change can also affect one's collection of chips. The old advice of not changing anything in the first year of a pastorate recognizes the danger of losing chips too fast and too soon. "Something as seemingly simple as changing the order of worship may cost a new pastor half his starting chips the first Sunday and create a misimpression of arrogance, insensitivity, and pushiness. It may take a year of sermons and hospital visits just to get back even," Leith says.

The net lesson of the chip metaphor is that a pastor with a chip deficit cannot lead a church for long. When the chips are gone, the pastor is likely to sense a call to another ministry. Or perhaps the church will communicate, "God wants you someplace else."

How do you assess your standing in terms of whether it's time to move on? You calculate how your defeats compare to your victories as viewed by the congregation. Then you take it to God. As Leith says, "Since it's his church and I'm his servant, the ultimate decision is his and not mine—win or lose."

In the end, most of the success of a pastoral transition rises and falls on the shoulders of the outgoing pastor. Pastors who can commit to regularly exploring the questions above as well as the larger question of whether or not it is time to transition will go a long way toward ensuring a great transition. In so doing, they will also write the sentences on the most lasting and important part of their legacy.

N E X T Steps

For Pastors: Go through the warning signs above. Do any of them resonate with your current situation? How many? How do you think you can start to address those warning signs?

For Boards: What two warning signs above stand out as the clearest danger to your current pastorate? Name three tangible steps that can be taken over the next ninety days to help solve the problems before they worsen.

5

Resigning "Young" to Start Another Ministry Chapter

And Does the Outgoing Pastor Always Need to Leave Town?

Pastor Francis Chan is exceptional in some ways. To date, he has penned four best-selling books—*Crazy Love* (which sold over a million copies in its first three years), *Forgotten God, Erasing Hell,* and *Multiply.* He is also a regular keynote speaker at the nation's biggest conferences for pastors and church leaders.

In other ways, Francis has followed the pathway of many other pastors. He went to college and then seminary, married and started a family, and became a youth pastor and then church planter. He's passionate about his faith and eager to please God, whatever the personal cost.

The question for this chapter is whether his example as the outgoing pastor of Cornerstone Church, Simi Valley, California, is unusual, or whether it is something that will become a more common pathway for other pastors. Francis planted the church and grew with it (at one point the church consistently hit five thousand in attendance), and in addition planted other churches along the way.

When pastors experience a place of growing influence, the vast majority tend to stay with it. Francis did not. After leading the church for sixteen years, he resigned. He was forty-three at the time. As his friend Mark Driscoll asked him in a public interview, "You've got a good thing going and you hit the eject button. Are you cuckoo? What were you thinking?"[1]

Francis answered that question in many different published interviews, addressing it from several different perspectives. He told one interviewer that he was fighting pride and arrogance. He told another he was afraid the church was becoming too much about him and not enough about the Holy Spirit. Other explanations he offered: he didn't want to stifle Cornerstone Church's leadership through too much dependence on him. He wanted to find another location that was more unchurched, more like Simi Valley was when he first came there. He felt the Lord's tug to a new type of ministry.

Indeed the church rebounded after his 2010 departure. Attendance dropped the first year by about 20 percent, but it has been climbing again since then.

Todd Nighswonger, executive pastor under Francis Chan, became senior pastor. He saw the resignation coming several months ahead. "Francis and I are good friends; we talk all the time—then and now," he said. "Francis comes back to the church and speaks on a regular basis."[2]

Francis eventually settled in San Francisco, doing ministry through a rescue mission called City Impact. As he explained, "I've helped start a ministry here where we just go door-to-door to the different apartments and build relationships with people by showing them grace, giving them groceries—whatever they need. We're just trying to go one door at a time, build relationships, pray for them, show them love and then lay out the Gospel for them."[3]

He also said about Cornerstone, "I did everything I could there, so let's move on and go somewhere else."[4]

Pastoral "Halftime"?

What's unknown is whether the way Francis left Cornerstone Church is an exception or the forecast of a new normal. This phenomenon has been popularized by Bob Buford and others as "halftime."[5] Ordinarily, this phrase refers to business people who hit a midpoint in their career and begin seeking "significance" rather than "success." That has traditionally meant leaving a business career to start a new, ministry-based vocation, which many have done.[6] But Francis Chan raises a new question: will the coming generation leave the "success" of their ministries for a different path far earlier than traditional patterns of career and retirement?

In the marketplace, there is evidence to support a new trend. Past generations saw people retiring at the company where they started. The "gold watch" given to employees for twenty-five years of service (or another seminal mark) was a norm. Now the times have changed in the business world. Study after study shows that younger generations are not only more likely to change employers but are also prone to entire career shifts, multiple times in life![7]

This doesn't happen only with people in their forties. Pastors in their fifties are also opting to retire from parish ministry and move into another ministry field, such as to a seminary, denominational post, parachurch role, or ministry they start to further something they're passionate about. Some are voluntary, as in the case of Francis Chan. Others do so under pressure.

Todd Nighswonger has heard many pastors raise such questions, saying that they too have thought and prayed about departing their own churches. "It's happened quite a bit—moments of pastors pulling me aside," he said. "They love their congregations, but want advice on how to make as loving a transition as possible."

> **Will more pastors who start young and experience growth then resign and move to other challenges?**

Pros for Staying Long

The benefits of staying a long time in one church are many. They include:

- **Growth.** While longevity doesn't guarantee growth, growth very rarely happens without a long-term leader.
- **Effectiveness.** The pastor's greatest effectiveness often occurs after about year seven, but a large number of pastors stay fewer than seven years. Some denominations reassign people every few years, but that is changing. More and more are open to allowing pastors to stay an additional term if they see a good match with fruitfulness.
- **Long-term discipleship.** Some of the best discipleship occurs when you can influence someone across many stages in life, from spiritual infancy toward spiritual maturity, from physical childhood into adulthood.
- **Addressing deep issues.** Dealing with deep-seated issues in a spiritual community requires time and trust that can take years to develop. The same is true about being a catalyst for community change as you develop deep credibility through long-standing relationships.
- **Long-term change.** Changing the culture of a church usually takes a long time for it to hold and then thrive.

Cons for Staying Long

But problems can also arise from staying in one place too long. Many of these can be overcome, but not always. They include:

- **Irreversibly graying congregation.** Most churches age with their pastor, the average age in a congregation being about five years younger than their senior pastor's age. Staying too long can leave the congregation with a median age that is too old to effectively welcome younger generations. This situation also makes it more difficult to woo a new, younger successor. There is nothing inherently wrong with a graying congregation—as long as it is a healthy congregation. A church can be made up of many older adults and still be dynamic and growing. In fact, in some communities pastors (whether the new pastor or the former pastor) need to have a vision and passion to reach the fifty-plus crowd, because those are the demographics of that particular area.

- **Calcification.** As the pace of change accelerates in today's world—a rate certain to continue accelerating—churches must fiercely protect their agility. Churches whose methods cannot change with the times will become less relevant. With a long-term pastorate comes stability, but stability unguarded becomes calcification. The culture of the church can stiffen, lessen the ability to change, become inwardly focused, and lose any missional momentum that was prevalent early in the senior pastor's tenure.

- **Habituation or lost effectiveness.** Human tendency is that the longer we are used to something, the harder it is on us when that thing is no longer available—even when it no longer works as well. The same familiarity factor happens with churches and pastors. A long tenure may lead to much fruit. Or it can create a church that is habituated to one style of preaching, one approach to ministry, and one personality of leadership—but with little fruit. A spin-off problem is that the church becomes so accustomed to its beloved preacher that the next pastor is set up for failure from the beginning.

Average Tenure of US Protestant Senior Pastors

1 2 3 4 5 6 7 8

Eight years on average across denominations

7.7 years is the average length of time US Protestant senior pastors stay at their current church. The larger the attendance, the longer they are likely to stay.[8]

Reasons Pastors Move On

Pastors who resign early, introducing the need for the succession process, may or may not have the same motives as those that drove Francis Chan's decision. Many reasons for leaving "early" may be good and godly, while others are not as noble. The range may include:

Souls with a holy discontent who do not stay anywhere for long. They are restless and never quite at home, spiritually and otherwise, no matter where they serve. Some are troubled souls. Some are serial starters, like the apostle Paul. Those who look up to such pastors as mentors sometimes wrongly interpret their mentor's journey as a prescription for what all Christians should do.

Runners. For some, what they're running to is not as important as what they're running from. They don't like what they're becoming or what their church is becoming, and moving on is the only solution they can envision.

Burnout victims. Pastors sometimes do a great job taking a church to a new level, transforming a church or relocating a church, only to find that they are burned out and ready either to take a break from ministry or move to a new pastorate.

Pastors who change. People change, and sometimes churches don't change with them. There are a myriad of stories about pastors who went to a church conference, sensed a renewed call to evangelism or to a new form of outreach, and went home only to find that their church wasn't interested in making that same commitment.

Pastors who thrive better at planting than maintaining. Some pastors are wired for entrepreneurial settings, but with each passing year find the church to be more established and cumbersome. So they also find their joy and effectiveness decreasing with each passing year.

Leaders with a mismatched call. Many pastors realize that ministry is different from what they thought it would be like. They discover that their calling is a better match if they serve in other forms of Christian ministry. Others leave the nonprofit world and find marketplace positions designed to influence society, such as in politics or in Hollywood.

Pastors who are outgrown by their congregation. Sometimes pastors lead a church to grow, only to realize that the new pastoral role required in a larger church is not a good match for their heart, spirit, and gifts. They decide to relocate for the good of the church. This is not necessarily a bad or unwise decision. Over time most leaders come to understand their personal "church size capacity." Sometimes described as the "Peter Principle," this means that people rise or get promoted to or beyond the limit of their adaptive competence.[9] When leaders take a church to the maximum of their ability, then it's usually best for the church, the leader, and the kingdom of God to relocate to another church to start the growth cycle over again.

Pastors who shift to a new ministry paradigm and depart to avoid causing division in their churches. One example would be a pastor who serves at a church built on a come-and-see, attractional model but later comes to embrace a distinctly different go-and-serve model. Another example is a pastor serving an affluent suburban congregation who becomes newly burdened to serve the urban poor but realizes it cannot happen without severe disruption and change in that congregation.

Pastors with private family issues. Sometimes the pastoral family faces such a significant medical or moral challenge—anything from mental illness to pregnancy out of wedlock—that they deem it better not to reveal their situation to the congregation. Instead the pastor resigns and moves on.

Pastors with a lack of self-awareness. This happens when pastors simply don't grasp why things aren't working out. So they resign, transferring the same problems to their next post. Sometimes a similar lack of awareness on the church's part means it cannot discern the situation either. Ironically, people today have often trained themselves to assess business situations in a healthier way than the spiritual and emotional issues surrounding a pastor's leaving.

Should You Stay after You Resign?

One of the most widely proclaimed pieces of advice is that the outgoing pastor needs to get out of the way, at least for a season. For most that means moving away geographically. Some denominations even require it. For example, many presbyteries (the local governing body) in the Presbyterian Church (USA) require a period of time away—often a year—for the outgoing pastor.[10] Others may continue to live locally but will intentionally try to stay away for a season by lining up speaking engagements, travel, or other ministry on Sundays.

> Outgoing pastors who continue to hang around usually remain much more in charge than they realize. Their stature and shadow can remain immense.

The most widely cited reasons for this strategy relate to control and influence. Outgoing pastors who continue to hang around usually remain much more in charge than they realize. They may have changed titles and may even have handed a symbolic baton at a transition ceremony at church, but their stature and shadow can remain immense. Even their nonverbal messages—what programs they attend, how long they applaud, whether they frown or smile—can carry great clout. Their spouse's behaviors can have the same influence. The net effect is that the successor pastor too often doesn't have adequate latitude, space, or sometimes authority to frame direction and build loyalties with the congregation.

However, in many good exceptions it has proved both helpful and fruitful for the outgoing pastor to stay. They often have goodwill in the community, they can make the "ask" of certain church members who have deep financial pockets, they know where the bodies are buried from earlier friction points in the church, and they usually have high-trust relationships with older and longer-term members.

Which pathway should you take, if you have the choice? Here are five short stories showing how different outcomes developed.

Christ Church—honoring the past unlocks the future. Dan Meyer, thirty-eight, became the new pastor of Christ Church of Oak Brook, Illinois, in April 1997, arriving from a church in San Diego. Only two months earlier, his predecessor, Arthur DeKruyter, had preached his last sermon at that church, retiring at age seventy after thirty-two years at the helm. The plan was for Art to retain his home down the street from the church building and attend worship six or more months a year, "snowbirding" the remaining months in Florida. Other DeKruyter family members also planned to stay at the church, some of them in active lay leadership roles.

With no interim period, how was Dan to navigate, especially with his predecessor's memory and shadow so close? "My experience is that you never go wrong honoring your predecessor," Dan says today, looking back on the transition. "If the predecessor's family is going to be around, the new pastor is also making a huge mistake not to cultivate that relationship."

Overall, the experience at Christ Church was positive. "It was wonderful for the congregation, as folks felt like this great man, who had been such a cherished part of the church's life, had not been banished or forgotten. Affirming his presence and legacy warmed the congregation and helped them accept me. Without Art's gravitas, affirming the right for new leadership to make changes, it might have been a lot harder to implement needed innovations when people were feeling anxious about them."

Dan also appreciated the private advice he got from his predecessor. "Like the book *The President's Club* points out, those who have sat before you in the head seat have a unique knowledge base, understanding the back stories to many issues," Dan said.

Both Art and Dan experienced some downsides as well. Inevitably, some people went to Art with concerns about the new era. "He was enormously gracious and affirmative of the need for new measures, but there were times when I think it was emotionally difficult for him to cope with the discontent of people he had shepherded over the years," Dan said.

The other big downside was preventable. "There came a time when he and I lost touch," Dan said. "I allowed too much distance to get between our occasional meetings and that led to some mistrust of one another's judgment or motives. Eventually we talked together and smoothed things through. I think we would have done better, however, if we had established at the start a third party whose purpose was to call us together if or when potential problems arose."

One of the biggest boosts Dan received in the transition was the commitment of the search team to the new pastor. "They were all deep and long friends of Art DeKruyter, but they transferred their loyalty and commitment to the new pastor," he said. And they didn't quit after Dan arrived. "They refused to give up on me in the early hard years. They had such credibility with the congregation at large that they could reassure people who were on the bubble about the transition. They were steadfast in saying to disgruntled folks that changes are needed, and that they believe God's hand is on this transition every step of the way. They did this publicly and privately. They never blinked. It was a major factor in our eventual success in passing the baton to a new generation."

Life Center—long overlaps can work. Fulton Buntain began ministry as a traveling Assemblies of God evangelist. He then became a pastor, coming to his third church, an Assemblies of God congregation in Tacoma, Washington, in 1965. Under his leadership, the congregation grew significantly in size and influence. He retired from Life Center, as it's known today, in 2005 at the age of eighty.

One of the thousands of people impacted over the years by the church's ministry was Dean Curry, whose parents were "radically changed by Jesus," as he describes it. This became Dean's first church. After college the church hired him to be the junior high pastor. At the time, Dean was twenty-two and Fulton was sixty-five. "Fulton invested in me. I got to take him to the airport and run errands with him," he said.

At twenty-nine, Dean became associate pastor. "I remained Fulton's sidekick until he retired at age eighty," he said. "He was my spiritual father, the greatest man I've ever known. In many ways he *was* my father, since my parents divorced when my mom was pregnant and I didn't even meet my biological dad until I was in my twenties."

Fulton never spoke of his future retirement until almost the moment he retired. "One day he called me into his office," Dean said. "He was seventy-nine at the time. He said, 'Hey, on Tuesday I'm going to tell the board that I'm going to retire.' But then he didn't raise the subject again, nor did the board for many months."

The board decided they wanted to interview many potential candidates, mostly former associate pastors. After a very confusing season that ultimately required denominational intervention, the congregation voted, and Dean Curry was installed as the new senior pastor.

"Through the turmoil the culture of honoring the pastor had been lost, and I wanted to reclaim it," Dean said. "I decided that we couldn't reach our city if we didn't have peace at home."

So Dean decided he would build a culture of honor there at Life Center. He insisted that Fulton stay in the same office. Six months later Fulton said, "You're the senior pastor so you need to be in this office"—but Dean then built Fulton a new office, which Dean intentionally made to be bigger than his own. Dean also invited Fulton to every board and staff meeting. He regularly honored Mrs. Buntain as well.

The congregation loved it. "Our income went up right away; our big givers gave even more. Fulton even helped me with fund-raising—and his presence raised thousands more." Dean heard more than once that some people who give financial gifts said they did so "because of him, not me."

Dean admits that it was not always easy having his predecessor around. "People went to Fulton and complained of various changes, and even he complained to me about them—but he supported me in front of others," Dean said.

When Fulton died at the seven-year mark of Dean's tenure, he still didn't always feel like the senior pastor. "I had three different people say, 'Would you pray for me? My pastor has died.'" Dean sincerely replied, "So has mine. I lost him too. He was a dad to me as well."

"I decided that love would win out," Dean said, looking back. From all evidences, it has. The church's growth has continued in attendance, conversions, and new ministries. "We're going to reach this city. This is Jesus's church, but he's given it to me for the next season."

Hillside—planning, passing the baton, and staying away often works. "After the transition was complete, I moved off the scene and stayed off the scene," said Dave Burns, referring to his role in the succession process after serving thirty-two years as founding pastor at Hillside Community Church, Alta Loma, California. The church is from the American Baptist tradition, where the pastor does not choose or recommend his successor. However, Dave was intensely involved with many of the processes that resulted in the final selection. He worked with the church's administrative board, staff, a search team he handpicked, and a search firm (Vanderbloemen) who together set up a process. "The groups were to be involved almost equally," Dave said. "As all these pieces worked well together, the church would have something significant."

One goal of the process was to avoid an intentional interim, if possible. "Such a person doesn't know the church, and so basically becomes pulpit supply handicapped in a neutral zone of not being able to do much of anything," Dave said. Another goal was to find someone with the potential to have a long run like Dave did, which meant the candidate would be much younger. Dave gave input on the lists of potential candidates, but when candidates came in, he stayed out of the interviews and the congregational meetings. The candidate they ultimately called, Aaron McRae, is twenty-seven years younger than Dave.

The envisioned timeline was two years, but the process took only one. During that year Dave pulled back in his preaching, with more of the sermons coming from a combination of staff pastors, young adults, and outside guests. Dave was usually there for announcements and to chat with people in the lobby. Some said, "He's checking out," but Dave could handle it. "I knew that when going through a transition like this, I would take some heat," he commented.

More important, he worked hard during that year to paint a picture of God's faithfulness in the past and to affirm that the church's best days were yet ahead. "I also headed off the power seekers who want to chart a new course," he said. And after Aaron came, Dave encouraged the creation of a mentoring structure so that Aaron could avail of the wisdom of the church's more mature leaders. And Dave validated him in front of the congregation, repeatedly saying in effect, "Here's why I would be excited if I were you."

Bethany—multigenerational pastorates within a family can sometimes bring stability. Roy Stockstill, an experienced pastor, began a new church in his Baton Rouge living room with a handful of people. Bethany Church took root and grew. Twenty years later, ready to retire at sixty-five, Roy reached out to his son, a missionary in Africa, as a potential successor. Larry Stockstill became the pastor and continued to grow the church with his dad sitting on the front row. He also led it to be multisite and to birth hundreds of cell groups. At one point the church's School of Leaders was training about five hundred new cell leaders per year.

Twenty-eight years later Larry, fifty-eight, passed the leadership mantle to his son Jonathan, age thirty-one.

The transition did not come easily for Jonathan, who was also a musician. "I wanted to plant a church, I wanted to continue doing music, and I had a record deal," he said. But that changed the day he was in his car and sensed a strong call from God. "I was exiting a certain spot on the interstate. I heard a clear word in my heart: 'Jonathan, I want you to pastor this church.' The courage and peace I needed came with it."

Jonathan's father now travels full-time, planting churches overseas. "Our entire mission budget is channeled through Dad's direction, through the organization named Surge," Jonathan explained. Larry also preaches every two months. "When he's not traveling, he'll sit on the front row, and Grandpa attends one of our campuses," he said. "Dad truly let go. Dad makes no decisions; he doesn't attend any board meetings," Jonathan said. Additionally, all of Jonathan's siblings—four brothers and a sister—are involved with the church. "It's what we knew in our entire life growing up."

"The benefit of all this family continuity is that the church community sees stability," Jonathan said. Indeed, these seamless family transitions have no doubt also helped the church's amazing growth trajectory to continue across three generations.

CityLife—finding and celebrating the distinct role of each outgoing pastor. Mark Conner is the third pastor of CityLife Church, a multisite, multicultural congregation in Melbourne, Australia, with over five thousand weekly attenders across its five current locations. Mark's book, *Pass the Baton*, describes the unique contribution of each pastor since the church's founding in 1967.[11] As one longtime member described it: "Richard [the first pastor] was the founder and gatherer; Kevin [the second pastor] was the builder and establisher; and Mark [the third pastor] is the entrepreneur and extender."[12]

Each outgoing pastor stayed at the church, took on a "grandfather" role, and remained busy, making active contributions both to CityLife and to the greater Body of Christ. Mark hopes to do the same at his eventual succession. Pointing out that some of God's promises to Abraham came true in Abraham's lifetime but others not until generations to follow, Mark draws application to a church's succession of pastors: "In the same way, God . . . wants us to play an important role in imparting his purpose and destiny into those who are coming after us."[13]

The Unspoken Stumbling Block: Problems When Spouses or Family Members Stay

During the more than one hundred interviews we conducted for this book, we heard a number of stories about pastors who transitioned from a church, perhaps to teach at a nearby seminary or even to retire, but whose spouse or other close relatives stayed behind, remaining in key positions at the church. In virtually every instance, it did not go well, but no one wanted us to put their story in print!

Leadership Journal published a true story of such a situation, though it was told anonymously. The writer said his first years as senior pastor felt like a perfect transition. He had been on the church's staff, and at the senior pastor's retirement he was called to become the new senior pastor. In his opening months he observed that certain members of the outgoing pastor's family felt they had a "sort of *carte blanche* in exerting control in the church" due to their relationship with the outgoing pastor. The former pastor's wife "was particularly challenging," according to the writer. "From day one, she saw my appointment as a threat to the status and control the 'first family' had enjoyed. Teaming up with the former first lady was her influential and successful son-in-law," a key deacon in the church. "He believed his status, prominence, and influence as a deacon was threatened by my new role."[14]

At first, the new pastor ignored the opposition, thinking it to be insignificant. After all, his relationship with the congregation had started out well. But he was naïve. Friction grew, exacerbated by several factors, including the former pastor's undefined role as pastor emeritus. The only named privilege of the role was to vote at elder board meetings when he was around, which he did in ways that made his successor feel unsupported.

By year five, the former pastor's wife would routinely leave the sanctuary when the successor pastor began his sermon. Congregants who supported the former pastor and his wife, including some key leaders, witnessed this behavior week after week but made no attempt to confront her.

The new pastor announced his intention to move on at the end of the year, but he was asked to leave before that. Why? The author's conclusion is that the warning signs were there, but he had failed to heed them. The new pastor had failed to honor the "queen" and "prince," and ultimately got fired.

Essentials If You Do Stay in the Church

Clearly some pastors do stay after stepping down. As the previous stories illustrate, for your presence to be positive if you do remain, you will probably need:

Agreement. Establish clear rules of engagement with your successor—what you will do, what you will ask permission to do, and what you will not do unless specifically asked to. One "must" is for you to both agree that you will contribute to a culture of mutually honoring each other.

Check-in. Meet together at least quarterly with your successor to strengthen your relationship and review or revise the rules you've agreed on. Be sure to ask not just about your own practices but also whether those of your spouse are causing any concern.

Specific niche. Have a defined ministry that you look forward to engaging in each week. Same for your spouse. It cannot be something general like "helping out at church wherever I see a need."

Write it down. The old saying "good paper makes good friends" applies well to pastoral succession. If you decide to stick around, having clearly defined guidelines for your role, written and signed by you and your board, will help memorialize the intent of your role in years to come. Like most contracts, the hope is that you will never need to refer to the document. But good contracts are written by friends who set boundaries for times when boundaries become hazy, circumstances unexpectedly change, or friendships are not functioning at optimal levels.

Have a long, clarifying talk with your spouse and family. If there is any one "hidden" key to the success or failure of pastoral succession that we have found, it's the essential role of the outgoing pastor's extended family. Having a serious, intentional talk with your family members before your transition is essential. It should cover their roles, their need to step out of the way, their need to support the new pastor, and any financial implications for life after you're no longer the senior pastor.

The business world is seeing a clear trend of younger people changing careers. This will also begin to be a new norm in the church world. Few pastors have anticipated this change, but the smartest ones will take the initiative to address the potential transition issues mentioned in this chapter—before they ever become issues.

 N E X T Steps

For Pastors: Do you have an annual check-in with a group of friends or colleagues that includes a serious "gut check" about your current passion for your present pastorate? If not, how do you think you can initiate that practice?

For Boards: If you had to choose one of the following terms to describe your church, which would it be, *more agile* or *more calcifying*? What action, if any, is necessary to modify your church's culture?

6

Four Church Cultures, Four Succession Styles

Plus One Cardinal Rule of Pastoral Succession

If you've been in or around church work for any period of time, you've probably decided there are a whole lot of different ways to do weddings but not one "right" way. Some ceremonies are black tie. Others are denim. Some use a unity candle. Some serve communion. But in the end, you really need only rings and vows (and sometimes just vows) to get the proverbial knot tied. Everything else is determined by context.

Similarly, in pastoral succession, no single model dominates. One successful succession model doesn't fit all churches.

Many churches we studied have fallen into the trap of cloning another church's succession model that "worked." Unfortunately, this one-size-fits-all approach often fails. Every church is unique, every succession scenario has its own complexities, and one plan doesn't fit all. As we've said before (and quite intentionally repeat here), pastoral succession is much more art than science. There is no single formula a church can plug and play for a guaranteed outcome.

In fact, the one cardinal rule for pastoral succession is that there is no cardinal rule for pastoral succession.

That being said, certain predictions can be made about how succession will work best at your church. In March 2013, the nonprofit company Leadership Network hosted an online video conference on succession planning. It was the first conference of its kind, so nobody knew what kind of attendance level or interest would arise. The conference contained some of our preliminary research, but more important, it demonstrated that there's a whole lot more interest out there than we ever imagined. The team at Leadership Network hoped for an attendance of one thousand. Instead, over 2,500 attended, making it Leadership Network's most successful focused online event to date. That popularity caused it to be rebroadcast, with similar strong viewership.

Among the most intriguing speakers was the nonprofit's CEO, Dave Travis, whose definition of "pastoral succession" we offered in the preface (page 10): *the intentional process of the transfer of leadership, power, and authority from one directional leader to another.* Dave also referenced a helpful model of viewing succession, where every congregation is classified as one of four different leadership styles. His model looks at how the church actually works rather than at the idealized state of where a church would like to be. To uncover the system of how things get done, he looks at power structures, asking: who holds the decision-making power for major decisions? That then determines how the culture makes decisions and expects decisions to be made.

According to Dave, each succession style (or model) is based on how the church's culture best matches two leadership issues depicted in the following figure:

- Left to right (x axis) looks at the level of a church's programming that directly involves the church's senior leadership. This moves from complex (left) to apparent simplicity (right), depending on how the church's programs are structured and supervised.
- Top to bottom (y axis) explores the location of power and decision making. This moves from group-based (top) to individual-based (bottom), depending on the level of teams, boards, committees, and systems that must work together to keep the church moving forward.

Every church can fit somewhere on this spectrum. Churches in each quadrant tend to handle decisions around succession in dramatically different ways. Understanding those differences can help lead pastors, church boards, and other decision makers understand and develop succession pathways for their unique situations.

Senior Pastor as Key Administrator

Old habits die hard. That's the story of succession at First Baptist Church, Orlando, Florida.

When Jim Henry became pastor of First Baptist in 1978, one of the hats he took on was that of chief administrator. He says the church was led by a "type of executive committee made up of laity who led or served in various facets of the church's ministry. They met on a monthly basis for reports and recommendations."[1] Over the years, as

Four Church Leader Cultures

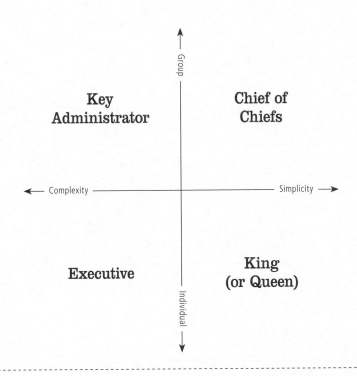

the church grew and became more organizationally complex, he led it to move to "a more pastor-led style, with heavy input from laity on major issues, with day-to-day matters left to the pastors."[2] In the newer approach, the church conducts congregational votes only "on calling of ordained pastors, budget, financial matters that pertain to borrowing over $500,000, and major building programs."[3]

Yet twenty-eight years later, when he resigned and moved into various semi-retirement ministries, he was not the one to choose his successor. Instead, consistent with widespread Southern Baptist pattern, a lay-led search team found the next pastor, and then the congregation voted on him. Jim had been an outstanding preacher and a strong leader who shepherded the church to significant and unprecedented growth, to relocate, and to construct several major buildings. But the congregation didn't treat him as a king when it came to succession; that power remained in a group (a deacon-commissioned search team to initiate the contact, interview, and recommend) and in the congregation (to vote). Thus in keeping with the figure above, this succession model blends organizational complexity with group-based decision making.

The successor, David Uth, came on staff as co-pastor during Jim Henry's final months. His first contact with the church had been through a phone call from a member of the search team.[4] He remains senior pastor to this day.

Senior Pastor as Executive

Chapter 5 told the story of Dave Burns, Hillside Community Church, Alta Loma, California. Although he had been there thirty-two years, the power resided with the elders to identify and call the next pastor. The Vanderbloemen Search Group conducted the search for his replacement and saw the model at work firsthand. Dave was not present for many of the meetings, the laity ran the process smoothly, and thus far the succession has been a good one. Dave's experience fits the "Executive" quadrant of the figure above with high complexity in the amount of the church's programming that directly involves the church's senior leadership and more individual than group orientation in terms of the level of teams, boards, committees, and systems that must work together to keep the church moving forward.

Almost all the seeker churches fit here, especially those that are now "second generation"—led not by the founding pastor but by someone who has followed that person.

Senior Pastor as Chief of Chiefs

Chapter 4 told of Tim Lundy's personal decision-making process as he decided to leave Fellowship Bible Church, Little Rock, Arkansas, where he served for eight years, and to accept a call at another church. Fellowship Bible's model was to have a directional leader as head of a three-pastor leadership team. Tim's predecessor at Fellowship Bible, Robert Lewis, had also been directional leader with a different senior team of two other pastors. Tim's successor is Mark Henry, who also leads a trio of pastors.

In this model, power is in a small group of chiefs where each one runs not only an area of the church but has prominence over other pastors and staff. In churches like this, including Fellowship Bible, the board often plays a prominent role. Many times a number of staff are elders. It is common in churches that match this model for almost half the governing board to be staff. Thus in keeping with the figure above, this succession model blends programmatic simplicity with group-based decision making.

Senior Pastor as Head of "Royal Household"

At age fifty-seven, Billy Joe Daugherty unexpectedly died. He had served as founding pastor of Victory Christian Center, Tulsa, Oklahoma. He was also the founder of

Victory Christian School, Victory Bible Institute, and Victory World Missions Training Center. Almost one thousand Victory Bible Institutes had been started in more than ninety countries around the world. He had hosted a daily radio and television broadcast, and he had coauthored several books. He also oversaw the Tulsa Dream Center, which provides food and clothing, and medical, educational, and recreational services to people in need. He had been diagnosed with a strand of leukemia one year before he passed. The strand transformed into lymphoma B cancer in September 2009, and he passed away on November 22, 2009.

One month later Billy Joe's widow, Sharon Daugherty, was elected president of the Victory Christian Center Corporation. This meant that, in addition to pastoring the large and influential church, she would oversee all of its other ministries. Previously she had played a very active role in the ministry, serving as co-pastor with Billy Joe.

The Daughertys have two daughters and two sons. All four children, along with their spouses, stepped up in the first year after their father died, each shouldering key administrative and pastoral responsibilities for their mother. Many continue to serve with her to this day.[5]

The model they represent is closest to that of a family business or "royal court," where it is expected that spouses and children will be the next to take over.

Sometimes the transition is gradual in family-led churches. Keith Butler founded Word of Faith International Christian Center in Southfield, Michigan, developing it into one of Detroit's leading churches. He and his wife, Deborah, have three adult children, all of whom are involved in the church—two as ministers and the other as an attorney.

In 2010, his son Andre, thirty-five at the time, was installed as senior pastor of the church, having served previously as pastor of one of the church's satellite campuses in another state. Keith devotes the majority of his time to out-of-state church planting and overseas missions.

Yet even though Andre has the title, his shift to everything the senior pastor role involves is partial, signifying a step-by-step transition. As of this writing, Andre's office is far smaller than his father's, the church website has a longer profile for the father than the son, and his father still oversees the overall money flow of the church. Andre is developing in his role as senior leader, but is clearly doing so under his father's oversight. In many similar churches, this is a helpful way for a rising generation to learn the ropes and develop their abilities.[6]

But more important than family succession in this model is the idea that the "king's and queen's" blessing is paramount for the next person to succeed. This is clearly seen in Keith and Deborah Butler's paving the way for their son Andre. But it doesn't have to occur within a family.

A non-family example is J. Don George, who was the longtime pastor at Calvary Church, an Assemblies of God congregation in Irvine, Texas. In 2010 he passed the leadership mantle to a young protégé, Ben Dailey, to whom he is not related in any way. The two are thirty-six years apart in age, and J. Don legitimated numerous changes Ben asked to make. Ben's first change was to ask if J. Don's longtime administrative assistant, who was the wife of a prominent board member, could move on. His second change was to dramatically change the worship style. By the end of Ben's first year a third of the staff was new, most close to Ben's age, representing a very different operation style than J. Don's. Yet because the outgoing pastor blessed all those changes, Ben remains as pastor—and to both pastors' delight the church has grown significantly since the pastoral transition.[7]

There are more "kingly" successions than you might think. Many are illustrations in this book, including high-visibility ones like Roy (grandfather), Larry (father), and Jonathan (son) Stockstill in chapter 5; John (father) and Joel (son) Osteen in chapter 8; and Robert H. (father) and Robert A. (son) Schuller in chapter 9. In fact, much like small businesses, family systems abound where a relative is assumed to be the hands-down first choice among any potential candidates.

Culture Trumps Vision

This model recognizes all the styles and quadrants as valid. Biblical justification can be found for all of them. Each is ideal for some organizations and some cultures. But not all will work with equal smoothness in your church.

Sam Chand believes that culture—not vision or strategy—is the most powerful factor in any organization. The heart of his insightful book, *Cracking Your Church's Culture Code*, is the oft-repeated line, "Culture trumps vision."[8] This idea applies to pastoral succession models as well. Just because you're attracted to a succession model in one church doesn't mean it will transfer well to another setting. A church's culture of where power is located and how leadership decisions are made commonly trumps an imported model that doesn't fit the existing culture.

Another set of helpful succession models can be found in chapters 4–8 of *The Elephant in the Boardroom*.[9] These too help a church analyze its culture and predict which approaches fit best.

Sometimes the Church Culture and Succession Model Change

That said, church cultures do change. For example, Abundant Life Christian Fellowship, Palo Alto, California, experienced a traumatic moral failure with one of its senior leaders. As part of the healing process, the church's remaining leaders led an intentional shift to a different type of pastoral model. The church moved from a setting similar to "Royal Head of Household" to one more like "Senior Pastor as Executive." When the failure happened, and time came to replace the hole created by the dismissal of the previous pastor, the board made a bold move. Abundant Life had grown to around seven thousand in weekly attendance before the fall. Afterward, attendance fell to around four thousand. Rather than look for a new, magnetic personality to lead the church, the board decided to take charge and change the model. They engaged the Vanderbloemen Search Group to find a new senior teaching pastor who would be the primary pulpit voice for the church, while leaving governance matters to the board. The new teaching pastor has been in place for a few years now, and the church is growing again. The transition has been very well received thus far.

There is no one way to do a wedding, and there is no one way to do a succession plan. Just as weddings fall into categories and types, so do successions. We hope that by identifying these four models of leadership, pastors and boards can know themselves a bit better before undertaking the unique process of pastoral transition.

_____ N E X T Steps _____

For Pastors: Which of these four models would you most closely identify with? Are you grooming someone who is a natural extension of that model?

For Boards: Historically, which model of these four best reflects your church? As you consider a transition, is your church in need of another transition within that model, or is a change truly needed?

7

Founder's Syndrome

What It Is and Why It Matters

Cornelius "the Commodore" Vanderbilt was the richest man in the world at the time of his death in 1877. Born to poor parents, he borrowed $100 at age sixteen to buy a sailboat and start a ferry and freight business. Eventually his estate was worth an unprecedented $100 million.

Yet thirty years after his death, no member of Commodore Vanderbilt's family was among the richest people in the United States. Then sixty-four years later, when 120 of the Commodore's descendants gathered for a first-ever family reunion, there was not even one millionaire among them.[1]

In addition, during the Commodore's heyday, ten Vanderbilt mansions lined Fifth Avenue in New York City, each an example of epic extravagance. Yet these homes failed to become the family seats their builders had envisioned. The first was completed in 1883 but was demolished by the wrecker's ball in 1914. By 1947 all of these grand halls had been broken to rubble, their contents sold with the auctioneer's gavel.[2]

Is there a spiritual parallel for pastors who found great congregations and the sizable facilities they often build and occupy? Is there a danger that, after growing a high-impact, influential church, a pioneering leader's legacy will decline dramatically or even end? What can founding pastors do today to have the highest likelihood that their churches will continue after they depart?

The Amazing Role of Founding Pastors

Some of the nation's best-known pastors had the privilege of founding the church they lead. They include Rick Warren, T. D. Jakes, Bill Hybels, A. R. Bernard, Guillermo

Maldonado, Craig Groeschel, Mark Driscoll, Andy Stanley, Steven Furtick, Perry Noble, Stacy Spencer, Creflo Dollar, Jamal Harrison Bryant, and Matt Chandler. In fact, in *Outreach* magazine's 2013 list of "Top 100" churches by size, founding pastors lead 45 percent (see appendix 2).

Often successors who are spouses or children of founders also have the stature of a founding pastor. Among many, they include Joel Osteen, Sharon Daugherty, Judah Smith, Jonathan Stockstill, and Rudolf McKissick.

Sometimes a significant-growth pastor functions as a founder. Ginghamsburg United Methodist Church, Tipp City, Ohio, was founded in 1863. When Mike Slaughter came as pastor over one hundred years later, attendance had never broken one hundred. Today the church numbers in the thousands, and while some of that original core are still part of the church, Mike is the only pastor the vast majority of the membership has ever known. Likewise the various programs and ministries are ones that have been developed under his leadership and direction.

The same could be said of Wilfredo "Choco" de Jesus, Max Lucado, Eddie Long, Floyd Flake, Ronnie Floyd, John Jenkins, Lance Watson, Jeffrey Johnson, Paul and Debra Morton, Deforest "Buster" Soaries, Charles Blake, Lon Solomon, and a host of others. They each came to a small, faithful, established church and led it to significant growth.

Sometimes a long-term pastor functions like a founding pastor. This book highlights many who have served the same church for thirty, forty, and even fifty years. As their long tenure shapes the personality of the church they serve, they come to function much like a founding pastor, especially if they led the church through an era of significant growth. As a result, they too face the huge challenge of how to not lose momentum or vitality when they step aside and someone else follows them.

And any of these great leaders may be tempted to stay well past the peak of their ministry effectiveness, but eventually they will move on and someone will need to fill their shoes. As Dale Burke quipped when asked what it was like to fill the shoes of legendary pastor Chuck Swindoll (introduced in chapter 1): "He is a wise leader, and took his shoes with him."[3]

More Like a Divorce Than a Wedding?

Successions from first-generation leaders to second-generation leaders are the least likely to go well. In fact, too often they end up much more like a divorce than a wedding. While the succession from a founder to the next leader should be a culmination of a legacy and a celebration of a new union between new pastor and church (a wedding), the reality is that the

> Successions from first-generation leaders to second-generation leaders are the least likely to go well.

outgoing founder is often a bigger part of the problem than the solution. When that happens, too frequently little can be done to avoid the church divorcing either their legacy pastor or their new pastor.

Across this book we've tried to hit a balance in our illustrations with roughly half stories of failed succession and half of successions that worked well, all with a valuable lesson to learn. Regrettably, too many of the troubled successions involved transitions from founding pastors.

Long Pastorates Can Be the Best

Long pastorates are typically healthy for churches. As leading consultant Lyle Schaller says, "While there is no evidence that long pastorates produce church growth, rarely does a congregation experience long and sustained rapid growth without the benefit of a long pastorate."[4] Likewise, "Short pastorates tend to encourage peaks and valleys in the congregation's growth pattern. . . . From the congregation's perspective the most effective years of a pastorate rarely begin before the fourth or fifth or sixth or seventh, and sometimes even the eighth year of that pastorate."[5]

Every church leader can identify the measurements that matter most for their context. For some it's baptisms, others salvation decisions, others attendance, others small group participation, others missionaries supported, and for still others congregational involvement in the surrounding community—just to name a few. Most churches can readily identify whether those measures are still increasing, have peaked or plateaued, or are declining. If those measures decline for years on end, unchanged by prayer or new strategies, then the normal reaction might be for the pastor to ask if it's time to pass the leadership mantle to someone else.

In fact, such metrics are often one of the best conversation starters. If presented and discussed in a loving, affirming way—never meant to embarrass—these realities can often be the key to changing the leader's mind about when to pass the baton.

Why do founding and long-term pastors stay far too long even when the church's effectiveness is clearly in decline? Chapter 3 raised three important issues that are foundational to all successions and that give us their possible reasons.

- No clear picture of what success would look like in a succession
- No idea what might be the next personal step upon leaving
- Lacking a sound financial base to feel safe in leaving

Those reasons are often pivotal, but other reasons often factor in as well. Several other factors contribute to failed hand-offs from founder to successor. The ones especially applicable to founding or long-term pastors include:

Unwillingness to face the emotional sense of loss. Few observers can appreciate how difficult it is for some pastors even to imagine someone else taking their place. Almost by definition, pastorates are roles where people place their entire identity in their job. No other vocation we know is as all-consuming. When the time comes to let go and allow another to step in, many pastors feel they have lost their identity and that someone replacing them is "better" than they are. That's a really difficult transition for anyone.

For founding pastors the identity issue is often intensified. They gave birth to the church and helped it grow. The church often becomes an expression of their identity.

Hope that they can do it again. Football great Brett Favre was first introduced in chapter 4. His story reminds us that often our greatest strength, unguarded, is our greatest weakness. The gifts needed to lead (and especially to plant) a thriving church are uncommon. They include exceptional initiative, bold leadership, magnetic charisma, and, of course, great preaching. These are rare gifts. It's been said many times that the fear of public speaking is more prevalent than the fear of dying. Comedian Jerry Seinfeld made this reality famous when he noted that most people would rather be the subject of a funeral than the one preaching it! Pastors who hold these gifts are also used to winning. They almost always have an unusually high degree of confidence, which adds to their ability to create a "win." That strength, unguarded, often leads them to the conviction that no matter how far along they are in life, or no matter how far in decline the church has fallen, they have what it takes to turn things around and get "one more win."

Pastors with these gifts often hear a voice that whispers in their ears, telling them, "You've got one more season . . ." And just like Brett Favre's famed career, too often things don't end well. Most people remember Brett's failed retirement more than they do his storied achievements. Especially in the case of a strong charismatic leader, very few—if any—staff or board members have the courage and authority to broach the subject with the leader.

Sometimes pastors misidentify this blind spot, trying instead to reenergize their churches with a building project or other ministry initiative. Then to be honorable, they stay at the church to finish what they started, but in reality they only make the downward spiral worse.

Fear that all they've done will be lost under the next person. Whether a church is made up of fifty, five hundred, or five thousand people, after its visionary founding pastor or long-term pastor departs, is it usual that chaos, decline, or even collapse will follow? Is a decline inevitable in attendance, impact, and such vital signs as conversions or baptisms? It seems there is a graveyard miles long filled with church leaders bearing similar stories of fruitful, long-term pastorates being followed by a failed successor. Hopefully, many of the stories in this book will affirm that numerous churches have found a better path, and your church can as well.

Fear of the unknown. For many people, pastors included, sometimes the known (staying) holds less fear than the unknown (moving on). Sometimes boards or denominational leaders take what seems to be the safe route (not talking about it) than what they fear to be the harder route (asking to discuss a transition strategy). As mentioned earlier, many senior pastors do not have adequate retirement savings and can't afford to retire. They have no idea how to fund life when their church paycheck ends, so they let that fear keep them from making a change.

Waiting on the right potential successor. Founders often feel as though they should mentor an internal person to replace them. Feeling responsible, they hold on, waiting for that right person. More often than not, if you will ask for help to spot potential successors—both candidates already inside the church and those somewhere "out there" but not yet found—you are more likely to find a successor sooner.

Enjoyment of the comfort level they've achieved. Another word for this might be entitlement. In many long-term pastorates where the pastoral family is constantly honored through material comforts, the temptation is strong to stay and enjoy those many perks even if the church is producing smaller and smaller crops of spiritual fruit. Too frequently, after pastors have given the best years of their lives to their churches, often making huge sacrifices, many begin to coast for their few final years—perhaps until their children finish school, perhaps until retirement, and so on. Sometimes they even realize the church is not best served by their leadership, but they ride on the goodwill they've built, knowing that it's highly unlikely they'll find another place of service with the same levels of familiarity and perks. While few pastors will go on record with these feelings, they are common and a real hindrance to a successful pastoral transition.

Some Believe They Should Never Retire

Many pastors court church volunteers with the oft-used line, "There's no retiring in the Bible. You're never too old to serve." It turns out they are wrong, at least for some roles.

In the Old Testament, God established a mandatory retirement age for priests when they were to step aside from the senior role, either retiring or moving to a role where they assisted (Num. 8:23–26). The community was then to provide for and honor these retired servants (Num. 18:31; Deut. 14:27; 18:1–8).[6]

Why were priests given a mandatory retirement age? Because after a while, the weight of carrying the tabernacle became too much for them. That concept seems like a good metaphor for today: after a season, the weight of carrying the burdens, fears, hopes, and dreams of the people of God can become too much. The pastor cannot carry the church forward, and it's time to let someone else do so.

As the appendixes to this book indicate, seasons of church growth are much more common for pastors in their twenties, thirties, forties, and sometimes fifties than for pastors in their sixties, seventies, or eighties. (Yes, there are indeed a number of pastors in their eighties out there.) Steven Furtick saw phenomenal growth at Elevation Church in his late twenties and early thirties, as did Perry Noble at NewSpring Church, and many others.

But Ed Young Sr. is seventy-eight at this writing, still takes the stairs two at a time, and leads a growing church.

You typically need wise counsel and clear metrics to determine if you are the exception. From your fifth year onward in a church, we urge you to prayerfully review several hard questions on an annual basis.

- Have I stayed too long?
- Am I still the leader this ministry needs?
- Should my church have a mandatory retirement age?

The Research Says Too Many Stay Too Long

Perhaps the most painful reality is the research that says too many pastors stay too long. In fact, when we were brainstorming titles for this book, one leading option was *It's Time to Go!* But we figured that title might not fly off the bookshelves.

Clear Decline before Pastor Moves On

Average amount of time a pastor waited to step aside after the church hit its peak in attendance, based on study of America's 17 largest churches from 1967 (see appendix 3).

Research by Leadership Network.

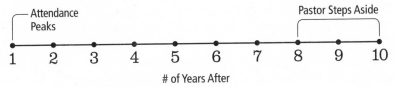

The Unique Challenge of Shifting from First- to Second-Generation Leadership

Phil Cooke, media consultant and author of *Unique: Telling Your Story in the Age of Brands and Social Media*, observes that too many people don't understand the incredibly important difference between first-generation leadership and second-generation leadership.

First-generation leaders are often Type A, make-it-happen people. Launching a new organization—whether it's a church, nonprofit ministry, or even a business—requires huge energy and passion. Phil observes that not only are first-generation leaders remarkably driven, creative, prolific, and specific, but they typically build a team around them that is great at execution. "The team tends not to be idea people, because they're not the idea generators; the leader is," he said.[7]

By contrast, the second-generation leader comes into an existing organization. The momentum has already happened and is hopefully continuing to happen. "As a result, second-generation leaders aren't driven by the same motives as the founder," Phil said. "Often they are more team-oriented and people-oriented." They're more collaborative and interactive. They like to exchange ideas with their team. They want players who help shape the vision.

The problem happens when first-generation leadership collides with second-generation leadership. "The difference can be dramatic," Phil said. Imagine a leadership team that for many years has been accustomed to their senior pastor saying "this is what I want" and "this is what needs to happen." Their job has been to put feet to those dreams. Now their new leader, a successor pastor, comes to the meeting and says, "I want your ideas about how we should do this." They are likely to mistake this openness for incompetence. In such cases, "It doesn't take long for a ministry to implode because that first-generation team can't get along with a second-generation leader," Phil said.

As a result, when a second-generation leader steps into a first-generation role, it's often best to bring a new team into that position, according to Phil. "Too often, a successor will use the previous leader's team, and that almost always results in failure," he said. "Every leader is different; all leaders need a team that complements their unique mix of gifts and talents. You usually cannot mix a second-generation leader with a first-generation leadership team and vice versa."

If the outgoing pastor does resign but does not actually let go, such as if the outgoing pastor lacks confidence that the new leader has adequate passion and drive,[8] Phil has a secret strategy for helping create space for the new leader to become established. "One of the most important techniques is *distraction*," he said. "I often will encourage a pastor or ministry leader to create a book (sometimes a major coffee table book) on his life and ministry—or the history of the church. That alone takes a year or two of focused attention. When that's finished, we schedule a preaching tour to promote the book. That's another year. This way, a new leader or successor has the breathing room to build a team, set in new policies, and begin work. So if you hire me and I suddenly suggest that you do a book on your life and ministry, you'll know what's coming!"

---------------- N E X T Steps ----------------

For Pastors: Succession following a long-term or founding pastor requires unusual amounts of humility from the outgoing (primarily) and incoming pastors. What are you doing to grow your gift of humility, and who can give you a candid assessment of how you come across?

For Boards: What provisions could be added to your church's bylaws to create both definition of a mandatory retirement age and an incentive to comply willingly? Clearly articulate the criteria for that mandatory retirement and any incentives you have in place, and then take them to your pastor for review and input.

Part 2

Be the Exception

8

Wisdom from Unlikely Sources

Transitions That Shouldn't Have Worked but Did

Some successions had incredible odds against them, and yet they seemed to have worked beautifully. To us, this is further evidence of how God works. Stories where God is at work seem to combine the supernatural, the amazing, and even the bizarre. Hollywood might find them too uneven to produce into a movie with clear plotline and full resolution. Yet God's pathways seem to delight in many surprises, all of which can bring him glory.

Stories like the five transitions we highlight in this chapter are clear reminders that God "is able to do immeasurably more than all we ask or imagine, according to his power that is at work within us, to him be glory in the church and in Christ Jesus" (Eph. 3:20–21).

After presenting these rather stunning case studies, we offer six tips of important principles to be observed.

Joel Osteen as a Most Unlikely Candidate

Lakewood Church in Houston, Texas, began quite humbly. And its first and only pastoral succession was uncertain. Yet from 2002 to 2012, Lakewood was the largest-attendance church in North America. To this day its television ministry reaches ten million households weekly, its sermon podcasts are consistently in the top ten ranking of all podcasts on iTunes, and its pastor has authored books that have sold millions, including five *New York Times* bestsellers. He also has one of the world's largest Twitter followings.

The church started after Pastor John Osteen received the baptism of the Holy Spirit and left his denomination that did not affirm his charismatic beliefs. In 1959 he started Lakewood Church in an old feed store on the poor east side of Houston. The church didn't grow past two hundred in attendance for its first dozen years. Yet over time, a caring atmosphere, quality leadership, and community outreach attracted people of all ages, religious backgrounds, races, and walks of life. The church outgrew its 234 seats. In 1972 it built a metal building adjacent to the feed store, seating 700. In 1979 it expanded the building to seat five thousand. In 1988 it opened a new campus nearby, seating 8,200, one of the largest sanctuaries in North America.[1]

In 1982, at the encouragement of his then nineteen-year-old son Joel, a freshman at Oral Roberts University, John started a television ministry. When Joel proposed it, his dad said, "That sounds good," Joel later recalled. "So we purchased the equipment and a year later we were on air."[2] The decision changed Lakewood—and the Osteen family—forever.

Joel left college at the end of his sophomore year to help his father launch the growing TV ministry nationally. For the next seventeen years, Joel produced his father's program, growing it into one of the world's most successful media ministries.[3]

Joel had opportunities to preach but turned them down. "For seventeen years, my father tried to get me up in front of people at his church. I said, 'Daddy, I am not a minister.' I couldn't even get up and make announcements," he said. Later, when he finally did take the platform, he indeed found it to be a challenge: "I was so nervous and I so dreaded doing it, I had to hold on to the podium because I felt like my hands would shake. My first thought was: *Why are all these people staring at me?*"[4]

In 1999 there was no succession plan when John was incapacitated from kidney failure. From his hospital bed, he asked Joel, then thirty-five and the youngest of his six children, to deliver the sermon for the coming Sunday. That would be Joel's first time to preach. At first, Joel did not want to do it, but afterward states he got a "gut" feeling he should. Six days later, his father had a heart attack and died. Joel reluctantly agreed to carry the ministry forward. As Joel stepped up, preaching finally found a home in his heart. Lakewood began to grow even further than his father had carried it.

Though Joel is the dominant preacher, and his wife, Victoria, is at his side as co-pastor, they are not alone. Joel's mother, Dodie, is on church staff, along with four of his siblings, plus most of their spouses and many other relatives.

In 2000 the church hired Cindi Cruse Ratcliff as director of music. That same year it went to two services. As growth continued it went to a third service. By 2002 attendance exceeded fifteen thousand adults and children. In 2002 Marcos Witt was named senior pastor of the Hispanic congregation, which by 2005 was drawing three thousand people to that fourth service. In 2004, Joel's first book, *Your Best Life Now,* launched, selling five million copies in the first three years (and Joel stopped taking salary from the church in 2005). In 2005 the church relocated to the Compaq Center, a converted sports arena in downtown Houston that could seat sixteen thousand.

Lakewood's explosive growth is something few could have predicted. The church's initial location was a terrible place to reach, with traffic jams and severe parking challenges. Joel had never preached before, and in fact turned down opportunities to do so. "I really never had a desire to be out in front of people and minister, even though my father tried to get me to do it many times. I'm naturally more quiet and reserved,"[5] he said, pointing out another contrast between him and his outgoing father. He shifted the direction of the ministry to be even more TV friendly and with a positive-emphasis-only theology. Joel made several shifts from his father's style, including shortening service length and intentionally preaching to a broader audience. Massive changes like this rarely work for the successor of a founding pastor, particularly one as well loved as John Osteen. The rarity of the success is only further compounded by John's death in office, a circumstance where most successions fail.

Yet Joel Osteen made headlines and history books. He demonstrates powerfully that sometimes even the unlikeliest candidates can become pastoral successors with amazing results. His favor in the city of Houston and the church at large is unprecedented. Despite Joel drawing critics from many corners, nearly everyone would agree that the transition from John Osteen to Joel Osteen as pastor of Lakewood has been nothing short of remarkable.

Successor Is Fifty-One Years Younger

It's somewhat amazing that Charles Jenkins is alive. The death threats he had received were not just idle words. One day he came out of his home to discover that all four of his tires had been slashed—not by vandals, but by disgruntled believers or church members who were upset that he would be their new pastor. Another time he and his wife were driving on a highway, felt an intense shaking, and pulled into a nearby mechanic shop to have the car inspected. Someone—likely another upset church member—had removed the lug bolts from one of the tires. Had the wheel flown off at highway speeds, the car certainly would have wrecked badly. "We could have died," Charles said.[6]

As Charles became the new pastor of Fellowship Missionary Baptist Church in Chicago, a historic and leading African-American congregation, he faced more than safety challenges. "I had all types of resistance. My character was challenged. My motives were challenged," he said. "As I anticipated encouragement and love, I got the exact opposite. There were nights when I came home and cried because of the opposition. Yet all I wanted to do was serve God."

Charles was just twenty-four years old when he followed a pastor who had been there fifty years and who had just retired at seventy-five. The man he followed, Clay Evans, had left an amazing footprint. He was a powerful preacher and leader who grew a great church, a civil rights leader during a turbulent era, and a pioneer in gospel music, leading the church to record twenty-two albums.

At seventy, he began asking the congregation to pray with him in his search for a successor. And when he spoke at various denominational conferences, he announced that he was looking for someone to take his place. Predictably, he was deluged with recommendations and applications.

Charles was still a student at Moody Bible Institute when the legendary pastor first heard of him. Charles, then twenty-one, had come to the church one afternoon, thinking that he was simply dropping off a proposal he had been asked to develop about youth ministry. To his surprise, he was ushered into a thirty-person leadership conference, where he was asked to present it. As Charles tells in his book, *Thriving in Change*, "At the moment I stood up, Rev. Evans later told me that the Spirit of God spoke clearly to him, 'That's your successor.'"[7]

For the next three years, Charles was groomed and trained to take over as senior pastor. "The first year, I was a sponge, listening to how he handled phone calls, learning from his interaction with various people, sitting in meetings, watching how he handled mail, even observing how we pay our bills. Largely, I was silent. Then in the second year, it became a gradual hand-off," he said.

Charles estimates that 75 to 80 percent of the congregation was seventy-five years or older, all looking to Pastor Evans for how they should feel about this new person who was still in Bible college. "Without him bestowing me with his mantle of credibility, they never would have given me a chance," he said.[8]

Although Charles may have said little, his heart and mind were spinning. During this preparation era he sensed that "for our church to reach our community, we had to make radical changes in strategy from the day I became pastor . . . We weren't going to be the relevant church God called us to be if we focused only on the elderly who currently sat in the pews."[9] So he met one-on-one with the forty established leaders in the church, affirming his love for them, seeking their counsel, asking them questions, and listening to their answers. He made allies of people who might have become adversaries. "To them, my willingness to listen earned the currency to make necessary changes," he said.[10]

Upon his installation, every part of the church was impacted by Charles's new leadership: structure, strategy, outreach, and staffing. He even shortened the worship service from its customary three to four hours to less than half that time. These widespread changes were a formula for potential disaster as a young leader took over from a venerated statesman leading a church with rich and established traditions.

Yet the church grew, including with young adults and young families. This called for more changes. Few came easily. For example, when it looked like the church needed a third worship service on Sunday morning, the only available time was when the adult Sunday school class met in the sanctuary. The class had about two hundred people, 90 percent senior citizens. This class was like an institution, having met there and at that time for forty years. Yet if these two hundred people could be flexible, they could make room for 1,500 others.

Charles first met with the staff and board. They affirmed that this was God's design for their church. He met next with the Sunday school superintendent and the head of Christian education. When they saw the need, they too became supporters. He then scheduled meetings with class teachers and small groups of influential people in their classes. As Charles explains in *Thriving in Change*:

> They didn't like it one bit, but in those conversations, they gradually realized the proposed move would help them accomplish their vision, which was to reach more people for Jesus Christ. That proved to be the key: helping them align their heartfelt desires to reach people with the vision for a third service. In these meetings, I shared my heart, and I used Scriptures. I explained how the proposed change would touch young people in our community, and I gave them some specific ideas for the continuation of their class. By the time I met with the whole class, I had already met with about half of them in these previous meetings, and they were vocal advocates for the move.[11]

When the move actually took place and the new service began, about twenty men and women refused to go to the place where their class now met. When Charles saw them sitting resentfully, he didn't get angry. He was well aware that the change had shaken up their world. "I sat next to each of them, one at a time. I put my arm around them and told them how much I loved them. We talked together, and I reaffirmed the need for the change and expressed my concern for their feelings."[12] Some still refused to go to the new room for their class, but the hostility lessened. Their friends who had made the move also ministered to them.

Over time the active but plateaued and aging congregation of two thousand has exploded with new life in Christ, new ministries to the city, new younger families, new younger leaders, and new momentum.[13] All point to a promising future, a new chapter for a legendary church. "We left cruise control and got the engines running again," Charles said. From every indication, the change of drivers has been a success.

Successor for Major Pulpit Had Never Been a Pastor

Houston's First Baptist Church replaced a larger-than-life, traditional pastor with someone who had never before been a pastor anywhere—and it worked.

John Bisagno had pastored the church for thirty years, then retired and became pastor emeritus in 2000 at age sixty-six. His successor, Gregg Matte, became the church's senior pastor at thirty-four. Under his leadership, the historic church founded in 1841 has moved to the cutting edge of ministry and experienced tremendous growth. But before coming to Houston in 2004, Gregg had never been a pastor. He didn't even own many neckties! He had founded Breakaway Ministries at Texas A&M University, growing it to what became the largest college Bible study in the nation. What started with twelve participants in his apartment grew to a weekly gathering of more than four thousand students each Tuesday night under his leadership.

The interim period between pastors was also an exceptional story. For four years, as the church looked for a permanent pastor, David Self, an associate pastor, provided leadership. Not only did the church continue to add new members and prosper financially during that time, but when the new pastor came, he asked David to remain on staff where he is the church's executive pastor today. Gregg has publicly stated that having David there was a real key to success. Plus John Bisagno and his wife, Uldine, continue as active members. In fact, Gregg occasionally asks his predecessor to deliver the sermon on Sundays when Gregg is out of town. Gregg refers to John as one of his biggest encouragers.

From No Succession Plan to Thriving Multisite Campus

Living Word Church in Pelham, Alabama, probably represents a lot of churches. A good man started it, reached people through it, ministered sacrificially, and along the way led them to acquire land and build facilities—in his case, including a 280-seat auditorium. He served as the church's only pastor for twenty-five years and abruptly died of a heart attack—without a succession plan. That left his widow and about forty members with some tough decisions.

Before his death, the pastor—who had envisioned a growing church—had talked with his wife about forming a partnership with Church of the Highlands, a fast-growing Birmingham church based about twenty miles away that had begun adding campuses around Birmingham. The widow called Highlands on behalf of her church, saying to Pastor Chris Hodges, "You can have everything if you don't sell it."

After the merger, Church of the Highlands took six weeks to renovate the building, expand parking, and add the technology for video teaching feeds. Highlands then sent a worship team to lead weekly services. Members who lived in the area were encouraged to attend that campus. At the four-year mark, Chris said it's their most successful campus. "One of the joining church's members told us that what has happened has been a fulfillment of their prayers for many years."

The story doesn't end there. The campus also hosts a Hispanic service, which now draws more than three hundred people weekly. It had been a small church meeting in a Pelham basement and was invited to join the new Highlands campus there. "We have the same vision, the same theology," Layne Schranz, associate pastor at Highlands, said. "We realized we could do more together."[14]

Changing Languages and Ethnicities

In the summer of 1979, Chicago's mayor offered job opportunities for the youth of Chicago. At age fourteen, Wilfredo "Choco" de Jesus applied, ready to clean streets. He was instead assigned to work at a little Spanish-speaking church in the very rough Humboldt Park area to help with a children's day camp. There he not only met Jesus but also his future wife—and her father, who was the pastor.

Choco remained active in the church, serving and being discipled. In 1992 he became an administrative assistant. Upon his father-in-law's retirement, he became the pastor at New Life Covenant, as it's known today.

Choco is a second-generation Puerto Rican who started a worship service in English, appealing to other second- and third-generation Hispanics, but also blacks, whites, and Asians in the changing neighborhood. The church today has two Spanish services and five English services. It has become the largest-attendance church in the Assemblies of God denomination, runs the nation's second-largest Dream Center (second in size only to the original Los Angeles Dream Center), and sponsors a wide array of social services designed to transform the community as well as the souls of its inhabitants for Jesus.

His father-in-law later said, "If I'd known it would go this well, I would have stepped aside sooner!"

Seven Surprises about Succession

After studying these five cases and hundreds more, we see patterns that are common surprises in succession planning. Much of the work of succession is counterintuitive, perhaps echoing God's assurance that his ways are not like our ways (Isa. 55:8–9).

Examining these patterns has led us to these surprises regarding succession planning.

God is in control and can transform even the most challenging situations into kingdom gain. Whether it's the death of a founder like John Osteen or the public moral failure of a national leader like Ted Haggard, God can birth a new era of healthy life for the congregation. What literally threatened death for Charles Jenkins changed to a life-giving new era for Fellowship Church.

Nearly everything rides on the back of the outgoing senior pastor. Exceptions are those senior pastors who ended poorly due to a scandal, conflict, or other significant breach of trust. But otherwise, if the outgoing pastor behaves well and appropriately supports the incoming pastor, almost any succession has the potential to work.

New pastors shouldn't dismiss the leadership and staff they inherited before taking a long look at them for the future. Gregg Matte could have followed conventional wisdom and replaced the existing interim leader. But his patience and testing of David Self as a ministry partner has led to uncommon success for the transition and the new chapter of ministry.

A perfect state is not required. You might think that successions work best when the church is healthy and things are going well. Perhaps, but successions have worked even in situations of catastrophe (extensive fire or hurricane damage), conflict, debt, and moral failure.

Succession might involve not calling a new senior pastor. In a number of examples, the succession process leads the church to consider a different sort of model for ministry, one where the role of the outgoing pastor is replaced with a new or modified role.

All successions are unique. If every church is unique, then all successions are unique. As much as we would like to write a singular blueprint that would solve all succession issues for all congregations, anyone who claims to know "the one plan" suitable for all succession probably doesn't know much about succession.

Bylaws about your incoming pastor should reflect qualities that your incoming pastor *must* have, not just your desires. The classic examples of this in searches are that (a) churches want a married pastor until they are reminded that Jesus and Paul were single, and (b) churches want a required level of college or postgraduate education until they are reminded that Steve Jobs and Bill Gates were dropouts, or that Jesus and many of the apostles didn't have a formal education. In his story above, we see that Charles Jenkins was only a student at Moody Bible when he was called, even though the bylaws required a seminary graduate.

After looking at the underbelly of many churches, we have been reminded of a clear truth: church staffs are all made up of people who need a Savior. Working with churches on succession day in and day out makes us more keenly aware than ever that the church is not staffed with superhumans; all people in the church, from followers to leaders, are broken sinners for whom Christ died. What God started, he will complete (Phil. 1:6). And no matter how dire your church situation seems, the ultimate Senior Pastor and Good Shepherd (John 10:14; 1 Pet. 5:4) has seen it coming and can see you through, not somehow but triumphantly.

NE X T Steps

For Pastors: Write down a list of your personal "ten commandments of being the outgoing pastor" (things you vow to never do or always do when it is your turn to be the previous pastor). Once written, share a copy with your spouse, close friends, and, ideally, a trusted board member.

For Boards: If you had to face a succession that required a different model of organization than your current one, what would the top three potential models be?

9

What Happened at the Crystal Cathedral and First Baptist Dallas

A Close Look at Two Failed Successions

Those who cannot remember the past are condemned to repeat it.

George Santayana, philosopher

Wise leaders in pastoral succession will learn from the past. Scripture is full of encouragement for God's people to learn from the models others have set. We're to observe both the wise leader and the fool (Prov. 3:35; 12:15), the sluggard and the disciplined (Prov. 24:30–34; 13:8), and those who prepare ahead and those who don't (Prov. 30:24–25; 6:6–8; 24:27). We're also to discern both the good and the bad from the examples of those who have gone before us (1 Cor. 10:6–11).

The graveyard of failed succession stories is miles long. Reversing the trend so that more transitions happen well begins with studying why that graveyard exists. Those entering pastoral succession planning would do well to learn from the past mistakes of other churches and leaders. There are singular events that may not apply to every church, but the more cases we studied, the more we saw patterns. And while singular anomalies aren't the best learning tools, there is power in learning from patterns.

The following stories are from two of the nation's most visible succession failures—good people seeking to follow God, yet something went severely sideways. We don't highlight them to gossip or to criticize. Any church can find itself in a similar mess. Instead, we try to go beyond the media sound bites with sources that help us understand the backstory of how each unfolded. Then we make observations about some of the principles and insights that seem to be at work across those stories, which represent patterns we have seen throughout our research.

Perhaps by learning from these heartbreaking endings, churches will avoid repeating history.

Crystal Cathedral Succession Plan Started Well, But . . .

On the surface, the Crystal Cathedral succession story seems simple. A young pastor named Robert H. Schuller launched a new church. With a growing congregation, a big vision, a television ministry that would eventually reach more than a hundred countries, and a rising reputation as one of America's most influential preachers and communicators, he built a landmark facility named the Crystal Cathedral, which he described as "the first church auditorium designed to be a television studio as well as the sanctuary of a worshipping congregation."[1] The ministry attracted thousands to its weekly worship services and to its spectacular Christmas and Easter productions. The church also developed a broad range of outreach ministries in the local area, including multi-language worship services, support groups for people facing a variety of challenges, and a K–12 school.

Over time the momentum slowed and financial challenges mounted. The pioneering televangelist eventually shared the leadership with son Robert A. Schuller and then with daughter Sheila Schuller Coleman. But financial contributions continued to decline and debts continued to mount, culminating in the church declaring bankruptcy, selling its property, and relocating a mile down the street. The church, renamed Shepherd's Grove in 2013 and under the leadership of the founder's grandson, Bobby Schuller (Robert V. Schuller), is now starting a fresh chapter and a new era.

What prompted such a dramatic reversal and severe financial collapse in one of the world's most recognized churches as the leadership baton passed from the founder to his offspring? How could the church that trained thousands of church leaders in successful church leadership take so many missteps itself?

Robert H. Schuller truly started the church from scratch. In 1955, armed with a $500 grant from his denomination, the Reformed Church in America, the twenty-eight-year-old church planter prayed, took out a napkin, and listed ten sites that might host his new ministry. He soon discovered that the first nine were already in use for other purposes. So he set his sights on the tenth: the Orange Drive-In Theatre.[2]

He decided to call the new congregation the Garden Grove Community Church. "I didn't think the name 'Reformed' would bring the unchurched people rushing in," Schuller later explained. He began preaching there from atop a snack stand with his wife, Arvella, playing a two-manual electronic organ that they pulled by trailer from their home every Sunday.

To attract people to his services, he canvassed the Garden Grove area, ringing over three thousand doorbells and inviting people to the new church by conducting a survey: Were they members of a local church? If not, why? What would they like to see in a church that would attract them to it? He used the information he acquired to develop the various programs his church offered to meet and fill human needs. He also placed advertisements in the newspapers with the slogan "Come as you are in the family car."

The next year, this entrepreneurial pastor outlined a plan for the church to grow to several thousand, generating enough revenue to support a staff of ten to twelve people. It was revolutionary, he said, because in those days mainline denominations planned only small churches—"no more than 200 members because that was all one pastor could accommodate."[3]

Schuller's approach to ministry was unusual for its time. Not only did he grow a large church, but he created a model that many others adapted. As *Leadership Journal* noted, he was among the first in the modern era to:

- Call his denominational church a "community church," since he felt most seekers wouldn't understand or relate to a denominational label.
- Call a sermon a "message."
- Use a nontraditional setting for church worship—in his case, a drive-in movie theater.
- Conduct door-to-door research, asking, "Why don't you go to church?"
- Use marketing strategies to reach unchurched people.
- Train pastors in leadership through an annual pastors' conference (it began in 1969 and was eventually named the Robert H. Schuller Institute for Successful Church Leadership).
- Televise a weekly church service, the *Hour of Power*, starting in 1970 and not missing a week for decades.[4]

"I didn't know I was going to get criticism," he said of his innovations. "I thought I'd get pats on the back."[5]

His vision seemed boundless. The church was renamed the Crystal Cathedral in 1980 when it completed a sanctuary designed by Philip Johnson, America's dean of architecture. It featured over ten thousand panes of glass, 2,890 seats, and a Jumbotron. The cost was $20 million (over $60 million in today's dollars). Breathtaking Christmas and Easter pageants featured professional musicians, live donkeys and camels, and costumed flying angels.

The more popular and long-lived the *Hour of Power* was on television, the greater the percent of church attendees who were one-time guests—loyal viewers who were in town for vacation. By the late 1980s, church attendance had begun to decline, but the pioneer, now in his sixties, kept building, adding a $250 million Family Life Center. The 234-foot-high, $5.5 million Prayer Spire was completed in 1990. A $40 million Welcome Center and museum opened in 2003. The majority of these funds came from *Hour of Power* revenues.

Schuller faced criticism for spending freely on buildings, but this level of his trademark "possibility thinking" was integral to his message, summed up in an aphorism inscribed on a Welcome Center wall: "I'd rather attempt to do something great and fail, than attempt to do nothing and succeed!"

Announcing a Succession Plan

Over time the elder Robert began grooming his son, Robert, for an eventual leadership succession. The son began regular appearances on the *Hour of Power* in 1976. In 1980 he founded a branch campus of the Crystal Cathedral in San Juan Capistrano.

In 1996 a succession plan was formalized when the elder Robert, then sixty-nine, announced that son Robert would be his successor, and subsequently appointed him as co-pastor in 2000. During 2004 and 2005, with the father now in his late seventies, the two went on a national tour of fifty cities involving some twenty-five thousand donors. It was organized to introduce the future heir to the support base for *Hour of Power* and to ask those donors to support him. At each stop, the senior Robert introduced his son as successor, typically with a standing ovation. "With that the transition was well grounded," Robert A. observed.[6] Then with much fanfare Robert A. Schuller was installed as senior pastor on January 22, 2006.

The succession plan contained ambiguities about who really would be in charge. The elder Schuller insisted all along that he was not retiring. Instead he announced plans to continue to preach at the church, and he had also formulated a twenty-year plan designed to culminate as he preached at the Crystal Cathedral when he turned 100.[7]

Then in October 2008, less than three years after the elder Robert handed over his medallion necklace and senior pastor role to his son, the founder told his congregation that his son would no longer be the preacher of the church's weekly, long-running Christian television program, *Hour of Power*. Why? According to a church spokesman, "It was suggested that he [the son] rotate with other preachers and he was opposed to that."[8]

The younger Schuller was more blunt in his interpretation. He said that he resigned because he didn't want to be pastor in "name only . . . The *Hour of Power* owns the Crystal Cathedral, and the owners, in effect, evicted me." He also attributed sibling rivalry to the decision for him to stop being the *Hour of Power* preacher.[9]

According to analysis by *Church Executive* magazine, several family issues led to this turning point. In becoming senior pastor, son Robert outlined several goals, including, "[1] install an impartial board not paid by proceeds from the ministry, [2] rework the *Hour of Power* to attract a younger audience, trying different methods of worship to develop a more meaningful spiritual encounter, and [3] have public financial transparency. This process would install a level of accountability. As of now the leadership is accountable to no one."[10]

Unfortunately, these goals became a family challenge because all five of Robert and Arvella's children, plus many of their spouses and other relatives, were on the church's paid staff. Some were on the board itself. The proposed changes were resisted by his father, Robert H. Schuller, key board members, and ministry heads of the church.[11]

Robert A. Schuller said he had foreseen the potential conflict a few months earlier when the church's board named one brother-in-law as CEO and another as president, all part of the Cathedral's Office of the President. Both of those people became his boss and decided that the *Hour of Power* needed multiple preaching voices.

At the resignation, Robert H. Schuller was eighty-two and Robert A. Schuller was fifty-four. The longstanding head of the church's Spanish-language ministry was named interim pastor.

Leadership Remains in the Family

The leadership mantle was soon passed to fifty-eight-year-old Sheila Schuller Coleman, the eldest daughter. She had headed the church's school and family ministries for many years. Press releases said that she was becoming "co-leader" with her father. "My call is to help my dad finish strong," she said as she was appointed senior pastor. "I want Dad to be here until the day he dies in this pulpit. . . . Dad is not retiring."[12]

By this point several other unresolved issues were also at play, though most didn't become public until later. One was financial, as the church had begun to spend more money than it took in. For many years the *Hour of Power* was the source of roughly 70 percent of the church's revenue. One hour of weekly airtime might cost as much as $4 million across its numerous channels and countries, but that expense was affordable as long as resultant donations exceeded that amount.

But in such a high-ticket environment, losses added up quickly when donations began to lag. According to the later bankruptcy filing, overall donations to the church were down 24 percent in 2009 alone. One of the lawsuits alleged that Crystal Cathedral Ministries borrowed more than $10 million between 2002 and 2009 from endowment funds that were meant to pay for specific items such as maintenance of the Walk of Faith memorial stones on the campus. The money, according to the claim, was then used for regular church expenses and salaries.[13]

"It wasn't the bad times that got us; it was the good," Gary Moore, a Crystal Cathedral board member during that era, told *Christianity Today* in 2011. "We over-built."[14]

Another issue was worship style, both in music and format; neither changed substantially as the decades went by. As the *Los Angeles Times* described it:

> The service is bright and easy, featuring an interview with an inspirational speaker and a liturgy heavy on motivational advice and light on Scripture. There is almost no congregational participation. It is a style that was perfectly tailored to the World War II generation settling into Orange County's new suburbs in the 1950s and 60s.[15]

The congregation had aged over time, both in the pews and on the airwaves, remaining consistent with a music style that appealed most to an older constituency. Robert A. tried to introduce a more contemporary flavor, and Sheila pushed even further, but neither was successful. In response, after both had exited, Cathedral literature emphasized that the church would continue to "feature the traditional music and message which is synonymous with the ministry's legacy."[16]

Meanwhile, the community around the church had become more diverse over the years. The church's Spanish-language ministry, launched in the 1980s, exploded in growth with the arrival of a new leader in 2009, the young and charismatic Dante Gebel. Sunday mornings regularly saw waiting lines for seating—not for the morning services, but for the church's Hispanic Ministry that met on Sunday afternoon. Between 2009 and 2012, when it departed for another location, the Spanish service grew from three hundred people to three thousand, far outstripping the traditional ministry led at the time by the founder's daughter.[17]

Another issue during this season was the elder Schuller's ability to give leadership. In various interviews after his resignation, Robert A. Schuller said his father's mental acumen had been failing for at least ten years. As he told *Charisma News*, "He's definitely had memory loss. He hasn't had control of his emotions very well. . . . He becomes confused about different things and my understanding is that's a form of dementia."[18]

By the time Sheila Schuller Coleman became pastor in June 2009, which also made her the Crystal Cathedral CEO, *Hour of Power* donations had dwindled to dangerous levels. Attendance at Sunday services had decreased from thousands to hundreds.

Then in October 2010, a once-unthinkable event occurred: the Crystal Cathedral filed for bankruptcy protection, saying it owed over $50 million to more than 550 creditors. Bankruptcy filings indicated that twenty family members were being paid a total of more than $1.9 million a year at the time. In the bankruptcy reorganization, Sheila remained as senior pastor at a reduced salary but stepped away from her role on the board.

In response to the debt issues, the board enacted a number of cost-cutting measures, including a March 2012 decision to fire a number of unnamed staff—which turned out to be Sheila's husband, who had been director of creative services, plus other Schuller relatives, along with other staff. In response, church founder Robert H. Schuller resigned from the board of directors. One day later, Sheila announced her own resignation, leaving to establish a separate church and citing her family's "adversarial" relationship with the church's board of directors.[19]

Back in 2004, Robert V. (Bobby) Schuller, grandson of the founder and son of Robert A. Schuller, had become the Crystal Cathedral's college pastor, developing a young adult fellowship. This was a paid position. A few months after his father's resignation, he resigned that role, departing to plant a church and run a nonprofit. In April 2012 Bobby was invited back as a visiting pastor. Then in 2013, at age thirty-one, he became pastor for *Hour of Power*, moving with the congregation to its new location as the world-famous Crystal Cathedral facility was sold. He initially served as an unpaid volunteer.

The bankruptcy proceedings eventually included a lawsuit from Robert and Arvella Schuller against the church. Their assumption had been that the ministry would compensate them indefinitely for use of Robert's intellectual property and for his role as a roving ambassador for the church. "In exchange for continuing to use my materials, the ministry granted my wife and me retirement pay that was intended to provide for us for the rest of our lives," he claimed.[20] But after the Crystal Cathedral entered bankruptcy, all payments stopped. (Another potential income stream—the royalties from his books—had always gone to the Reformed Church denomination or its schools.) In 2012, the senior Schuller lost the bulk of his multimillion-dollar claims against his former ministry; the bankruptcy court ruled that most of the claims were based on unsubstantiated verbal agreements and that there was a lack of clear or legal documentation.[21]

Lessons Learned from the Crystal Cathedral Story

What can be learned about succession from what is arguably the highest-profile church implosion of recent decades?

Every church is only one generation away from extinction. If there is a singular lesson from the fall of the Crystal Cathedral, it may be that no church is exempt from problems that inevitably accompany a rough succession. No matter the largess of the outgoing pastor, the size of the membership, the status and number of current and former donors, or the wide network of high-placed friends to the ministry, bad successions can be the death knell for a congregation.

Today's success formulas can poison tomorrow's succession. As witnessed in the changing demographics and worship styles surrounding the Crystal Cathedral, modeling future strategies around yesterday's successes can handcuff future leaders (even leaders from inside the organization) so they cannot make necessary modifications and changes that fit a new era.

High-control people have a hard time letting go. The very gifts that enable a pastor to lead become the temptation to stay beyond effective years. As Marshall Goldsmith writes of succession in the business world, "It's easy to fall in love with the baton of leadership. Whenever this happens, it is almost impossible to let go."[22] In the church world, such leaders are often far quicker to take on new preaching or additional leadership roles than to intentionally transition their own existing roles, especially in their local churches, into other hands. Leaders must address their own ego before and during a succession planning process to ensure a successful hand-off.

Hard conversations about succession often need to be scheduled in advance. Even setting an annual schedule to have that conversation is good. There must also be clarity regarding the roles and responsibilities in a succession plan, and both the board and the senior pastor need to understand who is ultimately in charge of setting the timeline and initiating the succession plan. If the church board is responsible, then the senior pastor must clearly understand, accept, and respect the leadership's decision as to when the succession plan should commence and conclude, even if they accelerate or modify the plan. In this case, could a board made up heavily of employees that included family members have lovingly challenged Robert H. Schuller's plan to preach until he was one hundred years old?

Succession conversations should start sooner than most would guess. All pastors in the stories of this chapter could have begun their succession discussions sooner and "now." Most pastors underestimate the advance time required to identify a successor. When the Crystal Cathedral's attendance peaked, the founding Schuller wasn't even sixty. In our research, this is not an uncommon age for peaking (see figure on page 83). It was not until the senior Robert was seventy-nine that the hand-off to Robert A. Schuller actually happened.

Senior pastors should spend more time developing the strength of their bench to create a potential leadership pipeline for every major leadership position within the church. Filling key roles with relatives may work under one senior leader, but does not necessarily ensure smooth transitions to successors.

Succession typically takes longer than most would guess. Pastors in this chapter also typically failed to understand that a reasonable transition period is best for a successor to be accepted and incorporated into the church's culture to establish a solid foundation for effective leadership and ministry. A Harvard professor once advised leaders in the business world that they "need 10 years to develop a great CEO."[23] Churches, especially high-visibility ones, may not need ten years to develop the next senior pastor, but they do probably need ten years to cultivate a strong culture of leadership development at all levels.

> Churches, especially high-visibility ones . . . probably need ten years to cultivate a strong culture of leadership development at all levels.

The more visible the church, the greater care should be given to public communication. Many pastoral successions have occurred of a near-seamless quality, but those rarely make the news. Instead, the higher the public visibility the more likely the public media is to report on its every misstep. The Crystal Cathedral's publicity was not only prolonged, prompting years of headlines, but it was exacerbated by the many people, from board members to grandchildren of the founder, willing to offer their opinion to local media.

Good Succession, Then Bad Succession at First Baptist Dallas

Before the Crystal Cathedral's bankruptcy and succession problems, perhaps the most talked about story was First Baptist Church of Dallas, Texas. It started like many other churches, having eight pastors during its first twenty-nine years. Each stayed from one to seven years.

Their ninth pastor, George Truett, led for almost five decades. He was installed in 1897. He came during an era of serious financial troubles—the lights had been disconnected the year before his arrival and the sheriff had threatened to sell the church due to its debts. Despite these challenging conditions, he led the church through an era of spectacular growth and expansion. Attendance grew to several thousand, becoming the largest congregation in the Southern Baptist denomination. During his era at First Baptist, the church recorded over five thousand baptisms, prompting one of his biographers to comment, "No church known to me has any such record."[24] As he rose to international prominence, especially through his presidency of the Baptist World Alliance, he developed the nickname "the Prince of the Pulpit." He remained there forty-seven years as senior pastor.

During his last six years he became ill with bone cancer, holding his final traveling revival two years before his death. In the last months of his illness, he spoke to the congregation by telephone, patched to a loudspeaker installed over the church pulpit, an innovation for that era.

Southern Baptist polity and practice puts succession decisions in the hands of the deacon board or a special committee of the congregation. Biographies of the church and pastor do not reference any discussions about succession or retirement during George Truett's ministry. His father had lived to be ninety-five and was quite active until within a year or two of his death, and likewise the son "entertained the lively hope that he, too, could live to ripe old age and continue preaching to the end. He hoped 'to die with his boots on' and in the thick of battle."[25] Indeed, he died in 1944 at seventy-seven. The city of Dallas virtually shut down so that thousands could attend his funeral.

The Problems Begin

The succession issue came to a head shortly after the funeral. The church had no associate pastor. The deacons struggled with pulpit supply. They had no experience with calling a pastor.

Yet within four months they called Wallie Amos Criswell, thirty-four, as pastor. Known as W. A., he served as senior pastor for fifty years until age eighty-four. The church was the entire continent's largest-attendance church. It set records in the Southern Baptist denomination in baptisms, and its membership rolls included an impressive array of nationally known Christians, including Billy Graham and Zig Ziglar.

Here was a church with a pastor for forty-seven years followed immediately by a pastor whose tenure hit fifty years. Both led the church to unprecedented growth in attendance, baptisms, financial giving to missions, and more. A little known fact, but one worth noting, is that despite a few bumps during transition, Betty Criswell and George Truett's widow forged a good relationship. While this may seem trivial or tangent to the subject, we have found that the relationship of the outgoing pastor's spouse to the church and to the incoming pastor and spouse is a key ingredient to successful succession.

Sadly, the transition to follow W. A. Criswell was rough and painful. In his early sixties, W. A. announced that he was looking to retire at age sixty-five.[26] That would give him a thirty-year run at the helm of First Baptist Dallas. After going public with his intentions, he began a search to develop a potential successor. At least two associate pastors were called with the expectation of succeeding this widely known preacher, but he ended up not retiring, and both potential successors moved on.

By this point W. A. Criswell's stature was like that of a founding pastor—he was the only pastor most people had ever known at that church. Mrs. Criswell was also honored as first lady, occupying many powerful roles such as teaching a weekly Sunday school class that was broadcast live on radio.

Then in 1986, at age seventy-eight in his forty-second year as senior pastor, W. A. Criswell had a vision of a co-pastor coming to join him in the work. The church unanimously voted for it. A committee went to work for two years and the local paper ran a front page headline: "Fiery Dallas Pastor Ready to Train Protégé."

Tension developed between the pastor and the deacon board. The former wanted a hand in the selection of his successor, while the deacons tried to follow the long-standing Baptist polity of a committee and congregational decision. Although W. A. influenced the selection of committee members, the committee gave no guarantees that it would call their pastor's pick.

Over twenty young pastors were invited to preach on Sunday nights. Some were called back to preach additional sermons. Over a two-year period, that group was narrowed to two finalists.

After months of gridlock, the committee voted to call one of the finalists, age forty-two. He had first been contacted by W. A. Criswell eight years previously to begin talking, exploring, and preaching at First Baptist to "see what God does." Although he was not the pastor's first choice, the congregation affirmed the committee's recommendation and extended the call. This person, Joel Gregory, who would become only the third individual in ninety-seven years at that church to be named pastor, accepted the call. His understanding was that W. A. Criswell would stay a few months and then retire.

An Unexpected Surprise

At the official transition itself, however, the co-pastor terminology was dropped, a surprise to the new pastor. W. A. decided to retain his own title as senior pastor, with the new person being called "pastor." He also continued to preach weekly at the worship service that was televised.

Tensions mounted between the two, and also between the new pastor and Betty Criswell. Points of friction ranged from the preaching schedule to dealing with what the new pastor believed to be a $9 million debt masked by methods of bookkeeping unclear to him. Joel met with key leaders to develop a strategy, and also with W. A., who did not commit to a specific retirement date.

Almost two years later, Joel Gregory abruptly quit, voicing a public resignation openly critical of both his predecessor and of the congregation's leadership for putting him and his family in "an intolerable situation." His resignation statement, a surprise announcement at the regular Wednesday evening church service in September 1992, explained that he accepted the call thinking that it was to be the pastor of the church, yet W. A. Criswell has recently "announced in several contexts his desire to continue in that role until his fiftieth anniversary"—two *more* years ahead. The statement concluded by saying that the agenda of "prolonging the incumbent's ministry rather than enabling the new pastor's" leads him to "immediately and irrevocably" resign.[27] He left broken, disillusioned, and disappointed, as did his family.

The next two pastors were O. S. Hawkins (1993–1997) and Mac Brunson (1999–2006). The former came with the understanding of being the senior pastor, and shortly after his arrival W. A. Criswell retired from any active leadership role in the church, never even attending a deacon's meeting. "He was, during my years there, my greatest asset and biggest supporter, as was Mrs. Criswell," says O. S.[28] Both successors played prominent roles at W. A.'s funeral when he died in 2002 at ninety-two.

The next successor—Robert Jeffress—grew up within the walls of this church: he was baptized there, married there, and ordained there. He got his first job out of college there, preached his first Sunday service there, and affirms that W. A. Criswell told him one day he would be the pastor there. Hired in 2007, he is still present as of this writing. He also led the church through a building program designed to significantly replace and update the facilities that was completed in 2013. That $130 million effort was "the largest Protestant church building campaign in modern history," according to the present pastor.

More Lessons Learned from First Baptist Dallas

What further lessons can be learned about succession from this church's story?

Talking about succession is a lot easier than actually doing it. It is a common practice to watch many pastors begin to talk about a succession plan—and even bring in or name a successor—only to decide not to retire. This is especially awkward when a first or second effort at passing the leadership baton does not go well; often the former pastor feels compelled to stay in control, as apparently here with W. A. Criswell.

Outgoing pastors must decrease so that incoming pastors can increase. Outgoing pastors must move out of the way for the incoming pastor to be effective. W. A. Criswell, despite his announced intent in his sixties, seemed unable to decrease. Whether through a geographic move or a visible change in role and title, the outgoing pastor must make room for the incoming pastor. When John the Baptizer prepared the way for Jesus by saying "He must increase, but I must decrease" (John 3:30 NASB), he was certainly deferring to God, who had appeared in the flesh, but he was also doing what all leaders should do as they transition from one to the next: intentionally moving out of the way. In larger churches, icon dependency is often a reality that must be addressed. In such cases senior pastors must shoulder the responsibility of shifting the congregation's attention and admiration away from themselves and instead to their successor.

Pay attention to the outgoing spouse. The success of the Criswell tenure was due to a lot of factors. But not to be overlooked is the good relationship Mrs. Criswell forged with Mrs. Truett. In our research, we have not found a succession that went well when the relationship with the outgoing spouse was contentious.

Written covenants trump verbal intentions. In both this story and the Crystal Cathedral's, verbal intentions were misconstrued. W. A. Criswell stated an intent to leave, but then he changed his plan. The Schullers recalled a verbal agreement about intellectual property, but had minimal written memorial of the agreement. While contracts are often viewed as needed only in adversarial situations, we believe smart churches will write down agreements about provisions for retirement, intended dates for transition, and other stated intentions about the process.

Everything rises and falls on the outgoing pastor. While not always the case, most of the churches we studied found that a successful succession rises and falls on the outgoing senior pastor. This is particularly true for larger churches and long-tenured pastors. But in churches of every size, including small churches, the attitudes and values sown by the outgoing pastor strongly influence how the next pastor will be received.

Behind-the-Scenes Truth about Succession

The stories above are painful. They are real. And unfortunately they're not uncommon. The fact is, churches are made up of and led by people who need a Savior. As we said earlier, we don't highlight these stories to gossip or to criticize. Any church can find itself in a similar mess.

Instead, our motive in telling these stories is to help churches avoid repeating unhealthy patterns. Through hearing these stories, we hope that the "lessons learned" sections of this chapter will help churches pay close attention to key dynamics that can become pitfalls during succession planning and execution.

Whether the church is little or big, and whatever its ethnicity, denomination, or geography, a poorly handled succession can hurt the church's momentum and reputation for years to come.

_____ N E X T Steps _____

For Pastors: Leaving a legacy as a pastor is a daily exercise in the lesson of letting go. What are five tangible steps you can take to let go a bit more this year, steps that can be measured by year-end?

For Boards: What are you doing to move toward asking for a succession plan from your current pastor, and what review process can you institute to ensure you don't end up approving a plan to allow your pastor to unilaterally make decisions that may not be right for the long-term future of your church, such as preaching until age 100 (as the Crystal Cathedral board did)?

10

The Term Limit Factor

What Might Prevent Your Church from a Multi-Generation Run

First Presbyterian Church of Hollywood, California, is a highly influential church that most Christians younger than sixty have probably never heard of. Back in the 1970s, its pastor at the time described it as "one of the greatest churches in American history."[1] We agree.

It was established in 1903 when Hollywood was a small community with a population of seven hundred and more orchards than homes, just beginning its growth era. The church had many great leaders over the years. One was Henrietta Mears, director of Christian education for thirty-five years (1928–1963), during which she established a legacy of Christian education and ministry that was unique in American Christendom and achieved worldwide renown.

The number of preachers spawned by her ministry is astounding; over four hundred young people went into Christian service under her leadership.[2] Her college department ministered to such future leaders as Campus Crusade for Christ founder Bill Bright, football Hall of Famer Donn Moomaw, and Louis Evans Jr., whose father served as senior pastor in the 1940s, leading the church's attendance to triple during his twelve years there. She also founded Gospel Light Press, a leading book and Sunday school curriculum publisher. Billy Graham, who frequented the church, said his ministry was transformed at the church's Forest Home retreat center.[3]

Over the years the church was a pioneer and innovator, from being an early user of radio (1924) to packing out the Hollywood Bowl for Easter services (1950s) to sending out dozens of missionaries from its membership. One of its pastoral staff helped develop what today is World Vision, one of today's largest Christian humanitarian organizations. Two have served as chaplain of the US Senate.

Attendance peaked during the 1953–1972 ministry of Raymond Lindquist. In the early 1960s, overflow congregations were the norm for the two Sunday morning services, using the church gymnasium via closed-circuit television. Lloyd John Ogilvie became senior pastor in 1972, by which time attendance had fallen from its historic high. He served until 1995, when he became chaplain of the US Senate.

Today the church averages 750 in worship attendance, impressive but far from the high attendances of the church's glory years—an era when the college/young adult ministry by itself was that size. The neighborhood around the church has certainly changed over the decades, giving the church continual challenges in how to be at the center of its community. But of greater concern is that over the last fifteen years it has not found or kept a long-term pastor.[4]

The current pastor has made great strides, but the track record of late begs a question: What can be done in pastoral succession so that there aren't as many "once-great churches we've never heard of"?

Frightfully Similar Stories across the Decades

We might expect churches to decline in the impact of their disciple making if there is a moral failure or other deviance from sound doctrine or sound practice. Yet it's not just scandal that moves a church from prominence to decline or death.

What about churches that have had strong heritages soundly rooted in Scripture? Why do so many seem like islands of health and spiritual vibrancy under one leader, only to decline across the decades and generations that follow? As the following figure depicts (drawn from appendix 3), a then-and-now comparison of the nation's sixteen largest churches in 1967 shows that in all but one case—Thomas Road Baptist—attendance has dropped. Some are small declines, but most are significant and even precarious drops.

What Happened to These Great Churches?

Henry Ward Beecher's church drew standing room only during the Civil War. Harriet Beecher Stowe, author of *Uncle Tom's Cabin*, a book that changed the opinion of a nation, came from a family of famous preachers. In 1847 her brother Henry, along with twenty-seven transplanted New Englanders, started Plymouth Church in fast-growing Brooklyn, New York, which at the time was nicknamed the City of Churches.[5] His mesmerizing preaching and fiery antislavery newspaper columns made him one of the first celebrities of that era of budding mass media. The congregation grew to be

Attendance Changes in Large Churches

-51% Average (median) decline in attendance at what were America's largest churches in 1967 and those same churches in 2013 (see appendix 3).

Research by Leadership Network.

1967   -51%   2013

one of the largest in the United States, one of the few megachurches of its era. It was the first US church with amphitheater-style seating, with capacity for 2,800. President Abraham Lincoln and other national leaders consulted with Henry Ward Beecher for spiritual advice, giving him such a reputation that a biography about him was titled *The Most Famous Man in America.*[6] Even a sensational though unsuccessful trial for adultery with his best friend's wife did not damage Beecher or the church's reputation to the point of lost momentum.

In 1934 Plymouth merged with another well-known congregation of the time. Today the church draws fewer than three hundred in attendance.

J. Frank Norris led the world's biggest church in the 1920s. Just under a hundred years ago, the nation's most visible pastor was J. Frank Norris. During his forty-three years as senior pastor of First Baptist Church in rapidly growing Fort Worth, Texas, the congregation became the largest in the world, both in worship and in Sunday school. The church had been founded in 1867. When he became senior pastor in 1909, worship attendance was about five hundred. By the late 1920s, average attendance was five thousand, a size it hovered around for a number of years.

Attendance continued to inch upward even after the pastor, who was outspoken on issues from the "evils of rum and Romanism" to confrontations with local politicians, shot and killed a man who had threatened his life. In a trial that made national headlines, he was acquitted.[7]

In 1935, while still active as senior pastor of the Fort Worth church, Norris accepted the pastorate of a second church—Temple Baptist Church in Detroit, Michigan. This church also experienced phenomenal growth, becoming the largest in its state. For some sixteen years Norris commuted by train and later plane between the two churches.[8]

The decline in each church began many years before the death of Frank Norris. He personally selected successors for both churches. Both were gifted and capable leaders, as were their subsequent successors, but attendance at both churches continued to gradually decline. Today the Detroit church has merged with another church, having declined so dramatically over the years that it could no longer sustain itself. Likewise, the Fort Worth church merged with another, relocated, and today draws a weekend worship attendance of about four hundred.

Dallas Billington led the biggest church of the 1960s. During the boom years of the automobile industry, a lay evangelist and Sunday school teacher who worked for Goodyear Tire and Rubber Company in Akron, Ohio, resigned to start a Sunday school and church. From fourteen people meeting in a public school in 1934, Akron Baptist Temple grew so rapidly that attendance five years later was running between 1,600 and 2,000 weekly, prompting construction of what became a series of worship areas and Christian education buildings. By 1950, the church had grown to a regular attendance of four thousand every Sunday. In 1969, according to an extensive study by scholar Elmer Towns, the church's Sunday school was declared to be the "World's Largest Sunday School."

Attendance peaked in the 1960s and began a long decline. Founding pastor Dallas F. Billington stayed in leadership until his death in 1972. His son, Charles Billington, followed as the next pastor of the church until 1996, when the church transitioned to the founder's grandson, Dallas R. Billington, who pastored until 2006. The leadership line shifted outside the family when Ed Holland took the helm as lead pastor. He has begun a significant turnaround effort in this historic congregation.[9]

The founding pastor put in the bylaws that he could name his successor, which the congregation would affirm. Charles used that same clause in appointing his son. The bylaws were then changed as a national search began for the man who became the present pastor.[10]

Do All Churches Have "Life Spans"?

Many other historical examples across all denominations and size ranges could symbolize the same situation: too many once-mighty churches have fallen. Or they have declined significantly. Some were "the" church in their region for effective Sunday school, others for ministry to single adults, others for small groups, others for community transformation, and others as an advocate for justice, serving as the moral conscience of their cities. Yet something happened in each as the disciple-making momentum and voice once gained was gradually lost.

Is that process inevitable? Many Christians have gone to the Holy Land or traced the journeys of Paul, only to find that the vast majority of the churches mentioned in the New Testament do not exist today and didn't even seem to have lasted long after the close of the first century. The book of Revelation opens with a message to seven churches in Asia Minor, none of which exist today. God told one of those churches—the one at Sardis—"You have a reputation of being alive, but you are dead" (Rev. 3:1). Yet the message to that church is then to "wake up," because its work is "unfinished" (Rev. 3:2). In other words, you're dead but you could live again.

This piece of Bible history raises the question of whether churches are destined to hit a peak and then never to sustain or return to it again. In other words, do churches have inherent limits to their life cycles? More specifically, how does pastoral succession contribute to that ebb and flow over time, and how can good successions increase or restart a church's vitality along its life cycle?

Is the question of pastoral succession always bigger than "Who will our next pastor be?" Is the more important question "Should our church have a long-term future?" If you answer yes to that last question, then you need to explore what kind of pastor you need to thwart the pattern of churches falling into decline as various generations pass through, and often as the neighborhood changes as well. It takes good leadership for a church to avoid self-imposing a term limit on its life span. The solution might even call for a leader who is charged to lead the church in a different direction than it's currently headed.

Many excellent books have been written to explore the idea of a church life cycle, both specifically about churches and the corporate world. The basic idea is that living organisms—plants, animals, and people—experience birth and then they grow, age, and die. So do organizations. "As they change, progressing along their lifecycle, systems follow predictable patterns of behavior. At each stage, systems manifest certain struggles—certain difficulties or transitional problems—that they must overcome."[11] In the business world, the challenge is to diagnose the appropriate interventions to create the breakthrough needed.

Our sense is that churches tend to follow a life cycle of birth to eventual death *unless* they interrupt and restart that cycle. It can be done, but "gravity" is against them.[12] The typical stages for a church are birth, growth, adulthood and maturity, a period of aging, and then death—or redevelopment. As consultant George Bullard says, "Throughout their life congregations go through the life cycle multiple times." He then mentions a church over three hundred years old that he led through a discussion on this topic. "The leadership group laughed and said that it was probably cycle number forty for them."[13]

Church Flexibility Affects Succession

We become less flexible every day that we are alive. If you've ever tried stretching exercises near a small child who is doing identical stretches, you know this is true.

With age, bodies lose flexibility and agility, and they become more rigid. Smart people stretch regularly to help maintain their agility. But even with regular workouts, it's an almost cardinal law of nature: age reduces flexibility. It's far too common to hear stories of aging athletes who know they should stretch more—and don't. Then they try an exercise they shouldn't—and get injured.

Churches are similar.

Young churches are typically known for their ability to turn on a dime, to change quickly. In a word, they are flexible. Growth can come quickly. Launching new initiatives can become regular and rapid. But as a church ages, flexibility becomes more difficult. Customs become mores, and sooner or later, when faced with a decision about change, someone eventually answers with a change-resistant attitude of "but that's the way we've always done things around here."

Unfortunately, churches, like people, sometimes don't realize their loss of flexibility as they age. They both tend to underestimate their need for regular "stretching" and overestimate their current flexibility.

We've seen far too many instances where a church that was once growing, agile, and able to change begins slowly to calcify. They underestimate their need to intentionally remain flexible. They overestimate their ability to undertake change.

Then a pastoral transition comes along. The search committee charged with finding a new pastor talks to candidates and tells them of the church's deep desire to change. A new pastor is elected and follows the charge given by the search committee, only to find that the church isn't nearly as ready or able to flex and change as assumed. Conflict arises, and the transition is no longer seamless.

> Unfortunately, churches, like people, don't realize their loss of flexibility as they age. They both tend to underestimate their need for regular "stretching."

The situation calls to mind Jesus's telling his disciples that new wine cannot be poured into old wineskins without the old wineskins bursting (Matt. 9:16–18). What is the answer? Should churches simply close after a certain number of years? Should churches concede that they will never change and that pastoral transitions are doomed to failure?

We think there is a brighter future—and another way. Steps can be taken to create a more seamless transition. Three major issues need to be addressed: where the church currently is, what the church can do to remain flexible, and what the church can do to prepare for coming change.

A church's life cycle has a new beginning with every new pastor, but very few pastors are skilled in turning around a church. This is especially so when the neighborhood around a church dramatically changes—whether the makeup of the people (racially, economically, and so on) or the character of the area (such as from residential to industrial). When the community around the church no longer matches the church membership, the church must face a fundamental question: Do we want to change our approach to match our new reality? Often, that change won't come without some change in pastoral staff.

The current state of the church's flexibility needs to be clearly and honestly defined for all parties. One set of steps that might be required is having the outgoing pastor do an honest assessment of the church's agility and flexibility. Have the congregation take surveys about their current flexibility. Take steps to ensure that the incoming pastor understands the true lay of the land.

> Too few churches change well with their neighborhoods, and often a new pastor is a key to such transitions.

Another issue that must be addressed is increasing the church's flexibility. While stretching cannot make an older body as flexible as a newborn, it can help keep the church flexible enough to change and grow. Smart churches will address this phenomenon on an annual basis. They will come up with strategic initiatives that will preserve a spirit of change and agility. One solution: keep planting churches.

Finally, it's important to remember that pastors and congregations each have a personal life cycle that influences the church's corporate life cycle. Newer churches tend to draw younger people. Long-established churches are more often dominated by an older age group. The average age in a congregation tends to be the pastor's age minus about five years—unless certain exceptions are put into place. Those "age diluters" might include a younger worship leader, a mixed-age preaching team, a worship host who is a very different age from the senior pastor, or other young faces who are regularly on the platform. (The same principles, using race rather than age, can also help a church that's trying to become more ethnically or culturally diverse.)

Remember that "younger" is not always the preferred option. Sometimes the culture in a church determines the type of ministry to reach that community. As a congregation becomes older and grays, it might be better suited for reaching out to segments of the population in the surrounding community that it would not appeal to in its youth. Also, graying pastors can reach people in graying churches.

However, if there isn't a pulse for outreach and evangelism to interrupt that phase of the church's life cycle, then when the graying issue is done, it leads to death and burial—or merger with another, life-giving church. The book *Better Together* shows one of the more graceful endings when a church hits a "term limit" and considers merging with another more flourishing church.[14]

Maybe This Future Instead?

Most people have bumped into a long-established church, small or large, that has stayed on mission and maintained its influence across many generations. According to Leadership Network research, Moody Church in Chicago is the oldest church that's been a megachurch for the longest time—for most of its life from the 1860s to today. That makes it a long-term exception.

The church started as evangelist Dwight L. Moody developed a Sunday school in 1858, originally meeting in a saloon. By 1860, the Sunday school had relocated and grown to more than a thousand attendees when parents of the children began to attend. It soon became the largest and most well-known religious outreach of its kind, with the result that President Abraham Lincoln visited the meeting one Sunday.[15]

Between its founding and the writing of this book, the church has had eighteen senior pastors, with an average tenure of just under nine years each.[16] The pastor since 1980 is Erwin Lutzer. Current worship attendance is 1,800.

Great churches are not exempt from decline. In fact, every church is only one generation away from extinction. The evidence is staggering and shouldn't be a cause for pessimism but instead a call to planning for succession and the long-term future.

Can You Envision Multiple Generations of Succession?

While most stories in this book are from the North American context that we authors know best, pastoral succession is certainly a global issue. Wherever churches exist, their leaders must deal with passing the leadership baton.

Warren's good friend Edmund Chan, a Singapore native who pastored Covenant Evangelical Free Church in that country for twenty-five years, has practiced each of the "ten commandments for succession planning" outlined in chapter 2. He even developed a plan that lays the foundation for a *third* generation successor after him. To him, one of a pastor's main roles is to mentor and develop leaders, and the real test of true leadership is found in the third generation—those who succeed the current generation that's being developed. As he argues in his book *A Certain Kind*, "third-generation thinking is crucial to solid leadership succession."[17]

Edmund acknowledges that what he did may be rare, but he affirms that it can help a church leadership to lay foundations necessary for future health and growth. "Often, we are too short-sighted," he said. "It is vital to commit ourselves to think long-term."[18] This perspective makes sense if the primary call of the church is to make disciples, as the Great Commission teaches in Matthew 28:19–20 and elsewhere. "Jesus linked discipleship to leadership development, and therefore we have built intentional discipleship training in everything we do," he said.

Covenant Church was started in 1979 with seventeen people. When Edmund became pastor in 1987, attendance was fifty to seventy. Deciding early on to develop staff from within, Edmund started a mentoring practice he continues to this day. His view was that "it takes time, pain, and most important, it takes leaders to develop leaders. People we lead cannot go beyond where we can go ourselves."

In early 2012, he put his years of staff development to the ultimate test. At age fifty-three, he resigned as senior pastor. "I gratefully handed over my role to two younger pastors I have personally mentored for over two decades," he explained. He took on the role of Leadership Mentor at the church, serving under the board and under the two new senior pastors (one for each of the church's two campuses).

Why step aside at that point? "Because this strategic succession plan to the second-generation of senior pastors in their forties is crucial in the light of grooming the third generation of top-echelon leadership for the church," he said. "The longer I delay the transition, the shorter a runway my successors would have to successfully transit to the third generation."

> "One of a pastor's main roles is to mentor and develop leaders. . . . Jesus linked discipleship to leadership development."
> —Edmund Chan

Prior to his resignation and role transition, Edmund took a year-long sabbatical. His protégés each led for a six-month stint as the acting senior pastor. Upon his return, Edmund commissioned an anonymous 360-degree evaluation on their performance to assess their leadership during his absence. "I had told myself that if their evaluations fell below a seventy-five percentile, we are due for a re-look at their leadership. To my delight, their lowest score was in the high-eighty percentile! Both their majority scores were in the ninetieth percentile."

It was then that he decided it was indeed time to hand over the senior pastor's job. "They were ready!" he said.

Now, following Edmund's model, these two pastors are already focused not just on mentoring others, some of whom may become successors to themselves, but also helping those they are mentoring cultivate yet another generation of Christ-centered leaders.

Looking ahead is one of the most difficult tasks people face. Auto accidents happen too often because drivers aren't looking down the road. Businesses fail because they don't anticipate changes in technology or customers' felt needs. But leaders who look way down the road come out winners more often than not. Ask great golfers why they hit their drive in a certain direction, and they will tell you it was in preparation for the next three shots. Watch a great chess master play, and you're bound to see a player who is studying the board for possibilities four or five moves ahead. Anticipating what's next may be difficult, but the payoff is huge. As hockey star Wayne Gretzky often said, "I don't go to where the puck *is*; I go to where it's headed *next*."

The same is true for churches. No church is guaranteed to last forever. As we have seen in this chapter, great congregations often collapse. Sometimes, the end of a church's life is inevitable. But we believe that if churches and pastors will enter their chapter of ministry thinking about and planning for multiple generations of health, the life span of congregations will lengthen and the kingdom of God will be the better for it.

NE X T Steps

For Pastors: What steps are you taking now to ensure success for the third and fourth generations of succession at your church?

For Boards: When is the last time you looked at the forty-year growth patterns at your church? Are you growing at a rate commensurate (or better than) your city's population? How does the average attendee age in your church compare with the average age in your community, and what are the implications both now and when your church experiences pastoral succession?

11

Messy and Unexpected Endings

When Succession Follows Adultery, Nasty Church Splits, or Other Challenges

If you're a pastor following someone who experienced a sudden or messy ending, you're not alone. Sadly, you're not even the exception.

The bad news is that messy and unexpected endings for pastors do happen. At Vanderbloemen Search Group, situations like this comprise maybe 1 out of 4 of the cases that come to us. We're not saying that's the actual ratio for all churches out there, because churches with challenging circumstances are probably more likely to solicit outside help. But having found successors in a lot of messy cases, we can report the good news that many new pastors have indeed led their congregations to break through some horrendous circumstances they inherited.

In studying scores of traumatic endings, we are seeing some clear lessons and themes emerge. Readers might question our motives for including not just happy stories but also some that show pastors and congregations at very low points. The last thing we want to do is write a tabloid that tears down the body of Christ. We are especially un-comfortable with how many stories of failed succession involve illicit sex or abuse of power. But we didn't go looking to stack the deck that way. While some successions are seamless—and hopefully this book can help more move toward that direction—too many others are birthed out of messy and unexpected circumstances.

As we walk you through the messiness so you can see patterns, hopefully you will learn what to expect should you go through a similar situation.

Moral Failure of Highly Visible Senior Leader Changes Everything Quickly

First Baptist Church, Hammond, Indiana, was the nation's largest-attendance church in the 1970s and 1980s. Senior Pastor Jack Hyles almost never missed a Sunday in the pulpit, although church attendance in the 1990s significantly declined from its

earlier high points. In January 2001, at age seventy-four,

While some successions are seamless, too many others are birthed out of messy and unexpected circumstances.

Brother Hyles, as he was known, had a heart attack. In February he died, and on March 7, his son-in-law Jack Schaap—his choice of successor—was installed as pastor.[1]

The transition went well as the momentum, the baptism count, and the attendance all grew. Then one Sunday in 2012, the fifty-five-year-old pastor asked a deacon to retrieve his cell phone that he had left on the pulpit. The deacon saw an incoming photo of the pastor passionately kissing a sixteen-year-old student at the college the church sponsors, who had just sent him the photo. Confronted, the pastor confessed to an affair with the girl. He was immediately fired as "unfit" to serve as pastor.[2]

The girl left the school and church, as did her family. The Schaaps began family counseling between the firing and his court sentencing. Church attendance and finances plummeted, and significant staff layoffs followed. A new pastor was installed in 2013.

Lessons Learned: Nothing brings harsh and constant media attention like a leader's hypocrisy, especially sexual hypocrisy. Notice how many people were affected: the girl, her family, the pastor's family, and the staff who got laid off because finances plummeted. Typically it takes only days (or weeks) for fallout to occur, but it requires multiple years to work through problems caused and to rebuild church reputation and attendance. Sometimes a church never comes back to its former status.

Sudden Death with No Succession Policy

Just twenty-seven years old, Zachery and Riva Tims started a church with five members, New Destiny Christian Center in Apopka, Florida. It grew rapidly into hundreds, and then thousands. As the primary preacher, Pastor Zach, as he was known, was open with his congregation about his own failings, including his previous life of crime and drug addiction.

In 2007, the father of four admitted to a year-long adulterous affair with a stripper. After three months of counseling, he returned to lead the church, which continued to grow. He and his wife divorced. In 2011 Pastor Zach, age forty-two, was found dead in a New York City hotel room from a toxic combination of cocaine and heroin. There was no foul play, said the police; it was a drug overdose.

The independent church's board of regents, board of directors, and senior staff worked together skillfully to handle the immediate crisis. They drew on staff and pastor's friends as preachers, hired a PR firm to handle the public media, brought in counselors for the congregation, and regularly communicated with the membership.

Among the most active in giving leadership was Paula White, a member of the board of directors who had moved to the area after her divorce from Tampa pastor Randy White. In the past, Zachery Tims had been on the board of her church, and she had served as his personal pastor.

Now what? The church's constitution had nothing about succession in its bylaws, simply that the vice president would take over the board—but no one had been named vice president. The church's legal documents didn't allow votes by the membership, so the church's board of directors became the search team. As they prayed fervently for guidance, they sensed God's leading to ask Paula White to become senior pastor. As one of their members said in a statement, "We were searching for someone who could understand the history of our ministry, one who had a close relationship with our members and our staff and one who knew the heart of our senior founder. We earnestly know that the Lord led us to select Pastor Paula White."

Paula White was installed four and a half months after the sudden death of Zachery Tims. Elder Marguerite Esannason, who had served with Pastor Zach for seventeen years and still serves on the board of directors, sees God's grace and provision throughout the process, as the church continued to receive new members, even during the transition between pastors. "I also learned that we need to have a strong, legally tight succession plan in place, spelled out in our bylaws," she added.[3]

Lessons Learned: Successions are messy enough in crisis, but especially when clear policies and procedures are not in place. Without clear policies for emergency succession, boards are prone to turn to people who are in close proximity and relationally "known," which is sometimes but not always the best move forward. Plans made during calm, clear periods will provide sure guidance during turbulent times when clarity is harder to come by.

Botched Instructions and Succession Fights Kill a Church

Four days after the death of Betty Peebles, pastor of Jericho City of Praise, Landover, Maryland, her son and the church board's attorney faced off in court. They were fighting over who would run the church's massive assets that included a ten-thousand-seat sanctuary, a $9 million office park, a $52 million independent-living facility for seniors, and a lucrative agreement to provide parking for Washington Redskins home games.[4]

The son is Joel Peebles, age forty-two at the time and his parents' only surviving child. He said his mother left him in charge, naming him to the church's governing board shortly after the deaths of his father (the founding pastor) and his oldest brother (the successor until his own death). The board produced conflicting documents to show otherwise.

The finances were a mess as well. Court depositions show the multimillion-dollar organization "never had regular financial reports." When asked if "there has ever been a budget," the church's financial officer answered under oath, "No."

The legal challenges played out in the *Washington Post* and on YouTube. Meanwhile, shoving matches erupted at church during the financial offering, as both sides tried to take the money. In early 2012, the board fired Joel as acting pastor, stripped him of membership, and escorted him off the property. Most members went with him, and since then the group has been meeting in high school cafeterias, hotel ballrooms, and an equestrian center, waiting for the legal battle to end.

Since Joel's ouster, only a few hundred people attend Sunday services at Jericho, and Joel's nomadic following has likewise dropped significantly.

Lessons Learned: Situations like this force the congregation to take sides or to move on to healthier places. The longer the issue is unresolved, the more attendance dwindles and financial obstacles mount, raising basic survival challenges. As Scott Thumma, a researcher who specializes in congregational studies, observed, "Too often, tension and conflict fill the void in the struggle for control of resources, leadership, and a new vision. Without prior planning, such transition times can easily result in the demise of the organization the various parties are fighting to control."[5]

Leader Makes Theological Shift

Rob Bell was twenty-eight years old in 1999 when he started Mars Hill Bible Church just outside of Grand Rapids, Michigan. It became the fastest-growing church in America at the time, drawing over four thousand by the end of the first year and almost ten thousand by the end of the second year. In coming years he became a popular author and also the producer of a creative video series that many pastors used for sermon illustrations.[6]

In July 2011, he released a book that immediately stirred national controversy. Titled *Love Wins: A Book About Heaven, Hell, and the Fate of Every Person Who Ever Lived*, it suggested that non-Christians may be saved and that hell may not be an eternal banishment. The book's implied theology unsettled many evangelicals.

In late November 2011, Rob resigned, announcing plans to move with his family to California to launch a spiritual talk show in Los Angeles. "The idea that we were forced out is absolutely untrue," he insisted, but he did acknowledge that a major attendance drop may be related to the publication of *Love Wins*.[7]

In August 2012, Kent Dobson was announced as teaching pastor. Previously, Kent had served as worship director. Rob had also studied under Kent Dobson's father, Ed Dobson, pastor emeritus of Calvary Church in Grand Rapids.

Lessons Learned: Messy transitions are not always centered around a moral failure. Rob did nothing illegal or immoral. However, his understanding of theology and his theological framework shifted, and it did so faster than the body of the church could digest. While Rob left well, it was an unexpected and messy ending, leaving a church leaderless that had been defined and led by a personality and an extraordinary preacher. Smart churches will learn to keep an eye on the body and its leader for theological or philosophical drift over the years, lest they find themselves with a leader who doesn't match their DNA.

Financial Scandal Closes a Church

The 1986 book titled *Jim & Tammy Bakker Present the Ministries of Heritage Village Church* highlights stories of God's blessing in and through the church pastored by the husband-and-wife authors. Eleven years later, founding pastor Jim Bakker was divorced and broke. He then authored another book, *I Was Wrong: The Untold Story of the Shocking Journey from PTL Power to Prison and Beyond*.

By that point the whole world knew about Jim and Tammy's extravagant living that included an air-conditioned doghouse funded by their ministry. A sex scandal had led to his resignation. Subsequent revelations of accounting fraud brought about his imprisonment on twenty-four counts. He also went through a divorce, with Tammy later marrying the man who had used $279,000 in ministry funds as payoff for the silence of a staff secretary at the church, with whom Jim had an affair.

The church and ministry ultimately closed with detractors saying that PTL stood for "Pass The Loot." Today Jim Bakker is back in ministry and still owes the IRS about $6 million.[8]

Lessons Learned: When a pastor is loved, congregations can be very generous. They can be sympathetic and even appreciative of material abundance that the membership can bestow on the life of their pastoral family. However, when a perceived impropriety or financial abuse comes to dominate the relationship, the tables tend to turn quickly. Both membership and public media often come to view the material excesses as greedy, shamelessly self-serving, and harmful to the body of Christ. Ministers guilty of financial improprieties are often dogged with that reputation, and also the debt, for the rest of their lives.

Even Long-Ago Public Statements Can Come Back to Haunt You

Jeremiah Wright of Trinity United Church of Christ, Chicago, came to national attention as the longtime pastor of then-presidential candidate Barack Obama. Under the microscope of media scrutiny, he made front-page headlines as YouTube clips of certain sermons were aired. In them he seemed to invite God to condemn this country, using swear words to do so.

Under great political pressure, the presidential candidate gave up his church membership and denounced his pastor's words. Jeremiah Wright's retirement was accelerated, and he resigned from the church at age sixty-seven after thirty-six years of leading the church.

The search brought in a successor, Otis Moss III, age thirty-seven at his installation. He is totally unrelated to Jeremiah Wright. He was called to the church as associate pastor prior to his predecessor's retirement to begin what was described as a "two-year transition walk," after which the official installation occurred. He has put major efforts into keeping the church out of further controversy and launching new initiatives—and has been successful at doing both.

Lessons Learned: The public knows and remembers only one thing about the outgoing pastor—a few words from just a few of hundreds of sermons he preached. Never mind that he came to the church when it had eighty-seven members and led the church to great growth. It almost doesn't matter what other good things he and the congregation did to make their community a better place. Those long-ago sermons will be his tagline in history, not the role he played as a positive faith influence on young parishioners named Barack and Michelle Obama. As a result, his successor has had to proceed with great caution. This lesson will only become more pronounced as sermons are more clearly categorized in the digital age. Likewise, with the advent of social media, a few slips of the tongue or mis-strokes of the keyboard are memorialized in a way that will require pastors to think very carefully about how they use their platform.

Founding Pastor Has an Affair Then Starts Another Church in Same Town

In 2004, Gary Lamb started Revolution Church in Canton, Georgia. The church was growing until 2009, when he had an affair with the church secretary, divorced his wife, and married the secretary. After being dismissed from the church, he started a new congregation in the same small town.

"My ego got out of control," he said. "I neglected my walk with God and my family. I lied to the board, the staff, and the church. I hurt a lot of people. I destroyed my family, I was selfish and egotistical, and it was all about me."[9]

His successor at Revolution Church, Jason Gerdes, was called to the church six months later when everything was still in turmoil. Jason was thirty-two and began to help the church process its wounds. "I told the church it was okay to be messy but not to stay there," he said. Most of all he had to rebuild their trust in God. "During one message I affirmed that they had lost their senior pastor but not their real Lead Pastor," he said. "Jesus is still their Good Shepherd. That solidified their sense that God never took his hand off his church."[10]

Brian Bloye, who with his wife, Amy, wrote *It's Personal: Surviving and Thriving*, pastors the church that sponsored Revolution Church. He worked with the board of overseers that attempted restoration. He supported Jason while trying to err on the side of grace with Gary, his family, and other parties involved. "The public is watching for how sympathetic and loving we are toward those who have fallen," he said.

Brian was especially interested in preventing the church from becoming bitter or hostile. "We want to move forward in a healthy way so that people will say, 'God has redeemed this. God gets all the glory,'" Brian said.[11] Thus far that is happening as the church has gone through much healing and has even built a new building due to all the growth.

Lessons Learned: Don't give up. Revolution Church could have easily folded up shop and called it a day after Gary's departure. Instead of quitting, they decided to go "all in" and find a successor. While the search was complex, the prayerful resolve the board showed opened the door to a new chapter of ministry.

Sudden Death of Pastor Accelerates Hand-off to Son

What is today called The Orchard Community, Aurora, Illinois, was going through a season of decline. Despite a new facility, morale was down, attendance had slipped, finances were rapidly disappearing, and worst of all, the surrounding community was not being reached. The pastor began to sense that the church needed a deep change.

In 2002 the long-term pastor brought his son, Scott Hodge, on staff to find a new path forward. Scott had a different style than his dad did, which was fine. As Scott recalls, "My father realized he couldn't turn the church around by himself. He had been doing ministry the same way for so long that he simply didn't know where to begin, what questions to ask, or what changes to make first. He needed help."

The easier changes came first, including a switch in style for both the worship service and teaching. They began using more of a team-based approach to leadership. These changes brought fresh energy and put a younger face on the church. They also led the church to change its name.

The bigger challenge was internal: changing people's values to prioritize outreach. Two tough years began as long-term members left and giving fell, throwing the church into survival mode, where the father didn't receive a paycheck for almost the entire period.

Then the clouds began to lift. Scott and his dad shared a sweet moment one Sunday morning. "Do you see what's happening here?" they rejoiced. "Look at all these people! We are reaching our community!" The room was filled with people who were encountering Christ for the first time in their lives.

Two days later his dad, age sixty, died of a sudden heart attack. A few months later Scott accepted the church's invitation to become its next lead pastor. At the time attendance was in the high three hundreds.

The church continued the transition and today is in one of its most spiritually vital eras. In Scott's words, "During the transition, I remember my dad saying to me, 'Scott, you are up here in your thinking and vision, don't let us pull you down to where we are, instead, pull us up to where you are.' Even though he was positionally in charge, it was important to him that I felt empowered to help lead us forward where I could." As God has worked, both Scott and the congregation have risen to that challenge.[12]

Lessons Learned: The death of a pastor can bring out the best in a congregation. The shared experience of grief, if processed well, can become a bonding force to help a church find a new way forward. Leaders who have seen good models and received healthy mentoring can rise to amazing challenges and thrive.

The Epidemic No One Wants to Talk About

Again, why tell such painful stories? Yes, some have great outcomes, ending with new life and an "only God" turnaround. Others proved irreparable both for the leader and the church. And for some, the jury is still out.

But hard succession realities affect churches large and small, old and young, east and west, denominational and non-denominational. We hope our frank writing will serve as a reminder that a change is needed in how people view and approach pastoral succession.

Perhaps by highlighting so many "reality" stories in this book, all verified to the best of our ability, we can contribute to a new reality in church, one where messy endings are far more the exception than the norm. That prospect gives us a lot of hope, and we hope it will do the same for you.

_____ N E X T Steps _____

For Pastors: Messy endings almost always result, at least in part, from clouded decisions made by tired leaders. Write out three new steps toward maintaining your patterns of daily, weekly, and seasonal (perhaps annual) rest. Share this list with a colleague, family, and, ideally, a board member.

For Boards: What three steps can your board take to ensure more rest for your pastor? What person on your board would run point with communications (to media, members, and the community) in the event of a sudden or messy end to your current pastor's tenure?

12

Unintentional Interim

How to Avoid Being the "Sacrifice Pastor"

Pastor Max Lucado has written over seventy-five books with a total of over eighty million copies in print.[1] After twenty years of leading Oak Hills Church in San Antonio, Texas, a heart condition required him to transition from full-time to half-time. The church board called Randy Frazee as the new senior minister. Max's title changed to Minister of Preaching to represent that his primary focus going forward would be the twenty to twenty-five weekends a year he would be in the pulpit.

Randy arrived just after Max had been voted by *Reader's Digest* as "America's Best Preacher."[2] On his first week in the pulpit, Randy noticed several tour buses in the church's parking lot. He asked one of the drivers what brought them to the church that day. "We come regularly," the man replied. "Part of our San Antonio visitor tour package is to bring people to come and hear Max Lucado."

Randy was a bit taken aback. He replied, "But Max is not preaching. I am."

"I guess it sucks to be you," the tour guide said, bringing blunt words to every insecurity Randy was feeling that day.

Few Can Follow a Legend Well

How would you like to be the pastor to follow Max Lucado? Or to follow Martin Luther King Jr., the pastor and civil rights pioneer so revered that today a national holiday honors him? Or to follow Robert H. Schuller, whose *Hour of Power* broadcast was for years the nation's most-watched one-hour religious church service, at its peak drawing 1.3 million viewers from 156 countries? Or John Maxwell, the former pastor known today as one of the nation's top motivational speakers and bestselling writers on leadership?

How long do you think you would last as the new pastor?

Actually, the issue is not limited to pastorates that follow celebrities or other headline makers. It happens in ordinary churches where the outgoing pastor has been at the helm a long time or has in some other way achieved a larger-than-life level of admiration. Churches small and large, "hidden" and spotlighted, experience the same kinds of pressure and challenges. They too can have equal challenges in making a succession work well. Maybe the scale and intensity differ, but the principles and lessons at play are largely the same.

Sacrifice Situations Develop in Three Months to Three Years

The phrases *unintentional interim* and *sacrifice pastor* are commonly used in discussions about pastors who do not survive the shadow cast by their predecessor. They refer to the idea that a new pastor arrives with every prayer-filled intention of serving for many years. Instead, these successors run into unexpected obstacles. Their tenure becomes short-lived, typically three months to three years. It ends painfully, far sooner than they had intended or hoped. Often the boiling point happens somewhere between year one and year two. Then it's just a matter of how long the new pastor can handle the heat and hang on.

We'll write more below on those who come to a church as an *intentional* interim. That's an entirely different animal. For now we're looking at what one street-smart person described as three stages: the new pastor can do no wrong, the new pastor can do no right, and the new pastor leaves. In other words, what happens to cause a succession to become transitional rather than lasting?

The Core Issue Is Whether You Have Enough Investment in the Bank

Chapter 4 used the metaphor of parish poker to describe the trust and goodwill most congregations grant new pastors as they arrive. Over time the pastor then gains or loses this relational capital.

The pastors who avoid the sacrifice pastor syndrome generally do so because they have discerned how much of this "pocket change" they need at any given time, and have functioned with at least that much money in reserve. For others, when the bank of pocket change has zeroed out, then so has their effectiveness and future at that church.

> Jesus was the only sacrificial lamb for our sins, so no church needs another one!

As Lyle Schaller says, "During that crucial first year it is possible to help people become aware of new possibilities, to begin to grasp a new vision and to help them look down a new road, but there is a limit on how many changes can be accomplished during the first year."[3]

Biblically speaking, Jesus was the only sacrificial lamb for our sins (John 1:29; Isa. 53:7), so no church needs another one—for any reason! Our conviction is that most sacrifice pastor situations didn't have to end that way.

Positive Examples of Following a Long-Term Pastor

We can share several successful transition stories for when a new pastor followed a long-term pastor.

Earning the trust of your predecessor. One of the most heralded examples in recent years of a highly successful succession is the hand-off between Bob Russell and Dave Stone at Southeast Christian Church, Louisville, Kentucky. Bob wrote it up in a very readable book, *Transition Plan: Seven Secrets Every Leader Needs to Know.*[4] Bob and Dave, sometimes along with Kyle Idleman, have likewise spoken frequently on the lessons learned through the process.[5]

One thread of their story is that Bob cultivated several preaching associates, one of whom—Dave—received wide affirmation as a potential successor. After a season of prayerful discernment and then intentional overlap between Bob and Dave, the official transition happened. One of Dave's early tasks was likewise to cultivate a number-two preacher as he began developing potential successions for down the road, or for an emergency hit-by-a-bus scenario. One of those leading preachers was Kyle Idleman.

As Dave and Kyle worked under Bob, he recognized their effectiveness, maturity, and potential for even greater impact. "One reason I left Southeast . . . when I did was because I sensed that if I stayed much longer, the church would lose the opportunity for Dave Stone and Kyle Idleman to lead them," he wrote after the succession. "These men were both capable and eager to lead. It would have been unfair to ask them to wait any longer. I concluded that the church would do better in the long term if I stepped aside."[6]

Honoring your predecessor. As a "non-family" example, J. Don George is the long-time pastor at Calvary Church, an Assemblies of God congregation in Irving, Texas. In 2011 he asked the church to elect Ben Dailey, a young protégé to whom he is not related, to the position of senior pastor elect. J. Don and Ben are thirty-six years apart in age. J. Don explained that in this new position, Ben would succeed J. Don as senior pastor whenever he vacated that role. The congregation then gave Ben a unanimous vote of approval for the newly created position. "In coming to this church, I had to be okay with the fact that I'll be known for the next ten years as the guy who followed J. Don George—and it's an honor to do so," Ben said. "Pastor George has been willing to spend all the influence he has accumulated over the years, like pocket change, on me—celebrating, defending, and building a culture of trust. If he wants to be here until he's ninety or one hundred, that's fine with me."[7]

Ben is so enthusiastic about honoring his predecessor that he pours out honor not only in person, but even in many personal illustrations in the first book he wrote, *Collide: When Your Desires Meet God's Heart.*[8]

Ben's first thirty-six months were marked by huge transitions. Prior to Ben's election as senior pastor elect, J. Don asked Ben to give him a list of his recommendations for change in Calvary Church. J. Don approved each recommendation, including numerous personnel changes, as well as dramatically altering the congregational worship style. The administrative structure of the church was also reconfigured according to Ben's recommendations. Ben is quick to say that he could not have survived the changes without his predecessor highly engaged in validating the changes. As Ben explains, "When Pastor George began to cultivate me as a possible successor, he believed that God said to him, 'When he comes to you, make him a son.' He has done just that. Every day I'm living that dream."

J. Don and Ben continue serving the congregation in their present roles as senior pastor and senior pastor elect. To the delight of both men, the church has grown significantly since accepting Ben's new position of leadership. When J. Don vacates his role as senior pastor, Ben will automatically and seamlessly assume that position. At that time the formal succession will be complete.

Listening to counsel. Anthony Michael Chandler followed a pastor who had served fifty-two years at Cedar Street Baptist Church, a historic and predominantly African-American church in Richmond, Virginia. The outgoing pastor, after a church-wide season of celebrating his ministry and retirement, came for the first two Sundays of his successor, during which he gave his public blessing to the new pastor. After that point he largely stayed away, giving his successor space to lead. Anthony in turn blessed his predecessor at every opportunity. "I honored his legacy and the work he did, mentioning his name at every chance I got and highlighting his successes," Anthony said.[9]

Anthony, pastor since 2007, has weathered his share of storms as the forty-one-year age difference between him and his predecessor required many adjustments by the congregation. Writing a book to chronicle lessons learned during the transition, he emphasized the importance of taking advice from the longer-term members. He tells, for example, of one of the early church gatherings, a banquet. The pastor was sitting on the dais waiting for everyone to be served. One of the deacons came up to him and whispered, "At every event, Doc would walk around the room and greet every table.... I'm not telling you what to do. I'm just saying." Anthony took the cue and followed his predecessor's example. "Without reservation, this same gesture is now working for me," he said.[10]

Successors Who Follow "Famous" Pastors

10
years

Average length of time the successor stayed in our sample of 100 famous-pastor successions (see appendix 1).

Research by Leadership Network.

Should You Use an Interim Pastor?

Many churches explore the option of whether to hire an intentionally interim pastor. This person plays the deliberate role of bridging between two pastors and helps frame the church's necessary transition between the past and the future. This is a crucial period in helping a congregation prepare for and adapt to the anticipated new personality, leadership style, and perspective on ministry represented by the new pastor. It is also a time in which the potentials of the congregation and expectations of new members become more evident.

An interim pastor is "one who temporarily assumes the leadership of a congregation that is without an installed pastor . . . someone who serves for a limited period of time between two permanent pastors."[11] These intentional interims are typically contracted to serve for a predetermined number of months. Rarely is it as short as three, more often nine to eighteen, and on occasion as many as twenty-four months. According to the Baptist General Convention of Texas' Intentional Interim Ministry, eighteen months is the average length from the start of the intentional interim ministry to the call of the new pastor.[12] Our sense is that the most common interim contract is for one year, but that term often lasts longer.

There is no clear, uniform answer as to whether or not an interim pastor is a good idea. This approach typically works best in older, established churches where the congregation knows it will take considerable time to find a successor and local preaching is not available. Interims also work well when the church is fractured or is in shock following a turbulent pastorate. They are also effective when a much-loved, highly regarded, often longer-term pastor has departed, creating a buffer time while the congregation adjusts to their loss. Sometimes interims accelerate the process by causing people to long for a new pastor bringing sermons with fresh material!

Here are some questions to ask, adapted from Scott Delashaw's book *How to Search for a Pastor in Today's Church*.[13] The higher the number of "no" answers to these seven questions, the more advisable it is to find an interim pastor.

1. Will you be able to fill your pulpit with a quality message week after week, potentially for months on end?
2. Does your church historically do well between pastors, such as not suffering a decrease in attendance?
3. Does your church have a way of handling both the administrative and the leadership development needs necessary for going forward between pastors?
4. Can your congregation capably form and process a Pastor Search Committee?
5. Was your former pastor with you for fewer than ten years?
6. Did your former pastor leave in a way that allowed time to process both the farewell and the first steps of planning for what's next (as compared to departing suddenly)?
7. Did your pastor's term end with an absence of turmoil, such that the church avoided hurt, damage, or division in a significant way?

Why Someone Becomes the Unintentional Interim

In the business world, 40 percent of new CEOs fail within the first eighteen months on the job.[14] This painful reality has birthed the occasional joke that CEOs are the most expensive temp employees in the world. Churches don't want to fall into that pattern. Understanding what triggers an unintentional interim situation can help the likelihood of its happening to be reduced.

Toxic situations. Sometimes a church's circumstances make an unintentional early ending for the new pastor seem all but unavoidable. Typically this develops after the new pastor arrives. The most frequent scenario involves the outgoing pastor, who had agreed to depart after a few months or to engage with the congregation in very limited ways. Something then changes for the outgoing pastor. In the worst cases, these predecessors decide they need to save the church from the new pastor and wage an active campaign to lobby for the new pastor's removal. Other times it's far more subtle. On occasion it's a well-intentioned plan to support the new pastor that backfired terribly. Some might feel that the successors to the Crystal Cathedral's Robert H. Schuller and First Baptist Dallas's W. A. Criswell (both introduced in chapter 9) fit here, but others might say they match one of the next three reasons better. The toxic situation sometimes involves the spouse of the outgoing pastor, whose influence is threatened by the incoming pastor.

Change comes too fast. Many successor pastors see the need to make certain major changes and receive endorsement to do so from various church leaders, but far underestimate the resistance that emerges, especially as unintended consequences surface. One unintentional interim we interviewed canceled the long-standing Sunday evening service due to its low attendance and asked the staff member who led it to resign from the church. He had received approval to do so, but misread both the level of pushback and fallout that various special interest groups would voice as well as the level of sympathy that would arise for the employee he had pressured to resign.

Ignorance of transition dynamics, low emotional intelligence, and/or lack of self-awareness. Some new pastors fail to help the congregation process their grief in losing the previous pastor. Or they show impatience or anger toward the congregation for not transitioning quickly enough to a new era or ministry model.

Bad cultural fit. Many would say that a good cultural fit is more important than a high level of competence—thus a good tissue match is better than great talent that's simply not a good fit for the DNA of the new church. Many times this happens because the church hires a "rebound girlfriend/boyfriend"—that is, someone who's exactly the opposite of its previous pastor. We all know that rebound relationships almost always end up being short, quickly forgotten flings!

Bad personality match. Search committees, whether consciously or subconsciously, will seek a candidate who demonstrates strengths that appear to compensate for areas of weakness in the previous pastor. Such overcorrection often leads to a candidate who proves to be a poor match for the congregation's personality and needs.[15] If a church has always valued and responded well to a pastor with strong shepherding gifts, but decides on candidates who are teachers and leaders more than shepherds, they may find they overcompensated to the point of an incompatible match.

Bad gift match. When pastors experience long pastorates, their congregations often "assimilate" their giftedness, becoming like their pastor. Then they expect the same with their next pastor. However, if the next pastor has a different set of spiritual gifts and doesn't deliver what the congregation expects and reflect their strengths, the new pastor usually leaves or is fired.

Lack of connection with the church's opinion leaders. As consultant Lyle Schaller says, "The recently arrived minister *must* earn the confidence, the trust, and perhaps even the passive support of the influential members of the congregation—including some who do not hold official office, but who possess permission-withholding power; such as local patriarchs."[16] In other words, connect with the church's opinion leaders, surround yourself with them, and go only as fast as they go. This may range from a powerful lay leader to a relative of the former pastor, such as the pastor's wife.

Not enough allies. Schaller says, "The new minister must identify potential allies within the membership. This process should include (a) identifying the unmet religious and personal needs of these potential allies, to which this congregation can develop a programmatic response and (b) identifying and affirming the distinctive gifts, talents, skills, and strengths of each of these potential allies, including some latent gifts."[17]

Lack of confidence and certainty of call. The incoming pastor needs to sense a call of God and a spiritual fire that the congregation is drawn to. While the Bible is clear that we shouldn't think too highly of ourselves, newly installed pastors must also not lack the confidence that God will do great things through them.

Clergy-killer congregation. Some churches have an emotionally unhealthy DNA. Typically they are energized by conflict and have a long history of chewing up pastors and a history of conflictive relationships with their pastors. Should the pastor recognize this before taking the assignment? Sometimes the church appoints a new pastor but isn't ready to move beyond the past. Sometimes the congregation needs major intervention to address its "clergy killer" tendencies before it can move forward.[18]

Remember How Randy Frazee Felt?

Max Lucado's successor, Randy Frazee, walked away from his conversation with the tour bus driver readily able to imagine why the man could decide that "it sucks to be you." But Randy fundamentally disagreed with that comment. Randy knew he was right where God wanted him to be. "I had to stop drawing my sense of identity from my performance," Randy reflected. "If I could just trust in my position in Christ, the entire congregation and I could together do more for the kingdom—and in the process have a lot more fun with a lot less stress."[19]

Indeed, he had already begun doing just that, kicking it off (literally) with a humorous visual picture to the congregation. Visiting the church shortly before it hired him, Randy publicly addressed what many recognized as the elephant in the room. Six inches shorter than Max Lucado, Randy asked him to come on stage. The two tried on each other's shoes, to no avail. Point made. A standing ovation ensued.

"If I come, Max is going to be Max. And I'm going to be Randy," he said then. "And we are going to stand side by side and partner together in this deal. . . . People want to believe in their ministers, that human beings can pull this off."[20]

Every arriving pastor will one day be a departing pastor. It's not a question of if, but when.

You perhaps would like to know whether that "moving on" time for you is next month, next year, next decade, or not until God calls you home. Looking at the factors that make your departure "unintentionally" early can help you discern ways to have a maximum-impact run and to prepare for that day when it is time to move on.

NE X T Steps

For Pastors: What actions can you take to double your listening and learning efforts with your congregation before making your next change?

For Boards: When starting your next pastoral search, what concrete steps will you take to gain a clear and realistic profile of the type of person that will best succeed as your new pastor?

13

Forced Farewell

What to Do If the Pastor Needs to Go but Doesn't

The following story is true, but we have kept it anonymous for reasons that will soon become obvious.

This small-town, mid-America church began in the early 1900s. Attendance was always quite modest.

In the early 1980s, the denomination sent in a redevelopment pastor who grew it from seventeen to seventy-one attendees over three years. He then moved to another extension church, and the congregation called a new pastor.

This new pastor had an amazing run, building on that surge of momentum. Year after year, the church grew. He led them through expanded ministries at every level—children, youth, adults—and through more than one building project, most finishing debt free. The church added multiple worship services and developed an excellent staff team.

By 2006 the church was averaging a thousand in worship, all in a town with an official population under ten thousand. The church was widely known and respected as a lively hub of ministry and fellowship. The pastor's reputation was solid, with no hint of sexual or financial improprieties. The pastor had come to the church at age thirty-one, and at this point was around fifty.

A slow but gradual change followed that peak year. The pastor became distracted, lost energy, and began to coast. The church's elders, who helped us compile this story, are still not quite sure what happened, but the excitement lessened. The baptisms and reports of conversions became fewer in number. Attendance dropped by about one hundred year after year.

The elders met repeatedly with the pastor, encouraging him to find his fire again. Over time, the elders began to ask him about his future at the church. He saw no need to leave before he reached retirement age, quite a few more years down the road. Some of the elders felt otherwise and agreed that it was necessary to make a transition over time to a new lead pastor. As they began bringing in candidates to be interviewed, things got so bad between the pastor and the elders that a mediator was brought in to try to help them work through major issues of mistrust brought to the forefront because of the imminent transition of power.

The public story is that this pastor began talking with his elders about the process of preparing for his succession, and then at the twenty-five-year mark of his ministry there, he joyfully completed the two-year process of transitioning to a new pastor. He shifted to a new position on the church staff, teaching some classes and preaching occasionally. He received a sabbatical for the six months that followed the naming of his successor as lead pastor and returned with a much lower profile, as the new pastor was now the lead player. After a number of months in that role, he stepped down completely.

Sadly, the insider story is that it was a forced transition. The reality is that the long-standing pastor welcomed the new pastor only because he had no choice. Attendance was down to around six hundred at the point of succession, with many people aware that the church was not in the same place it had been just a few years previously.

Behind the scenes, the transition was bittersweet at best. The outgoing pastor felt he had failed. His sense of self-worth also took a hit: here he was, still in prime earning years, but feeling like others were telling him he was done. To this day, the outgoing pastor does not agree that new leadership was required for the church's future.

Forced Termination for More Than 1 out of 4 Pastors

A painful number of succession cases take shape because of a forced departure. According to one study of thirty-nine denominations, 28 percent of US Protestant clergy experience forced termination during their career. That's sobering: more than 1 out of every 4 pastors. The main reason for this statistic is conflict. The study also found that forced termination is also associated with high levels of depression, stress, and physical health problems, as well as low levels of self-efficacy and self-esteem.[1]

American Protestant churches employ approximately 1.2 million paid staff. Of those, roughly three hundred thousand are clergy.

> People will remember how you leave long after they forget what you did while you were there.

Clergy Terminated by Force

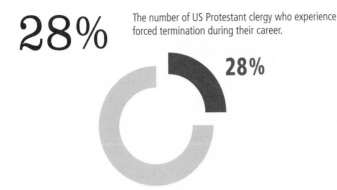

28%

The number of US Protestant clergy who experience forced termination during their career.

28%

If those clergy each average forty years in ministry over their lifetimes (a very high estimate), that 28 percent numbers as many as two thousand pastors experiencing a forced termination in any given year.

When the pastor is forced to leave, it touches serious nerves in the pastor. In chapter 3, we pointed out that succession is made much easier whenever the outgoing pastors have (a) a clearly defined identity they are passionate about pursuing post-pastorate and (b) adequate financial security.

Forced succession threatens both pieces of that puzzle. Outgoing pastors are often left (a) questioning their sense of self-worth and (b) challenged by their lack of net worth financially. That leads to a dynamic that, in a good case, can be highly tense, and in a bad case, can be like backing a threatened animal into a corner with no way out.

We've seen good pastors end their tenure poorly, all because of a force out. As we tell people all the time at Vanderbloemen Search Group, "People will remember how you leave long after they forget what you did while you were there."

It Doesn't Have to End Like That

What options does a pastor, board, or district leadership have in situations where the pastor, church, or both have lost momentum, as in this chapter's opening story?

In many denominational circles, the district superintendent or bishop can call for a pastor's resignation, and the pastor is morally and legally obliged to comply. This can happen for many reasons, including a scandal of some sort. But the reason could simply be that the ministry supervisor senses there is no longer a good fit between the pastor and the congregation.

Sometimes the termination is prompted locally. In many churches, both denominational and non-denominational, the constitution or bylaws allow for the congregation or its board to ask a pastor to step down. The most risky of those situations is when there is no outside religious authority that can enforce a decision that one or more parties are contesting.

A case in point was a pastor who came to a church when its attendance was less than one hundred. Under his dynamic leadership, the church became one of the largest-attended churches in the Pacific Northwest. At roughly the twenty-five year mark of his ministry there, multiple allegations of sexual misconduct arose. The pastor maintained his innocence throughout a protracted battle with members of his congregation, area pastors who weighed in, and the local media who month after month highlighted the latest police report or other accusation.

Ultimately the pastor did resign, admitting only that his credibility in the community had been seriously damaged. Six months later, a successor was announced. That successor stayed eight years. The next successor came in 2007, with worship attendance less than half its peak. That pastor, who is more than thirty years younger than the pastor who fell, is still leading the church today, and it is now experiencing new life and new momentum, even if it has not yet regained the full size and impact of its peak days.

This is another example of how a poorly handled succession can cripple a church for years to come—but also how God can bestow "a crown of beauty instead of ashes, the oil of joy instead of mourning, and a garment of praise instead of a spirit of despair" (Isa. 61:3).

Pathways to Helping a Pastor Exit

What are the different pathways by which a pastor's reluctant or unwilling resignation can be secured? Much depends on the church's relationship to a denomination, if any, and the constitution and bylaws of the congregation. General options include:

Intense and appropriate prayer leads a pastor to resign. In a small church where Warren was a member, the pastor was clearly unhappy. He increasingly isolated himself from most lay leaders in the congregation. Several other problems were serious enough that many feared a forced resignation was in the offing. Instead, a group of elders and former elders agreed to pray for him and asked to meet with him to support him in prayer. No one mentioned anything at those meetings about a potential resignation, but that's just what he did a month later.

The board sets expectations early. Upon hiring the pastor, make clear what the markers of stagnation are and what will be the indicators that the time to go has come. Writing down expectations early can create an ending that isn't viewed as messy but simply "necessary" for going forward, as the book by Henry Cloud, *Necessary Endings*, aptly describes.

The board encourages the pastor to find a new identity and move toward it. This is often something the pastor feels a calling and passion for. Perhaps it's being passionate about a mission project, and the church heartily supports it. Funding that new role for a year or two could be far less expensive than a messy termination.

The board asks a search firm to help the pastor discern a new identity. Whether you do it yourself or bring in an outsider, a discernment and prayer process is set up to help the long-term pastor imagine a new-chapter identity, something your pastor is passionate about. Most have a pet ministry project, so provide them a pathway to financial security by funding it. This is often a great way out.

The board pays for its pastor to become a certified interim pastor as a graceful exit plan. Many denominations offer this sort of training. Release your pastor to this ministry, framing it as a promotion and honor.

The board forecasts to the pastor that a forced retirement or termination may happen. This happens most often after a considerable season of tension between board and pastor. If an outside consultant or search firm is brought in, they are instructed, "You negotiate for us. We want our pastor to be able to leave quietly and with as much dignity and honor as possible."

The board votes to release the pastor but negotiates it quietly behind closed doors. This conversation conveys clearly and respectfully to the pastor, "You have been fired." However, such discussion is handled confidentially, never going beyond the board. Typically, the board sets up a severance package, paid over time and leveraged so that if things go sideways with the outgoing pastor's behavior, the money stops. They offer that option to the pastor who then publicly resigns, receives affirmations from the congregation, and moves on.

Denominational leadership steps in to release the pastor. Usually this is done quietly and with efforts to protect the dignity, reputation, and future employability of the outgoing pastor.

The congregation votes to release the pastor. Sadly, congregational votes are usually the roughest way for a pastor to depart, and they often leave a divided church behind. Words are often voiced at such forums that leave wounds and painful memories on both the pastor and the congregation.

An annual review is scheduled that includes discussion of potential succession. Many churches have a personnel team or parish-pastor relationship team. It can be appropriate for them to include this topic in their review to explore whether a plateau has happened and if a retirement discussion needs to move forward. This means a true performance review needs to happen, not just the "wink and a handshake" that too often occurs. When performance monitoring and evaluation are done properly, the news of termination should never really come as a surprise to any staff member.

Talking about succession needs to become a normal conversation between boards and pastors. Once it becomes a regular, anticipated part of a pastor's tenure, anxiety levels drop, and clear thinking can lead to a plan before one is needed—and long before a situation reaches crisis level. We are seeing this start to happen in more and more churches, and we are hopeful that is the beginning of a trend. If these conversations become standard practice, we are certain the number of forced successions will reduce. The fruit will be a healthier future for pastors, boards, and churches throughout God's kingdom.

NE X T Steps

For Pastors: Do you have someone in your life who will speak honestly with you about how your ministry is doing? Schedule an annual meeting with that person (or group of people) and proactively ask whether the church is better off than it was a year ago.

For Boards: Forced exits should never be surprising to the outgoing pastor. Have you had a conversation with your pastor about what might be grounds for termination? What markers, besides moral failure, might be grounds for a forced exit? How do you set metrics for those markers? Set the markers, and set an annual meeting with the pastor to discuss them in a safe environment.

Part 3

Transition Well, Finish Strong

14

Where to Find a Successor

Staff, Multisites, Former Interns, and Recommendations from Friends

Many fine books, including ones listed in "For Further Reading" (page 207), guide a search team that functions after the pastor is no longer there. This chapter is written to a different audience: the senior leadership team of a church where the pastor is still in place. The goal is to help you design a potential succession pathway for when the time comes, whether next year or next decade.

Finding and grooming leaders for succession is one of the chief tasks of leadership. In many cases the outgoing senior pastor can shape or influence the process. Even if you are allowed to have a hand in selecting your successor, this responsibility is far too large for anyone to shoulder alone. It needs to be shared at several levels—a partnership of senior leadership team, board, and, where applicable, denomination.

The best starting point to find a successor, after prayer, is to pull your arms around the "givens." What qualifications and process do your constitution and bylaws outline (and do they need clarification or revision)? If you're part of a denomination or tradition, is there policy or expectation about how potential successors are to be contacted or chosen? What issues of belief, character, training, and experience are essential? What is the history and culture of your church regarding succession? Which of the succession models outlined in chapter 6 is the closest match to your situation?

The Bigger the Age Difference, the Greater the Likelihood of Change

Any candidates for succession will want to know what the church's vision is, whom it is actually reaching at present, what its strengths and potentials as well as its weaknesses are, where it is going, and where it wants to go. If the current leadership lacks clarity on these present realities, then senior level discussions of those issues are necessary.

Realize that the congregation will become more like the next senior pastor. Everything about your pastor, both now and in the future, attracts people who identify with that life stage or lifestyle—amount of body art, educational level, marital history and age of children, race and ethnic heritage, even hobbies.

The age difference between the outgoing pastor and the incoming pastor is one of the biggest predictors of how much the congregation will change over the first several years of the new pastor. The greater the age difference, the bigger the implied mandate for change in who makes up the congregation. In appendix 1 we examined a number of completed large-church successions and found that the average difference in age was about one generation.

Age Difference between Outgoing Pastor and Successor

22
years

Age difference between the outgoing pastor and incoming successor in our sample of 100 famous-pastor successions (see appendix 1).

Research by Leadership Network.

Incoming Pastor — **22 years** — **Outgoing Pastor**

At the time of succession, the outgoing pastors ranged in age from the forties to the eighties. They had served thirty years as senior pastor on average. Two-thirds had overlap between outgoing and incoming pastors, but on average there was a thirteen-month break between outgoing pastor and successor. While many churches want their sixtysomething outgoing pastor to be succeeded by a thirtysomething, the table in appendix 1 suggests that a fortysomething successor is the more likely reality. History also suggests that it is inevitable that a successor of a different age will bring a different style and approach.

Internal Candidates Are Often the Best Matches

When you're ready to begin naming specific potential succession candidates, the best starting place is usually to look at "family" members, which are more formally defined as internal candidates. This is especially helpful when the church is healthy, growing, and wanting to continue its current DNA, mission, and path forward.

Internal candidates aren't just those you can promote from within your congregation but also people who have had some kind of direct relationship with your congregation. Advantages of internal candidates are that you both already have a sense that the chemistry is a good fit. They already understand a bit about your church's DNA and your community. They have already developed some degree of trust and respect among the congregation. They know the family and the systems that run it, and their transplanting into the body will have a much higher probability of being a good "tissue match."

Even Smaller Churches Have "Internal" Candidates

If you're a smaller church, internal candidates are people the church knows and who know the church. Options include guest preachers who have been well received. These may range from the youth pastor at another church who spoke to your congregation last year to a denominational leader who has relatives in the area. Consider parachurch leaders who have presented their ministries or the leader of the Bible college group that gave the passionate testimony on their efforts to end sex trafficking.

Chances are that you've got a larger pool of internal candidates than you initially think. However, if you're a church with minimal outside relationships, it's never too late to start developing them!

Larger Churches Can Start with Staff or Former Staff

Larger churches will have even more options. Consider associate pastors present and past, from youth leaders to counselors. If your church has sponsored interns, consider the brightest lights among them.

The larger the church, the more possibilities there are toward finding a successor among internal candidates. One recurring theme in smart churches is to look to former associate pastors to see if there is a possible successor, similar to Tom Pace's personal experience. Tom worked from 1982–1987 as the pastor to youth at St. Luke's United Methodist Church of Houston, Texas. He had long felt called to preach more and to serve beyond that particular role.

Tom's senior pastor, Jim Moore, encouraged Tom to move on to have these opportunities. Jim later shared with Tom his hope that Tom would be the next pastor of St. Luke's, planting that possibility in his heart and mind.

In the years that followed, Tom served as senior pastor of several different churches. One was a church plant, and others were established churches. One was in inner-city Houston and others were more suburban.

During all these years, Tom maintained a relationship with Jim as a mentor, keeping in touch maybe once a year. When Jim began to think about retirement, not only did he remember and suggest Tom, but other voices at church who remembered Tom also recommended that he be considered for the senior pastor role.

The St. Luke's personnel team asked if the bishop would consider Tom. She was glad to have someone within her conference to consider. The church looked at other candidates, but ultimately wanted Tom to come back to St. Luke's.

Jim was not on the search committee, but he did offer his recommendation of Tom. And he also made it clear to the congregation that he accepted the calling of Tom. One of the defining moments in the transition occurred on a Sunday morning when Jim announced, "I'm no longer your pastor, and I won't do your weddings or your funerals. Tom Pace is your pastor: he will do them. I will come back and be your friend, and would love to be your friend forever—but I won't be your pastor anymore." He spoke clearly to the congregation about the change in roles. Then after resigning in 2006, Jim moved to Dallas where his children live.[1]

If Multisite, Give Early Consideration to Campus Pastors

Multisite churches have the additional staff role of campus pastors, which is proving to be a sometimes viable option in succession planning. As multisite consultant Jim Tomberlin says, "Although there are currently few instances of campus pastors succeeding their senior pastors, many are in position to become the next senior pastor of their church."[2]

The benefits, Jim says, are that multisite campus pastors are more likely to

- Buy into the mission, vision, and philosophy of the church.
- Already be known by the church family.
- Possess the DNA of the church.
- Have been mentored and coached by their senior pastor "up close and personal" over a long period of time.
- Understand how the church functions and "dys"-functions.
- Help the church have a smoother transition because the relationships are already established and therefore will have fewer "surprises."

- Be less risky, because the personal, family, community, and cultural fit has already been proven.

When Jay Passavant, founding pastor of North Way Community Church in the Pittsburgh area, began to think about succession, a young pastor was brought in to share leadership and teaching responsibilities. He seemed to have potential for the successor role that Jay anticipated at the thirty-year mark of his leadership, still some four or five years out. However, this more "personal" approach did not go well and was mutually terminated.

With the succession window now much closer, Jay convened a "succession team" including key elders and staff members who would champion the process. Jay was a member of the team, but delegated leadership to others to ensure equal voices. The team agreed that the first place to search was within their own pool of campus pastors, something that had been growing since the initial succession steps had been taken. Four candidates were in this pool, ranging in age from thirty-two to forty-eight. In addition, a highly respected executive training firm agreed to evaluate each candidate from a totally neutral perspective in terms of leadership style, administrative skills, and potential strengths and weaknesses. This process took about nine months, but the results proved outstanding.

The executive pastor was eventually chosen to be the successor, but two of the three remaining campus pastors are still on the team and in the pipeline for greater roles in the future. Post-succession, Jay went on to create a church consulting firm, but is still loved by the congregation, meets regularly with his successor, and preaches periodically in the church he founded. Since Jay released the reins to his successor, North Way has increased financially and numerically and has launched another multisite campus. These are all confirmations of a successful succession.

Sources for Outside Candidates

If you cannot identify candidates from your internal network, do you have time to begin developing such a pipeline? If so, chapter 2 offers suggestions about developing your bench through intentional leadership development.

If you need to explore outside candidates on your own, one of the best places to start is to prayerfully seek out the recommendations of people in the congregation and friends who know the church well. If you follow this approach, be certain to be clear about where the church wants to go and what it wants to accomplish. Hiring is an anxious thing, and while hiring someone a friend knows may feel less anxious, it may not be the right match for you.

It is at this point that many churches consider hiring a search firm, such as William's organization (see "What Our Organizations Can Do for You" on page 182). Many if not most times when Vanderbloemen Search Group is retained, we are handed a list of internal candidates, as well as tasked with finding outside candidates.

Your familiarity makes internal candidates look so good, especially when you're anxious, even if it's not the best person. By hiring someone to give an outside opinion you validate your process. Sometimes the denomination does this well, and sometimes they lack time or expertise, especially churches "different" from the norm such as those that are bigger, more contemporary, and urban.

Is Your Succession Plan Strong Enough to Handle Surprises?

Since his first days as CEO of Lockheed Martin in 2004, Robert J. Stevens and his board of directors began planning his succession. Their approach was not just about finding the right candidate for the right spot to lead the world's largest defense contractor. It was about building an entire group of leaders, a team that could work together for the long haul—and would develop future talent at many different levels.

The importance of a top team with that much experience was underscored when Robert's designated successor, who was due to take over in a matter of months, abruptly left the company under a cloud in 2012. Without a delay, Robert and the board promoted Marillyn Hewson, a thirty-year veteran of the company, to president and CEO, and elected her to the board of directors.

Then, just as succession was a topic at Robert's very first meeting with the board as a new CEO in 2004, it was also a topic at Marillyn's first board meeting. As Robert explains, "Our board was very—and I think appropriately—insistent on recognizing that succession planning isn't optional. It's essential."[3] Even when the unexpected happened in the succession plan, "because we developed a deep reservoir of talent, the change was seamless," he said.

Robert summarizes the company's succession plan as a leadership program on steroids. But it's far more than a general plan to grow and develop talent from within and to network with gifted leaders on the outside. "Everything has a model. Everything has a structure to it," Robert said.

Part of their approach was to regularly review progress on the succession plan. More than once, he presented the succession model to the board, where together they made refinements. They also named specific people as they populated the model at various stages, starting with questions like, "Do we have talent internally?" and "Should we go get talent from outside?"

Their plan not only recognized the company's present needs but anticipated its future ones. They looked at the kinds of talent needed, what kind of company Lockheed Martin is today, what kind of company it needs to be in the future, and how that translates into the dimensions of leadership and professionalism.

They also benchmark themselves against other organizations in their industry. They looked at the age of the other CEOs when they announced their retirement, how long it was between their announcements and their actual retirements, and how much transition time there was with the new CEOs. They also studied whether the CEOs stayed on the board, and if so, in what role. "We did that within our industry, and we looked beyond our industry," Robert said.

Do they adjust the model over time? "Yes. It's interactive," Robert said.

While businesses and churches differ at key points, Robert demonstrates that succession planning can be done well, even when surprises occur. He also models well the idea of imagining that his company has many viable years ahead. "It's not about me. It's not about the board. It's about the health of this enterprise," he said. "So we're not going to fail in our duty to make sure that these enterprise goals and commitments are transitioned generation to generation."

> How strongly do you believe the legacy of your leadership significantly affects how well the ministry continues to thrive after you are gone?

If succession planning is possible in one of the world's largest companies, it certainly can be done in churches large and small. The challenge for churches is less about methodology and more about commitment and perspective: How strongly do you believe the legacy of your leadership significantly affects how well the ministry continues to thrive after you are gone? That legacy starts now, while you are still at the church, as you build a culture that values shared leadership, team development, and empowerment of others, both volunteer and paid.

As Laurie Beshore at Mariner's Church, Irvine, California, said, "Hire staff or recruit volunteers with your successor in mind. Always be on the lookout for your replacement."[4]

Candidates to Probably Avoid

Whether you seek candidates internally or externally, here are some candidates to consider avoiding.

- Someone who served at a great church but has a poor track record in other contexts. Just because you're in a great church doesn't mean you can lead or create one.
- Your best friend, and your assumption that friendship means a good DNA match.
- A pastor who has served several churches, none of which have gone anywhere for years, but you're convinced that in *your* setting, everything will thrive.

- A pastor with no experience in a church your size or slightly larger.
- A pastor with a lawsuit or one that seems imminent.
- A pastor who's had high staff turnover at previous churches.
- A pastor who has incurred an exorbitantly large amount of debt relative to church size and then left the church with little headway on debt reduction.
- A pastor who bends personal theology or practice in order to fit yours.
- The pastor at the smaller church down the road who wants to merge his church with yours. (Mergers always work best when a joining church and a lead church come together, as explained in the book *Better Together: Making Healthy Church Mergers Work.*[5])
- The pastor's son or daughter, who is also in ministry at the church but whose gifting is so different that they lack the leadership skills you need and also the potential to develop them.
- A pastor with a track record of not getting along with the board or staff.
- A pastor who has been a great teacher but hasn't led anything of significance and/or has no ability to lead or cast vision (unless all you want is a great teacher).
- Someone with an agenda to remake the church into something that isn't consistent with your current DNA or history.
- A pastor who has been a caretaker (maintainer vs. builder), even in a larger setting, when you need a builder (and the reciprocal situation).

Should You Keep Strong Staff or Let Them Go?

One reason leaders across the board, including pastors, don't plan for succession is because they know it has implications for people they care about and leave behind. The issue of what to do with existing staff is almost always a tricky part of the succession question. For example, should the loyal, knowledgeable administrative assistant to the senior pastor stay on with the new senior pastor? Is it best for strong personalities on staff—from the youth director to the senior associate pastor—to remain after the transition or to move on?

Decades ago it was widespread practice, sometimes written and sometimes not, among churches with staff for the arrival of a new pastor to mark the day that most staff (director level or above) submitted their resignations. The logic was to make clean transitions so that new pastors could build their own teams. In many of those situations the new pastor didn't act immediately on those resignations, saying instead, "I'll hold them in my desk drawer for six months. At that point I'll either accept them or tear them up."

In hiring new staff, Willow Creek's Bill Hybels emphasizes three elements: competence, character, chemistry.[6] When all three align well, candidates have a much higher rate of being a solid cultural match for the position. The last one—the personal chemistry between people—is the hardest to predict. It takes time to assess and develop. The same principles apply for inherited staff.

This issue applies to the senior pastor's assistant as well. Continuity of base knowledge from one administration to another is extremely helpful, but not if the chemistry fit is stressful or strained. You can't assume or guarantee chemistry. Your successor will need above anything else a high trust relationship with good mutual understanding. Some would say that the ideal admin can finish the pastor's sentences (but does so only when necessary or asked!).

If you are the outgoing pastor and have full-time staff members, be assured your resignation announcement will trigger questions for them about their own future at the church after you depart. Not only will various ones ask "Does the church want me to stay?" but also "Do I want to stay?"

The sooner that someone—you, the board, or the personnel team—can address such questions, the better. You want to avoid a great staff person seeking employment elsewhere under the assumption that staff are supposed to move on, only to discover too late that this assumption was inaccurate.

Another issue involves internal staff who want to be considered for the senior pastor role you are vacating. The most common approach is to frame it like this: internal candidates can apply, if polity allows, but if you don't get the job, you resign.

The bottom line: don't make it up as you go. Have your board or appropriate body develop a policy if none exists. Make sure it's articulated in a safe context where people can ask honest questions without being judged as disloyal or out of place.

There is no single model for where to find successors, and in no way would we say that the possibilities we've listed are in order of importance or are a procedure that must be followed. Rather, we've tried to give you a list of possibilities and pools for candidates. In the end, you must turn over every rock, look everywhere you can, and trust that God will guide you to the best candidates possible. With a prayerful approach to the process, you may find that you have more candidates available than you would have initially guessed.

NE X T Steps

For Pastors: What are three action steps to be taken over the next ninety days to develop internal leadership? What former staff members could be your successor? Schedule a call (at least annually) with each of them to check in.

For Boards: What three responsibilities can you take off your pastor's "plate" so that he or she can pour more time into leadership development?

15

The Money Question

What It Really Costs to Finance a Pastoral Succession

This is perhaps the only book on pastoral succession written to pastors to help them anticipate their own eventual succession. As we explained in the preface, we wrote to pastors knowing that many of their board members will also read *Next*. Our dream is that as board members figuratively look over their pastor's shoulder, they will pray through and process these important issues together.

In chapter 3, we wrote about pastors needing to prepare for their own financial future so that when God prompts them to move to another church, pursue a new ministry challenge, or at some point retire, they are free and ready to do so. In this chapter, we write about what a pastoral succession will cost the church budget. This information is crucial for both pastors and boards to know. To communicate it, we're temporarily changing our audience, writing to board members with the pastor looking over their shoulders.

We start with emphasizing how high the stakes are: the most expensive hire anyone can ever make is hiring the wrong person. A bad hire is expensive in every enterprise, but it's even more expensive in the church.[1] Severance payments can be costly. Momentum will most certainly be lost, hampering the church's mission. Reduced momentum is usually accompanied by reduced tithing. Other costs of a sudden and new search mount quickly as well. Smart churches will make every effort possible to mitigate the likelihood of a bad succession by planning early and reviewing often.

Basic Costs for a Typical Search Team

Can "basic" succession costs that are core to most church transitions be calculated and scaled by size? Stories and lists of expected succession costs follow and are framed by the generalization that, typically, expenses usually run higher than the church originally envisions.

As the first of two examples (one larger church and one smaller church), St. Andrew's Presbyterian in Newport Beach, California, has experienced an unusually smooth succession from their legendary pastor, John Huffman, to their new pastor, Rich Kannwischer. Attendance didn't experience large drops during the search, there have been very few bumps along the way, and the church hasn't missed a step as they have gone from one pastor to the next. Today, the church is thriving, growing, and filled with energy and vision, all while Rich and John enjoy a great relationship.[2]

Even with this healthy scenario, the costs added up.

Prior to the actual search, the board spent a long period of time exploring the possibility of promoting a candidate from within the existing staff. However, they concluded that this was not how God was leading. The transition planning at St. Andrews lasted about three years from John's public announcement of his intention to step down until Rich's first Sunday in the pulpit as the new pastor. Once the formal search for a pastor began, the search committee incurred many expenditures to visit prospective candidates or to bring in candidates for an interview, which often included spouses. Each of these candidate explorations involved airfare or mileage, hotels, meals, rental cars, and other costs.

St. Andrew's search ended in success, but only after a process that took nearly thirteen months. During those many months, the search team met over twenty-five times, and that was only the final phase of the selection process. The nine-member committee took extensive time away from family to attend meetings, participate in phone calls, and listen to a myriad of candidates' sermon samples. The costs incurred could have been radically reduced with more planning and perhaps outside help.

The small church in metro New York City where Warren is a board member completed a pastoral succession during the writing of this book. Its attendance was about one hundred people. The previous pastor had served for five years and then suddenly resigned and moved away on less than one week's notice. The denomination intervened immediately to help with the awkward farewells and launch what became a surprisingly smooth transition process. The approach was to engage a two-days-a-week interim preaching pastor contracted "for up to 18 months or until a new pastor was found." Various governance board leaders took on extra responsibilities during the transition period.

The process actually took twenty months. The church board had to work through a number of issues before it felt ready to launch a search. These included crisis management for the first few months. The church brought in a Christian counselor who led sessions on helping the congregation grieve the sudden loss of their previous pastor. The board then sorted through a profile of who the church is, where it is heading, and what kind of pastor it needed next.

After denominational training, the search team conducted initial candidate interviews by phone, listened to sermon samples over the internet, and brought in the leading candidate and his family for two different visits. His previous church was two hundred miles away, so he drove, receiving reimbursement from the church for mileage, hotel, and meals. Once called and appointed, the church paid moving costs for him and his family, with volunteers awaiting them at the parsonage when the moving van arrived. They had stocked the refrigerator, put flowers on the table, and were ready to help with anything needed for setting up the pastoral family's new home.

The primary expenses were a generous departure gift to the outgoing pastor, salary for the part-time preaching pastor, candidate expenses for the in-person weekends, and moving costs. These added up to roughly the salary amount the church would have been paying if it had a full-time pastor all along. Even in this simple and smooth succession, the costs maxed out what the church could pay.

The Costs Are Often Even Higher

The costs associated with the two church succession plans we've described were for relatively smooth and healthy transitions. Sadly, that's not the norm. Ordinarily, succession plans are not seamless, and too often they are not healthy. Consider the following, more typical scenario, which would carry all of the costs listed above, as well as added wrinkles.

Ordinarily, pastoral succession involves a lapse between the departure of the former pastor and the arrival of the new one. We estimate that time range to be from twelve to twenty-four months. Typically, the larger the church, the longer the pastoral search time range runs.

> Typically, the larger the church, the longer the pastoral search time range runs.

The biggest variable in succession plans is that during the many months between pastors, the church also loses its spirit of momentum. Revenue falls markedly. Worship attendance leaks downward. Young families newer to the church drift off to other congregations. Ministry initiatives are put on hold until the new pastor is found. If it's a larger church, vacant staff positions remain unfilled because candidates want to wait for the senior post to fill before signing on, and the same is true for most potential new volunteers. Existing staff members become restless due to the lack of a clear visionary leader at the head of the organization. If it's a smaller church, key volunteer roles remain open as the church's limited volunteer energy is focused elsewhere.

Pastorates were once
viewed as lifetime
positions with 8 out of
10 pastors staying in
one church for life.

Pastorates were once viewed as lifetime positions with 8 out of 10 pastors staying in one church for life. A study of the graduates of Yale College from 1702 to 1775 shows that 79 percent of those who were ministers served one parish from ordination to retirement. The majority served for more than thirty years, and a mere 7 percent had more than two parishes.[3]

Nowadays, clergy turnover is more common. Mismatches seem to happen far too often, and too many churches are left inert during the process.

Hard Costs Add Up Quickly

The financial stakes for a succession plan are often far higher than most churches initially estimate when you consider the typical hard costs.

Parting gifts to outgoing pastor or salary paid as part of separation agreement. When a senior pastor departs, churches tend to err on the side of generosity. Even in unhappy separations, they are apt to offer a severance payment higher than the one-month-salary-per-year-of-employment level often paid in marketplace severances. In happier departures, the generosity often goes beyond that, especially in larger churches. For extremely long-term pastors who led the church to significant growth, the stakes are often even higher. It is not unusual for a larger church to continue paying the full salary of a founding pastor who has served the church for several decades of continual growth, especially if that pastor has spent an entire career at the same church and made minimal to no financial preparation for the future. Three months is rather standard for subordinate staff in a good departure. In either case, however, it is typically much less than that in an unfortunate departure or in smaller churches.

Written separation agreements are typically useful. In positive good-byes, they help preclude misunderstanding. (Is the laptop computer the pastor's or the church's?) In strained relationships, they help preclude further tensions and also make necessary legal statements. They also help anticipate the unexpected. Separation agreements contain language about speaking well of each other, families included, so if the pastor's teenage son or daughter begins writing nasty things about the church on Facebook, then the final payments to the outgoing pastor can be paused until that situation is remedied. Separation agreements should always be written and signed by both parties after a period of review.

When using a separation agreement, our advice at Vanderbloemen Search Group is that it should never come as a surprise. It should be hand delivered, always with a witness observing the interaction. It generally comprises a long list of conditions ranging from details of final paycheck to a waiver that allows church leaders to disclose details of the departure to prospective employers who inquire. It should begin something like this: "Thank you for your services to [CHURCH]. This letter, upon your signature, will constitute the agreement between you, [NAME], and the Church on the terms of your separation from employment with the Church. . . ."

(If you need an actual separation agreement, the Vanderbloemen Search Group is happy to provide one for you for free, which you can have your legal counsel review to ensure compliance with local laws in your area. Email support@vanderbloemen.com to get started; also see "What Our Organizations Can Do for You" on page 182.)

Ongoing support or salary. This is quite common for a long-tenured pastor or to the widow of a former pastor, especially if the pastoral family did not make adequate financial preparations for their years after serving your church.

Such agreements have the potential to become the tail wagging the dog. The idea of pledging long-term or lifetime support is increasingly an issue that causes the new generation of leaders to curse what they inherited. They are aware that some settlements are quite large and take needed resources out of the church budget for years. Sometimes the church genuinely might not be able to deliver on it over time. Our recommendation is that whatever is paid out needs to be done so over time so that the church has some leverage over the outgoing pastor (and family) for a period of time. For gifts given purely out of goodwill, it's best to include conditions or stated review points. For example, "Our intention is to pay this amount monthly for two years, at which point we will review both the church's circumstances and yours." You don't want your desire to be generous to mitigate their motivation to find other avenues of gainful support.

Weekly preacher/teacher. Some churches will have no cost for pulpit supply, relying on capable lay teachers or existing staff within the congregation who will not expect honorariums. Most churches, however, will need to prepare for honorariums. These amounts vary widely. A smaller church bringing in a local preacher, such as a hospital chaplain, parachurch minister, retired pastor, or preaching professor from a nearby seminary or Bible school might pay a few hundred dollars each week to preach for the church's single worship service. The going rate for honoraria increases with church size and the number of church services. For itinerant guests, travel and lodging costs also become a factor. These costs also apply to interim pastors, an approach discussed later in this chapter.

Travel related to interviewing candidates. Airfare or mileage, hotel, meals, and other travel expenses can add up quickly, especially as most churches don't call the first candidate they check out. Fortunately, with online sermon podcasts and streaming video feeds in today's technological world, the cost of a search is greatly reduced. Free video interview services like Skype have also proved to be helpful and cost-effective for a candidate's initial interview before a face-to-face meeting as the next step.

Moving costs for new pastor. Even in heavy volunteer churches, there will still be hard costs like moving vans, food, and lodging while a new pastor is in transit.

Higher salary for new pastor. This may not apply to your church's situation. However, it is common for retiring pastors to have declined raises for years, which leaves the church with a salary that is below what the market bears and requires a budget change so that the new pastor can be paid at a competitive level. We've also seen well-paid, well-tenured pastors replaced by young leaders who are paid much less. More churches than not should be ready to pay more to attract and retain a high-capacity leader. [4]

Updates to pastor's office and new equipment, such as a computer. These one-time costs can range from a few hundred dollars to thousands if major redecorating or updates are included.

Dips in giving by the congregation. Typically, giving will decline between pastors. Oddly, after a moral failure, the giving tends to increase for a brief time. It's almost as if the congregation has a "survivor's syndrome," banding together in the wake of a crisis. Everyone pitches in at the beginning. Knowing this and being able to capitalize on it by showing a clear plan forward could make a big difference as a church enters an unforeseen succession period.

Staff departures. During a senior-level transition, other staff will also move on, resulting in financial hard cost implications for the church.

Search firm. The typical fee to retain a search firm is 25 to 40 percent of the pastor's first year's salary-plus-housing-allowance, as well as travel costs for search firm visits.

Advertising for the position. For churches that don't use a search firm or denominational help, these costs can range from hundreds to thousands of dollars.

Publicity costs. Development of printed and video materials to support your search, advertising that describes your church and the type of candidate you desire, can range from hundreds to thousands of dollars, depending on the quality of the production.

Other consultants. You might use several consultants along the way, such as someone to advise on a debt reduction campaign.

Pastor's fund. Some churches have a pastor's fund, which is a separate fund often created by wealthy patrons of the church for discretionary use for any cause or project the pastor wants to support. In such churches, this fund is sometimes stocked or replenished in preparation for the arrival of a new pastor.

Soft Costs Can Be Even Higher

Soft costs might include

- Lost momentum.
- People leaving the church the longer the time without a lead pastor.

- Volunteer time given, usually by the best volunteers, to a search instead of missional work.
- Collateral impact on other staff who leave, eroding discipleship, outreach, or other ministries.

Cost of Interim Pastors

Chapter 12 looked at the pros and cons of interim pastors. In this chapter, we will discuss their cost. Usually, interim pastors receive a fixed salary or fee, whether part-time or full-time. Their responsibilities typically involve preaching, administrative leadership, and oversight of pastoral care. Interim pastors are rarely as strong in leading as the pastor who has just departed from the church.

Churches typically do not save money on salary costs during an interim time. You might expect that the interim makes less, but in many cases, they make the same when factoring in all related costs. Even if their remuneration is lower than the previous pastor's, the church's overall costs may be even higher if relocation or temporary housing expenses for the interim pastor are involved.

Insurance and Assistance with Personal Financial Planning

Another expense to consider is insurance premiums. Many churches take out a "key man" life insurance policy on the lead pastor, especially if the church has any level of indebtedness or a capital campaign in process. If a lead pastor were to die, the proceeds of the policy could be used for a variety of needs: to help pay any church-incurred medical costs on your pastor (maybe you helped fund hospice care, for example) or administrative costs (maybe you needed to hire outside pulpit supply during your pastor's lengthy incapacitation). Perhaps it could offset any downturns in giving by the congregation or fund an interim pastor. Additionally, the pastor's family is ordinarily a beneficiary to part of the policy. In the overall scheme of succession, smaller costs that might not be considered add up quickly. Smart churches will compile an exhaustive list of expenses and then set aside appropriate funds before considering a succession plan.

If a primary reason many pastors hang on to their job too long is a lack of finances for retirement (see chapters 2 and 3), church boards or compensation committees may want to offer their pastor help with financial planning. We recommend that the pastor be free to choose who the planner is. Otherwise, it might feel meddlesome to force the pastor to use someone inside the church with expertise in this area. Perhaps the church could offer whatever they have budgeted for financial planning back to the pastor as an additional retirement fund donation if the pastor chooses someone inside the church who will do the work for free.

The total cost of succession should lead churches to begin planning now, saving now, and forming a relationship now with outside entities that can help them navigate the succession process.

Avoiding Lawsuits Related to a Succession

We devoted many pages of this book to the topic of following a predecessor who had a messy ending (chapter 11). Sadly, too many of these unfortunate endings by a predecessor require extra finances.

One of the most expensive church costs is dealing with a lawsuit related to a succession. It can be an overwhelming expense for a church, both financially and in energy or focus. Our friend and nationally recognized church law attorney David Middlebrook of the Church Law Group[5] has offered these ideas for church leaders to minimize the likelihood of a lawsuit during times of pastoral transition.

Proactively address succession issues before they occur. Get over the fear and reluctance to engage your church and its leaders in discussing the topic of ministry succession planning as a sound legal and risk management practice. Make it an annual board agenda item or item for discussion in your church's business meeting.

Review existing employment agreements. Ensure that the organization honors its commitments to the departing pastor. Make sure any future employment agreements are reviewed and revised to adequately and comprehensively address how the organization will formally relate to a new leader regarding benefits, intellectual property ownership, and so on.

Assess your formal emergency succession planning. Do your governing documents—especially your articles and bylaws—adequately and clearly express the steps to be taken for an unplanned departure of the lead pastor or other senior executive ministry leaders? Silence or ambiguity in an emergency situation such as with a permanent disability or some other issue concerning a senior leader can lead to litigation.

Discuss how your church will address a planned departure of a pastor or senior executive. Ideally, a planned departure has a one- to two-year transition period. Do your articles and bylaws adequately and clearly address the steps to be taken for a planned departure? Will you appoint an automatic and specifically identified successor? Will you establish a succession planning committee? Will there be an interim pastor to assist the congregation in making a successful transition to a new leader? As with an emergency situation or unplanned departure, silence or ambiguity with a planned departure can lead to litigation. Set a specifically known departure date to ensure adequate progress.

Communicate as much as seems wise about why the pastor is leaving, letting church staff or board members be the first to receive such communications.

Make sure governing documents, articles, and bylaws adequately express and empower the process your church will be engaged in and the people most involved. Ensure that the process you have identified is clearly articulated and that the voting requirements, if any, adequately express the quorum required to take a vote (majority, super majority, and so on).

Bring membership rolls and the list of corporate officers up-to-date. Ensure your membership and any corporate members lists are current to avoid litigation over who is entitled to do what during the succession planning process.

Ensure that succession, whether internal or external, is based on performance and merit and not heredity. Resist automatically advancing the founder's or current senior pastor's son or other family member to a position of leadership. This advancement can be done, but it requires a proper leader and a thoughtful, well-designed process to avoid potential problems. An orderly and thoughtful evaluation process can help ensure that board members are protected against litigation related to the failure to exercise the duty of care when selecting a new leader.

Adequately address the broad range of departure issues and incoming leadership issues to avoid practical problems. Does the departing pastor or senior executive have adequate retirement savings? Are there future employability concerns? Are departing payments and benefits consistent with IRS rules on reasonable compensation and antidiscrimination rules with respect to health and retirement benefits? Is your proposed total compensation package for a new leader adequate enough to recruit and retain the quality of leader your church needs to continue to fulfill its God-given mission? Is it also consistent with IRS rules on reasonable compensation and antidiscrimination rules with respect to health and retirement benefits? Have you addressed a sabbatical policy? Have you addressed issues and concerns that were experienced during the tenure of the departing pastor or senior executive?

Work to ensure that the actual transfer of organizational control is effective. Communicate. Communicate. Communicate. Ensure that the particular culture of the organization is considered and respected. Work to coordinate the appropriate timing of announcements, the naming of a successor, the participation of any stakeholders, and so on. Respect the various emotions and passions of individuals that are different from those of the leaders most involved in the succession process. Ensure compliance with and documentation of compliance with the articles and bylaws. Be especially careful to document quorums and votes throughout the process.

Create separation agreements and new employment agreements that follow legal best practices. Both agreements should include provisions for confidentiality and a Christian mediation and arbitration clause to best guard against litigation in secular courts.

Congregational Giving Trends during a Pastoral Succession

The authors of *The Elephant in the Boardroom* advise, "Once a new pastor arrives, giving does not immediately rebound and may take six months to return to its previous level."[6] A typical example is Eastside Foursquare Church, Bothell, Washington. In 2011, DJ Vick, who had been on staff at the church for eleven years, succeeded Jim Hayford, who had served as senior pastor for fifteen years. Jim stayed active in the church, launching a ministry called "West of 50" to provide pastoral care for the spiritual needs of older men and women.

Even with a transition to someone already known, giving increased initially during the first year, which hadn't happened in a decade. At the transition, Jim was sixty-seven and DJ was thirty-three. Predictably, DJ began drawing a younger crowd, one whose economic life stage was at a lower level than that of older individuals in the congregation. By the two-year mark, there was light attrition, though the church is beginning to stabilize with fresh vision.[7]

Our friend Jim Sheppard, coauthor of *Contagious Generosity* and CEO of Generis, which helps churches and ministry organizations accelerate generosity toward their God-inspired vision, underscores the impact of a pastoral transition on congregational giving patterns.[8] "More than almost any other single factor, a change in the senior leader will affect the giving level of a church, for better or for worse," he says.

This is because giving tends to be tied to the mission and vision of the church as well as the ability of the top leaders, especially the senior pastor, to articulate it clearly. "If the previous pastor was held in high regard, there will likely be initial uncertainty about the new leader. In this case, people will be making up their minds as to whether they want to remain part of the church under the new senior leader, and it will take a while before giving levels rebound," Jim says. Confidence levels clearly have an effect on the giving level of the church, and newcomers don't give at nearly the same level as established members.

What happens financially when there is a season between the two permanent pastors, such as with an interim pastor? "The main role of an interim pastor is to stabilize the church during the time of transition and prepare the people for a new leader. When an interim pastor can do this and assuming the search for a new leader does not drag on, giving levels will likely remain stable," Jim says.

Jim does not generally see giving levels change immediately when the new pastor is announced. "Certainly, there is great anticipation until the name of the new leader is revealed, but that event does not typically have an effect on giving," he says.

"The period when the new pastor arrives and the first few months thereafter is a key time," Jim says. People are making up their minds as to whether they will "buy in" to the direction of the church under the new leader. If a leader makes an immediate positive impression on the people, it is not unusual to see a positive bounce in giving.

"Whether or not that bounce is short-term or long-term, is dependent on what happens over the six to eight months after that," he says.

Not all pastoral transitions are seen as a bad thing. According to Jim, "When leaders overstay their season at a church, such as when ministry momentum is stalled or there is a lack of enthusiasm among the people, the arrival of a new leader can be seen as a good thing and giving might even go up, at least in the short-term."

As the old saying goes, "Everything rises and falls on leadership." This phrase is often quoted, but its truth is never more apparent than when there is no leadership. Without a leader, churches lose focus. Momentum slows. Morale drops. Giving falls, and seats open up in services. Everything falls, and nothing except anxiety rises when there is no leader. Rarely will the church's income rise during a lack in leadership.

A Final Financial Caution to Outgoing Pastors

Outgoing pastors too often leave their post without thinking thoroughly about their own finances. If you're an outgoing pastor shifting to employment other than another church, take care to budget carefully. If you're leaving the world of ministry, you're likely giving up the tax exemption that comes with a clergy housing allowance and perhaps many benefits that a church covers but a new employer might not, such as your spouse's health insurance, continuing education conference money, and various expense accounts. Other perks from a hefty book allowance to a church-provided cell phone and computer might not be provided by your new employer. For your own budgeting, it's important to realize all the fringe benefits with which your church position may have helped you.

The Value of Outside Help

While few cardinal rules in pastoral succession exist, one clearly surrounds finances: when all parties weigh the costs, the need for thorough advance planning will become all the more clear. Exceedingly few pastors and churches take a hard look at the cost of a pastoral succession. Wise churches will take an annual look at these costs, and wise pastors will weigh the cost for their personal lives.

And sometimes outside help is needed.

Finding a key staff person for your church or ministry is as serious as an organ transplant: you're bringing an outsider into your church body to run a major system. If hiring a new pastor can be compared to a heart transplant, then transplants are critical enough to warrant specialized help. If the operation goes well, your ministry will find a new and hopefully higher level of life. If the operation is rushed, goes poorly, or ends in rejection, things can get downright unpleasant.

Whether you use a staffing search firm, denominational help, a board of overseers, a transition consultant, or a combination of these, your third-party assistant brings an objective set of eyes to the process. It's the same reason surgeons don't operate on themselves or their own family—they are too tied to the patient to do the job well. Likewise, churches often need someone with objective counsel and who has emotional detachment and expertise in the search process.

> Finding a key staff person is as serious as an organ transplant: you're bringing an outsider into your church body to run a major system.

An experienced outside firm, coach, or denominational leader can also perform a tissue match between the church and the pastor who will serve her. Excellence in search isn't just about finding a talented person. It's about prayerfully finding the right talent for your situation. A capable outside party can cultivate a "donor" list of candidates for your search far beyond your own ability. This outside helper becomes highly informed and involved with both parties, knowing both your DNA and the DNA of various candidates to achieve a successful tissue match, just as a successful transplant doctor would. This provides an optimal context for you to find the right match for your staff need.

NE X T Steps

For Pastors: Have you taken time to calculate what your lifestyle would cost annually to maintain if you were not in pastoral ministry?

For Boards: How have you budgeted for your next pastoral transition?

16

Preparing for the Next Pastor

Setting Up Your Successor's First One Hundred Days for Success

The first one hundred days of a pastorate are pivotal to a successful succession, and you influence your successor's first one hundred days far more than you realize. The keys to that success begin with how the outgoing pastor sets up the incoming pastor's launch. This is true even if you have no role in the selection process. It's also true if you will already have moved away when your successor arrives.

If you've been in ministry for a while you've heard your share of stories about moving. It's rare, but some pastors move to a new city and arrive at their new home to find the refrigerator stocked and a team of people available to help. That's the equivalent of what you want to do for your successor in ministry: "stock the fridge" and leave "a team of people to help" so that the first one hundred days have the best chance to be a maximum success.

In this sense, finishing well is not just about you, but about also putting energy into helping the church get ready for the person who comes after you.

"Succession planning is one of the hardest . . . processes to get right. We've seen the headlines all too often about messy, protracted, clumsy, embarrassing, and highly visible succession failures."[1]

That quote is not about pastors but about marketplace organizations, where the report also says that 50 percent of organizations with annual revenues of $500 million or more report they have "no meaningful succession plans." The article then raises a question applicable to churches: "If 50 percent of the big organizations who have the budget and resources to devote to succession have no salient succession plans, then you can only imagine what the scenario looks like for smaller companies. Big or small, is your organization one of them?"[2]

Stated more bluntly, corporate CEOs are often tasked with succession from their first day at work.[3] If the business world treats the issue with this level of importance, shouldn't churches?

Sadly, the answer in too many cases is that religious organizations are worse at this than corporations. The Evangelical Council for Financial Accountability helps its members set a gold standard in various management practices. It recently surveyed 1,595 CEOs and board members. Out of twenty self-assessment questions, the statement that received the fewest affirmative answers by far was "Our board is well-prepared to name its next CEO."[4] While they may say succession planning and selecting the chief executive is the number one job of the board, their practices show otherwise.

If you want your successor to start well, you must help your church prepare for that day.

Biggest Transition Help Came from Predecessors

Woodbury Lutheran Church, in an eastern suburb of Minneapolis-St. Paul, has had three senior pastors since its founding in 1967. The first pastor served for thirty-two years and then retired. His successor served for twelve years. Then just prior to a planned retirement, he was elected as a district president in his denomination.[5]

The current pastor, Tom Pfotenhauer—son of the founding pastor—came on staff as associate pastor in 2008 at age thirty-one. As the senior pastor announced his upcoming retirement, the church did a national search, seriously considering several candidates before calling Tom to be senior pastor in 2012. "Doing a full search gave integrity to the process," Tom said. "It also helped confirm to me that their call was the Holy Spirit's leading."

Continuing, Tom commented, "The succession process here was a night and day contrast with a previous church I had served. The pastor there was also retiring, but the church council [governance board] did not take the adequate steps to prepare for his retirement. As a result, there was turnover in staff and a significant drop in attendance."

Fortunately, the process was different at Woodbury. According to Tom, "They took it very seriously here. As the pastor's likely retirement approached, the council put together not only a search team, but a separate transition team that included a couple of people with training and experience in the field of human resources to help pave the way for the next guy."

The transition team worked hard on a plan to bring the new pastor on board. For example, they came up with about thirty topics for the incoming and outgoing pastors to talk about: who are the influencers, what are the sacred cow traditions, how does the church do Christmas and Easter, and so on. They also set up meetings for the new pastor to dialogue with various leadership groups in the church.

"The idea was to make sure I was surrounded by people and resources that could help me be successful as the new senior pastor," Tom said. He stepped into leading a church that was multisite, had recently merged with another congregation, and was anticipating a capital campaign for its next chapter of ministry. The transition strategy lasted about six months, at which point the transition team dissolved according to plan. "They were also a great group for me to use as a sounding board," Tom said.

Was this careful strategy really necessary once it turned out that the new pastor was someone who had grown up in the church and had been on staff for several years? Tom's answer is absolutely yes. Even though he clearly had the insider's head start and home court advantage, he felt the transition helped make his opening months go far better than he could have navigated on his own. "For instance, I'm still getting clarity on how decision making occurs and on addressing ministry silos that exist," he said. "How to work in unity and unison may take a few years to figure out."

In Tom's view, the biggest help in the transition came from his two predecessors. "Both pastors recognized that the church is not theirs but God's. This gave them an understanding that they should do whatever they can to help the next person be successful here—and they have! That means that the church continues to be about Jesus, and not about positions or people in authority." This attitude has freed Tom to lead to the maximum of his abilities.

Looking back on his first months as senior pastor, Tom appreciates all the intentionality in the hand-off process. Attendance and finances both held steady in the transition, and the church has a healthy sense of anticipating what's to come. "The Holy Spirit is really directing this, and we've been good at being open to the Spirit's direction," he said. "We've been blessed in the transition, with no major hiccups in the first one hundred days."

Happy Good-byes for Healthy, Positive Transitions

Leadership Network recently sponsored "A Day with Jim Collins" for twenty pastors and leaders.[6] Jim is a longtime friend of Leadership Network and is the author of six books, including *Built to Last, Good to Great,* and *How the Mighty Fall.*[7] Jim's opening words to these pastors? "Your church cannot be great if it cannot be great without you." He started the conversation by reminding them that at some point, their address will change.

William Bridges, an authority on change and transition, helps us understand the emotional side of those transitions. He argues that the single biggest reason organizational changes fail is that no one has thought about endings or planned to manage their impact on people.[8] His argument is that changes don't do you in. Rather, transitions do you in.

He explains the way the concepts differ. *Change* is situational. In churches, change is the move to a new location, the retirement of the founder, the reorganization of the roles on the pastoral team, or the decision to shift to a more contemporary approach to worship. *Transition* is psychological. It is a process people go through as they internalize and come to terms with the details of the new situation the change brings about.[9] In church, transitions might be the adjustments associated with the new pastor, a new preaching style, new working relationships, a new order of worship, or anything else new or different that comes with that new pastor.

One of the earliest marks of transition is the sense of loss known as grieving. We grieve for the loss of all relationships we consider significant. It can affect our entire being. It can often be addressed. Many counselors explore the five stages of feelings associated with grief that were popularized by Elisabeth Kübler-Ross: denial, anger, bargaining, depression, and acceptance.[10] Her final stage "is about accepting the reality that our loved one is physically gone and recognizing that this new reality is the permanent reality."[11] Not all people go through each stage, nor in that order, nor in any linear fashion. "The nature and intensity of feelings caused by a loss relate to the individuality and uniqueness of the relationship," cautions one writer.[12] Some say the final phase of the grieving process is accommodation. This occurs "when the bereaved person gradually moves on, re-entering the everyday world and lives with the loss of the loved one."[13]

The longer your tenure, the more likely you are to go through a period of grieving. This should be discussed and the good literature on the topic accessed. But you are not the only one to grieve. The congregation does too. One excellent book on pastoral succession starts with a reminder of the universal pain people feel in loss, and how it affects their behavior:

> Just six weeks after they had left Egypt, the Hebrew people began to grumble about their new leaders, Moses and Aaron. The exodus, which had begun with great drama and fanfare, soon deteriorated into murmurs and complaints.
>
> Ministry transitions today aren't much different. No matter how greatly anticipated the change, the question isn't really *if* dissatisfaction and opposition will arise; the question is *when*.
>
> Pastoral transitions are tough; there's no way of escaping it.[14]

In our work at Vanderbloemen Search Group, we've seen many churches take longer than the norm in their search solely because they aren't emotionally ready to hire a pastor. You want to help your church prepare to grieve, but the sign of healing and readiness for the next stage will be when they shift more energy from grieving your departure to anticipating the next pastor's arrival.

Here are ways you as the outgoing pastor can help the congregation process their feelings as you depart and as your successor arrives.

Offer at least one public and broad good-bye. It is important that members from every corner of congregational life can say good-bye to the entire pastoral family.

Invite people to express feelings. It helps people begin to grieve their loss if they can voice personal feelings through laughter, tears, and other emotions.

Celebrate the good times. Even if leaving was not your idea or if you're walking away from a bad situation, take inventory and celebrate what you can. Voice some life lessons that you've learned and are thankful for.

Be gracious. If you refuse to let people make a big deal of your leaving, you're not doing them a favor; instead, you're depriving them from blessing you and in turn being blessed themselves. Being gracious means accepting someone's gift of kindness without reservation. Let them say good-bye.

Don't burn bridges. Fight the urge to vent any frustrations other than in a private and appropriate context such as a formal exit interview. As you part ways, walk away quietly, gently, and with integrity. Most people will regret saying too much and not forgiving enough.

Here are ways church boards can help the congregation process their feelings as they say good-bye to a pastor and prepare for a new one.

Encourage pastors and their families to verbalize a personal good-bye. The congregation needs to hear expressions of appreciation, memories, and other words from the heart. Those are often pathways to healing of hurts for both the pastoral family and the congregation.

Set a short but defined period for the good-byes. For example, the church board might designate forty days for celebrating Pastor Smith's retirement.

Know you're going to grieve and be okay with it. As the book *The Emotionally Healthy Church* emphasizes, you aren't a growing or maturing Christian unless you connect your spirituality with the emotional side of your life.[15]

Honor the pastor's spouse. Be sure to have a separate, dedicated good-bye process for the spouse of your outgoing pastor.

Further the pastor's legacy. In addition to any monetary gift for the outgoing pastor, take up a special offering to give to a mission effort close to the pastor's heart. Give a gift in your pastor's name. An example of this is planting a church in an area of the world where the pastor and the church's mission department have been active during the pastor's tenure. But hold the memorials. Delay naming a room or area of your church as long as your pastor is still alive.

Bring in people who have helped them. If finances permit, fly any significant spiritual mentors/overseers into town for a surprise good-bye during your celebration time—including their families, if possible.

Send your outgoing pastor on a dream trip. One church bought their pastor great tickets, travel, and lodging for the US Open, knowing that he loves tennis.

Commission a professional photo or portrait. Have the outgoing pastor sit for a portrait to be hung somewhere in the building. This can be very meaningful, and the pastor's family will love having a copy for their home as well.

Family Matters More Than You May Realize

If you're an outgoing pastor going to a new ministry, and if you're married, it's important to help your spouse end well. At Vanderbloemen Search Group, perhaps the biggest change in our interviewing over the years relates to the spouse of the candidate we are talking to. We've learned that this is a dynamic not to be overlooked.

Pastors who are making a move to a new job are leaving specifically to go to a new adventure, and the lion's share of their energy is almost always on the new work and the new place of ministry. The spouse, however, is often left with pulling up roots, leaving friends, and oftentimes leaving family behind. While these dynamics don't doom a transition, they certainly affect it. Some years back, Lifeway Research ran a study asking the question, "How far do Baptist pastors live from their mother-in-law?" The answer: not far. So we spend time in interviews exploring what, if any, effect a move will have.

Likewise, when a pastor is retiring, we have found that a whole lot of focus is placed on the retiring pastor but not enough attention is given to the retiring pastor's spouse. Traditionally, especially for women, much of the spouse's identity is tied to the job and role of being the pastor's spouse. Leaving that behind is harder for many than they think. Smart churches foresee this, and do all they can to honor the retiring spouse, perhaps even helping the spouse identify future roles in the community or nonprofits to help direct energy in a positive, helpful fashion.

Honoring the Past Unlocks the Future

The book *The Elephant in the Boardroom* says that the first principle for a successful transition is this: honor thy predecessor. The default succession plan for kings of the Old Testament was often assassination. They would obliterate the previous king and the fruit of his life. Instead of trying to wipe out the past, wise pastors choose to celebrate the great legacy inherited from one or more predecessors.

The same need for honor applies to you as the outgoing pastor in how you speak about and treat your successor.

Seamless transitions are rare, but they do happen, even in extreme circumstances. Most of the time, the seamlessness can be traced back to a key principle: when the past is honored, future possibilities are unlocked. No two pastoral successions are identical, but some clearly go better than others. An excellent example of a smooth, long-term transition occurred between the fifth and sixth pastors at Peachtree Presbyterian Church in Atlanta after an era of great growth and the sudden death of someone who had been at the helm for twenty-eight years.

In 1976, the church called thirty-six-year-old Frank Harrington to be its fifth pastor. He arrived determined to grow Peachtree's membership and ministry as well as its giving level and generosity. Indeed he did, across a long tenure of twenty-eight years. During Frank's era, the church became the largest in attendance and largest in membership of any Presbyterian church in the country. Sadly, in 2000 Frank died suddenly from apparent pneumonia.

> When the past is honored, future possibilities are unlocked.

Deeply grieving the loss of its beloved longtime pastor, the church approached the future at a deliberate and methodical pace. The session asked the church's theologian-in-residence to preach weekly and assist with evangelism activities while the church looked for an interim pastor. Two months later, he was asked to be the interim pastor with primary responsibility for preaching while another staff pastor was given the role of head of staff with responsibility for day-to-day operations.[16]

According to one published report, no retirement or succession plan was in place, and no such plan had been officially discussed. Attendance dropped, giving slipped, and membership dived, accounting for 10 percent of the total denominational membership decline, reported in 2000.[17]

Twenty months after Frank Harrington's last Sunday in the pulpit, the church's sixth pastor was installed. Victor Pentz was thirteen years younger than his predecessor. In a previous church, he had followed a thirty-year predecessor, but this time was not the same. He was now following someone who had died suddenly while in office. Further, the predecessor was an icon of Southern culture, while the incoming pastor was a fourth-generation Californian who had at one time run a beach evangelism ministry. "I may not have been born a Southerner, but I got here as quickly as I could," he often jokes.

Newcomer Vic Pentz had a wide range of emotions to deal with. "One was sheer relief of the new pastor coming," he said, "but they were also grieving." He found the church to be extremely gracious toward him. It was a joyful beginning for him as well. "It was like following someone who built a Rolls Royce, and now I get to join with a marvelous community who enjoys driving it," he said.

One approach Vic used was to mention his predecessor frequently in sermons. "We also memorialized him such as in a scholarship for young preachers, named a couple of buildings after him, all to celebrate what Frank had been to this church," Vic said.

Vic was an undergraduate history major. His goal was to learn more about the history of this church than any human being. "I tell the stories of this church, which builds trust because you're constantly showing appreciation to those who went before me. If I can tell those stories with authenticity and appreciation, that connects me with people's souls. They're much more willing to be part of my leadership," he said.

But he didn't try to become a junior Frank Harrington. "I did not invite people to compare me to him," Vic said. "I had no interest in being just like him."

Vic also became a student of the culture of Peachtree Presbyterian. "First and foremost, they wanted someone who could preach to the kind of congregation that Peachtree Presbyterian was. Then, far after that was to lead staff well, building a team."

Over time, the congregation came to see their new pastor as one who had vision and passion like his predecessor, though not necessarily in the same way. "Our personalities were very different, and our backgrounds could not have been more different," Vic said. "But both of us love to preach, we relate well to leaders, and we have a conservative, evangelical, and assertive outreach."

Vic had his share of surprises and challenges, as did the congregation. Perhaps the biggest involved one of the most frequent issues in the transition of a long-term pastor: building a new sense of team from the remaining staff. "After several years, even bringing in specialists, I realized that I needed a new team," he said. "We had twelve pastors when I came, and by the five-year mark, eight of them were gone. Today, I love bringing together my leadership team and dreaming the next six months in a collegial way."[18] One of those pastoral team members is Frank Harrington's daughter.

The church has come to embrace their "new" pastor, even in his bold initiatives. One example was in a 2009 sermon that discussed abortion, the US president, and the sanctity of life. "I make a promise to you now and I don't want you to keep this a secret," the pastor pronounced. "Peachtree Presbyterian Church will care for any newborn baby you bring to this church. We will be the family to find a home for that child, and there's no limit on this. You can tell your friends, you can tell your family, and you can tell the whole world."

A week later, he reflected on that sermon to the local newspaper. "I seem to have touched a nerve by saying that to the congregation," he said. "I had people handing me checks as they exited the building."[19]

On the date of this book's publication, Vic Pentz will have just celebrated his fourteenth anniversary as pastor of Peachtree Presbyterian, and the church is growing, continuing to be the largest in its denomination.

Will You Set the Stage for Whoever Is Next?

According to one study, the average American Protestant minister moves about every eight years. Those in denominational appointment systems, such as United Methodists, move about every five years. Pastors who are free to choose their own jobs have led an average of 2.7 churches over their career, compared to an average of 4.1 churches among those who are assigned placements.

Pastoral succession is a universal and inescapable reality in the life of a pastor. You'll do best if you can come to say, as Scott Thumma, introduced in chapter 11, recommends for pastors: "This is bigger than me and if I don't have a responsible plan to move the congregation beyond me, then I'm not doing my task of ministering to this community."[20]

Perhaps the real test of whether or not you believe that statement is how far you'll go in setting the stage for your successor to experience a wildly successful first one hundred days.

NE X T Steps

For Pastors: What can you do to learn about the history of your church? Read the minutes from all board meetings in the church's history. What patterns of innovation can you find and how can you leverage that history for future innovations?

For Boards: Does your board have a "transition team" ready to help new staff on board? How can that team set up a plan for introducing new pastors and team members to the community, the church, and key people in the congregation?

17

Thinking Long Term

There Is No Success without Succession

When William Vanderbloemen was a young pastor, John Maxwell said something to him that stuck. He told William, then in his early thirties, to begin now to prepare for the end of his career. He said, "Smart people—including pastors—spend their early career years creating options for their latter years. What are you doing to create options—for income and where to spend energy?" John was challenging William to begin thinking about the idea of legacy.

Maxwell later wrote in *The 21 Irrefutable Laws of Leadership*, "Achievement comes to someone when he is able to do great things for himself. Success comes when he empowers followers to do great things for him. But a legacy is created only when a person puts his organization into a position to do great things without him."[1]

Good pastors focus their life on producing good fruit for God's kingdom, as John 10, John 15, 1 Peter 5, and other passages teach. But the wisest, greatest, and perhaps most effective pastors focus extensive time and energy on what their legacy will be when their life is over. This is a call to think beyond immediate fruit.

Our friend (and noted pastor and author) Geoff Surratt paints a vivid picture of this reality in a humorous fable about two people who each set out to become the best possible apple farmer.[2] They studied every book they could find about apple growing and talked extensively with other apple growers. While they both started with similar efforts to cultivate their apple tree, each imagined a different outcome and so each took a different trajectory. One focused on growing the perfect and exemplary apple tree, but the other farmer went further: he focused on the fruit from the tree, using it each year to plant other trees.

The first farmer grew a great tree, received numerous invitations to speak to growers' conferences about the secrets of developing his tree, and even wrote a bestselling book about it. Then the life cycle of the tree maxed out, and it stopped growing. His tree not only became the same as most other trees, but he had no answer to the question "What's next?" for his role with the tree or for whoever might follow him as the next apple farmer.

As the second farmer's tree began to produce fruit, he used it each year and planted a different row of new trees. Over time, an entire orchard developed, and he even began mentoring other young growers, helping them start their own orchards. Recently, he turned his orchard over to his children and now looks forward to spending the next few years helping other apple growers full-time.

Focusing on the Wrong Outcome

Geoff's point is that the first apple farmer focused on the wrong outcome. He spent his life growing a great tree, but he never looked beyond his era as a tree farmer. His legacy would have been very different if he had been visionary enough to think about a legacy that outlives one tree.

Good pastors focus their life on producing good fruit. But the greatest and most visionary pastors and church leaders share a common wisdom: they plan not just for their current "tree" but also for the time beyond their own tenure.

What would happen if that wisdom and vision were talked about among church leaders from day one of their tenure? What if seminaries and pastoral internships made "Securing Your Legacy" a required course? What could happen?

If the culture changed, the exception of good succession planning might become the rule. The change would lead to a healthier church overall.

What Will Your Legacy Be?

At present, there aren't enough tree planters and tree growers who think intentionally about legacy. That will change as a few exceptional leaders are forming a model and movement to think differently and, in turn, set the pace for others.

That perspective requires not weeks, not months, not even one or two years to develop, but rather a ministry attitude to start *now* and carry it forward in everything you do. That perspective isn't one that wonders when to think about succession but is a mind-set that always thinks about succession. A long-term view enables you

That perspective isn't one that wonders when to think about succession but is a mind-set that always thinks about succession.

to develop an attitude like our friend Lee Powell, founding pastor of Cedar Creek Church in greater Toledo, Ohio, demonstrates. "In ten years I'll hand off the baton," he said. Lee already has ideas of what he might be doing instead, driven by his big heart for the many leaders his church has been developing—church planters, multisite campuses, missionaries, and pastors of other churches. "I hope and pray that I'll be so busy building into the lives of those pastors," he explained. "Besides, if I stay too long, I might hurt the church."[3]

Others Are Setting the Model

Jubilee Christian Church is a predominantly African-American congregation in Boston with over five thousand people in attendance. Founded in 1982 by Gilbert Thompson, it is now pastored by his son, Matthew Thompson. It was such a gradual and smooth succession that there wasn't even a date or initially a public ceremony to mark the transition.

Gilbert Thompson has mentored his son each step of the way. One of their discussions particularly significant to Matthew involved a vision his father experienced as he brought his son into leadership. As Matthew tells it, "In the vision, the Lord asked my dad, 'What is the proof that your church has a future?' My father replied, 'It's growing.' But God did not accept that answer. 'No, that's proof only that the people are alive,' God replied. My father then asked what the proof should be. The Lord answered, 'The church will produce itself into the next generation.'"

That idea became foundational for Matthew. "If God is going to transform our city," he said, "we not only have to hand the baton well in this church but also reproduce what we do into other churches."[4]

That sort of legacy thinking could become the new norm. Thinking past our own careers, focusing on how we will pass the baton, planning for our own succession—these could be the markers of pastors interested in fruit for the kingdom. It is a fruit that will endure. As Jesus said, "I chose you and appointed you so that you might go and bear fruit—fruit that will last" (John 15:16).

Every race has a beginning point and a finish line. No runner begins a race without knowing the destination and without having a plan to finish. The best way to run a race is to start with the end in mind. If you know where and how you want to finish the race, you can make a plan on how to run it. That's what John Piper did as he reached a transition point after thirty-two years at the helm of Bethlehem Baptist Church in Minneapolis. His successor, John Meyer, summed up their perspective well when he said, "We tried to make this transition not about finding a man but about fulfilling a mission."[5]

That's what pastoral succession is all about. It's starting and finishing well because *there is no success without succession.*

Join a movement by thinking about what's *NEXT* long before you have to. Model the idea of finishing well that includes the setup for a solid baton pass. Doing so will make more of a difference than you can imagine, for you, the church you presently serve, the community of other churches and pastors you influence, and the many successors who will follow both you and them.

What Our Organizations Can Do for You

Vanderbloemen Search Group

If you think you need help when you're faced with a transition or succession, you're not alone. Most transitions involve people who have never faced this challenge. Where do you turn for help?

Vanderbloemen Search Group is uniquely equipped to provide assistance during your transition. With hundreds of transitions under our belt, from churches of all sizes and over seventy-five different denominations/tribes, Vanderbloemen Search Group has unique experience to help you. Additionally, Vanderbloemen Search Group has the unusual ability to combine years of pastoral experience with the best training of corporate executive search experience to bring you and your church assistance without parallel during your succession.

Whether you're a church facing transition or a pastor considering your own future, we would be glad to visit with you about your transition and to explore whether or not we might be a good solution for you. Contact the Vanderbloemen Search Group by emailing info@vanderbloemen.com or calling 713.300.6995.

Leadership Network

Leadership Network (www.leadnet.org) fosters innovation movements that activate the church to greater impact.

We work with a select group of influential churches to pioneer and propagate key innovations across denominational and tribal lines. Then we share those practices to influence and change thousands of other churches. Leadership Network, a ministry organization, was formed in 1984. Its global ministry includes programs around the world.

Leadership Network conducted a four-hour online video conference with interviews and stories from leaders dealing with succession and transition. You can access those video archives at http://churchleadersuccession.com/.

Leadership Network does limited onsite consultation and video meetings with churches and leaders in this area of succession. To inquire about those services please email dave.travis@leadnet.org. For general inquiries, contact Leadership Network at client.care@leadnet.org or 214.969.5950.

Acknowledgments

William Vanderbloemen

Any success I have with this book and our work at Vanderbloemen Search Group begins and ends with the Savior. I could never do what I do now had he not ordered each of my scattered career steps that have led up to now. All thanks be to God through Jesus.

My wife, Adrienne, is the epitome of a steel magnolia, and her support, wisdom, and insight helped me launch, grow, and run our firm. I turn to her for counsel before all others and trust her discernment above anyone else's I know. She was crucial to the formation and writing of this book.

Also key to the writing of this book is the team at Vanderbloemen Search Group. Their collaborative skills led us to a title, a plan, a great sounding board, and an honest group of critics who helped us bring you this work. Their work with hundreds of churches across the globe made much of our research possible, and the excellence of their work is what propels our firm's growth. My colleagues Tara Marrone and Katherine Prudhomme spent countless hours helping us with the fine details and compilation of data. Holly Hall's marketing expertise and creativity helped us stretch and get the word out about the book. Thanks to all for their work.

Finally, a special thanks to my coauthor. Warren Bird is a prince of a man and a superior writer and researcher. His attention to detail was a fantastic complement for me.

My prayer is that our combined efforts help churches for a long time and ultimately play a part in helping the bride of Christ along the path of perfection.

Warren Bird

I echo William's spirit and his opening words of thanks to God. My wonderful wife, Michelle, has journeyed with me through this, my twenty-sixth book. She is an invaluable sounding board and treasure of patience and grace. I married way above my station in life.

It was also a delight to work with William and his staff. I cannot speak highly enough of their insights and other feedback. I too give a special shout out to Tara Marrone,

Katherine Prudhomme, and Holly Tate for long, diligent hours of managing many different aspects of shaping the manuscript.

This book would also not have been possible apart from my work with Leadership Network, so a special thanks to its founders, leaders, and support staff.

William and Warren

More than one hundred people gave of their time for us to interview them. Most are pastors who experienced succession and were willing to go public with their stories so that others could learn. We made every effort to contact everyone quoted to ask them to review the material about them and the churches they serve. We spoke with many others who didn't feel comfortable in having their story told but wanted us to hear it to shape the advice we would convey in this book. To all of these people, we are profoundly grateful.

We want to thank the many friends who served as liaisons, introducing us or vouching for us so that we could interview pastors we might never have been able to otherwise. These "church spotters" and "door openers" included Dave Travis and Todd Rhoades at Leadership Network, plus our friends Wade Olinger, Ed Stetzer, and Elias Dantas.

This book is immeasurably better because of numerous true friends who took time to read earlier drafts and suggest improvements, many with follow-up phone calls or other conversations. Our three reading groups included Michelle Bird, Carol Childress, Gary Fenton, Kent Fillinger (twice), Carl George, Bill Giovannetti, Amy Hanson, Scott Harris, Tammy Kelley, Deanna Kotrla, Greg Ligon, Jay Mitchell, Preston Mitchell, Gary Moritz, Dan Ohlerking, Andrew Omotoso, Lisa Plunket, Jeff Quinn, Dale Schaeffer, Nicholas Smith, Joel Smith, Erik Thornton, Scott Thumma, Jim Tomberlin, Elmer Towns, Nhiem Thai Tran, Dave Travis, Lovett Weems, and Meredith Wheeler.

We also received serious research assistance from several important sources. Leadership Network's research database was invaluable, with special thanks to careful work by Christy Ceparano, Esther Thompson, and Kelly Kulesza. Glenn Lucke and the Docent Research Group deserve serious props for their input and first-class research. Several individuals did specific projects, including Laura Chambers (United Methodist), Neil Clements (intern), Kent Fillinger (Christian Church movement), Rich Houseal (Church of the Nazarene), Kristina Lizardy-Hajbi (United Church of Christ), Martin Smith (Evangelical Lutheran Church in America), Richie Stanley and Clay Price (Southern Baptist churches), Scott Thumma (non-denominational churches), and Ida Williams-Smith (Presbyterian Church USA churches).

Warren's statistical consultant is Marc Glassman PhD, a source of much wise advice. The book's legal advice in chapter 15 comes from David Middlebrook and Steven D. Goodspeed, attorneys-at-law at Anthony & Middlebrook in Grapevine, Texas.

Finally, the Baker team has done a great job. Chad Allen's wise counsel as our editor was a key ingredient to the book you hold.

Appendix 1

Succession Ages for Prominent Large Church Pastors

(See Especially Tallies at Bottom)

by Warren Bird

Pastor's Age at Transition	Outgoing Pastor	Church Name, City, State	Number of Years There as Sr. Pastor	This Person Was Pastor #	Year This Pastor Left	Months Until Successor Began	Successor's Name	Successor's Age at Transition	Successor Stayed Until
86 (born 1898)	Norman Vincent Peale	Marble Collegiate Church, New York, NY	52	40	1984	0	Arthur Caliandro	51	2009
86 (born 1927)	Chuck Smith Sr.	Calvary Chapel of Costa Mesa, Santa Ana, CA	48	2	2013	0	Brian Broderson	55	2013
85 (born 1909)	W. A. Criswell	First Baptist Church, Dallas, TX	46	10	1990	0	Joel Gregory	43	1992
85 (born 1926)	Jack Hyles	First Baptist Church, Hammond, IN	42	14	2001	0	Jack Schaap	44	2012
80 (born 1925)	Fulton Buntain	Life Center, Tacoma, WA	40	7	2006	0	Dean Curry	37	Still there
80 (born 1928)	G. L. Johnson	Peoples Church, Fresno, CA	45	3	2008	23	Dale Oquist	49	Still there
80 (born 1914)	John Rawlings	Landmark Baptist Temple, Cincinnati, OH	43	?	1994	0	Harold Rawlings	59	2001
80 (born 1926)	Robert H. Schuller	Crystal Cathedral, Garden Grove, CA	37	1	2006	0	Robert A. Schuller	52	2008
78 (born 1928)	Earl Paulk	Chapel Hill Harvester, Decatur, GA (church now named Spirit and Truth)	46	1	2006	0	Donnie Earl Paulk	33	Still there

Pastor's Age at Transition	Outgoing Pastor	Church Name, City, State	Number of Years There as Sr. Pastor	This Person Was Pastor #	Year This Pastor Left	Months Until Successor Began	Successor's Name	Successor's Age at Transition	Successor Stayed Until
77 (born 1921)	John Osteen	Lakewood Church, Houston, TX	40	1	1999	0	Joel Osteen	35	Still there
77 (born 1932)	Fred Price, Sr.	Crenshaw Christian Center, Los Angeles, CA	36	1	2009	0	Fred Price, Jr.	30	Still there
75 (born 1925)	Clay Evans	Fellowship Missionary Baptist Church, Chicago, IL	50	1	2000	0	Charles Jenkins	25	Still there
75 (born 1932)	L. H. Hardwick	Christ Church, Nashville, TN	57	1	2007	0	Dan Scott	54	Still there
75 (born 1877)	J. Frank Norris	First Baptist Church, Ft. Worth, TX	43	7	1952	0	Homer Ritchie	25	1981
75 (born 1929)	Wyatt Tee Walker	Canaan Baptist Church of Christ, New York, NY	37	3	2004	24	Thomas D. Johnson Sr.	50	Still there
75 (born 1938)	Dan Yeary	North Phoenix Baptist Church, Phoenix, AZ	20	4	2013	0	Jason Whalen	39	Still there
74 (born 1938)	Tommy Barnett	Phoenix First Assembly, Phoenix, AZ	33	7	2012	0	Luke Barnett	42	Still there
74 (born 1931)	Adrian Rogers	Bellevue Baptist Church, Cordova, TN	32	6	2005	4	Steve Gaines	48	Still there
73 (born 1915)	Tom Malone	Emmanuel Baptist Church, Pontiac, MI	47	1	1987	0	Frank Holman	58	1993
73 (born 1909)	Lee Roberson	Highland Park Baptist, Chattanooga, TN	40	1	1983	0	James Faulkner	37	1991
72 (born 1938)	J. Don George	Calvary Church, Irving, TX	51	1	2010	0	Ben Dailey	36	Still there
72 (born 1918)	Gardner Taylor	Concord Baptist Church of Christ, Brooklyn, NY	42	9	1990	0	Gary V. Simpson	27	Still there
71 (born 1940)	Vernon Armitage	Pleasant Valley Baptist Church, Liberty, MO	41	6	2010	0	Merle Mees	50	Still there
71 (born 1926)	Arthur DeKruyter	Christ Church of Oak Brook, Oak Brook, IL	32	1	1997	0	Dan Meyer	38	Still there
71 (born 1932)	Gene Getz	Chase Oaks Church, Plano, TX	22	1	2003	0	Jeff Jones	37	Still there

Pastor's Age at Transition	Outgoing Pastor	Church Name, City, State	Number of Years There as Sr. Pastor	This Person Was Pastor #	Year This Pastor Left	Months Until Successor Began	Successor's Name	Successor's Age at Transition	Successor Stayed Until
71 (born 1915)	Bob Wells	Central Baptist Church, Orange, CA	30	1	1986	6	Robert Knutson	44	1998
70 (born 1938)	John Ed Mathison	Frazer Memorial United Methodist Church, Montgomery, AL	36	15	2008	0	Barry Carpenter	58	2009
70 (born 1919)	Winfred Moore	First Baptist Church, Amarillo, TX	30	16	1989	24	Ben E. Loring	45	1994
70 (born 1903)	Homer Lindsay Sr.	First Baptist Church, Jacksonville, FL	33	24	1973	0	Homer Lindsay Jr.	42	2002 (died while pastor)
70 (born 1930)	Don Schaeffer	Grace Church C&MA, Middleburg Heights, OH	38	1	2000	0	Jonathan Schaeffer	35	Still there
70 (born 1889)	Oswald Smith	The Peoples Church, Toronto, ON	38	1	1959	0	Paul B. Smith	38	1994
69 (born 1903)	Dallas R. Billington	Akron Baptist Temple, Akron, OH	38	1	1972	0	Charles Billington	45	1996
69 (born 1941)	Knute Larson	The Chapel, Akron, OH	26	3	2009	0	Paul Sartarelli	51	2013
69 (born 1931)	Nelson Price	Roswell Street Baptist Church, Marietta, GA	35	5	2000	24	Ernest Easley	46	Still there
69 (born 1939)	O. Damon Shook	Champion Forest Baptist Church, Houston, TX	27	2	2005	20	David W. Fleming	41	Still there
67 (born 1932)	Frank Barker Jr.	Briarwood Presbyterian Church, Birmingham, AL	39	1	1999	0	Harry Reeder III	51	Still there
67 (born 1934)	Clayton Bell	Highland Park Presbyterian Church, Dallas, TX	27	?	2000	0	Ronald Scates	?	2013
67 (born 1938)	Jim Henry	First Baptist Church, Orlando, FL	28	28	2005	0	David Uth	48	Still there
67 (born 1934)	Frank Pollard	First Baptist Church, Jackson, MS	6	19	1980	15	Earl Craig	41	1984
67 (born 1941)	Jeremiah Wright	Trinity United Church of Christ, Chicago, IL	36	3	2008	0	Otis Moss III	37	Still there

Pastor's Age at Transition	Outgoing Pastor	Church Name, City, State	Number of Years There as Sr. Pastor	This Person Was Pastor #	Year This Pastor Left	Months Until Successor Began	Successor's Name	Successor's Age at Transition	Successor Stayed Until
67 (born 1946)	John Piper	Bethlehem Baptist Church, Minneapolis, MN	33	14	2013	0	Jason Meyer	36	Still there
67 (born 1944)	Leith Anderson	Wooddale Church, Eden Prairie, MN	35	4	2011	18	Dale Hummel	53	Still there
66 (born 1934)	John Bisagno	Houston's First Baptist Church, Houston, TX	30	27	2000	0	Gregg Matte	34	2004
65 (born 1937)	Walt Gerber	Menlo Park Presbyterian Church, Menlo Park, CA	28	26	2002	10	John Ortberg	46	Still there
65 (born 1934)	Jack Hayford	Church on the Way, Van Nuys, CA	30	1	1999	0	Scott Bauer	45	2003
65 (born 1924)	Harold Henniger	Canton Baptist Temple, Canton, OH	40	4	1989	0	Jim Henniger	44	1995
65 (born 1942)	John Kieschnick	Gloria Dei Lutheran Church, Houston, TX	33	2	2007	0	Greg Finke	44	2011
65 (born 1907)	Raymond Lindquist	First Presbyterian Church, Hollywood, CA	19	3	1972	2	Lloyd John Ogilvie	42	1995
65 (born 1931)	Greg Dixon	Indianapolis Baptist Temple, Indianapolis, IN	41	2	1996	0	Greg Dixon Jr.	41	Still there
64 (born 1932)	Paul Walker	Mt. Paran Church of God, Atlanta, GA	36	8	1996	0	David Cooper	40	Still there
64 (born 1948)	Dave Burns	Hillside Community Church, Alta Loma, CA	32	1	2012	0	Aaron McRae	37	Still there
64 (born 1905)	Harold John Ockenga	Park Street Church, Boston, MA	33	12	1969	0	Paul Toms	45	1989
64 (born 1944)	Bob Russell	Southeast Christian Church, Louisville, KY	40	2	2006	0	Dave Stone	45	Still there
63 (born 1946)	Betty Peebles	Jericho City of Praise, Washington, DC	16	2	2009	0	Joel Peebles	42	2012
63 (born 1908)	Adam Clayton Powell Jr.	Abyssinian Baptist Church, New York, NY	34	18	1971	3	Samuel Proctor	51	1989
62 (born 1897)	A.W. Tozer	Southside Alliance Church, Chicago, IL	31	5	1959	3	Elmer Murdoch	31	1964

Pastor's Age at Transition	Outgoing Pastor	Church Name, City, State	Number of Years There as Sr. Pastor	This Person Was Pastor #	Year This Pastor Left	Months Until Successor Began	Successor's Name	Successor's Age at Transition	Successor Stayed Until
61 (born 1934)	Glen Cole	Capital Christian Center, Sacramento, CA	17	1	1995	0	Rick Cole	37	Still there
61 (born 1942)	Howard Edington	First Presbyterian Church of Orlando, Orlando, FL	21	15	2003	20	David Swanson	41	Still there
61 (born 1937)	Bob Moorehead	Overlake Christian Church, Kirkland, WA	28	2	1998	8	Rick Kingham	46	2007
60 (born 1950)	Dennis Leonard	Potter's House, Denver, CO (formerly Heritage Christian Center)	25	1	2010	0	Chris Hill	41	Still there
60 (born 1933)	Richard Strauss	Emmanuel Faith Community Church, Escondido, CA	21	4	1993	0	Dennis Keating	40	Still there
60 (born 1934)	Chuck Swindoll	First Evangelical Church, Fullerton, CA	23	2	1994	15	Dale Burke	41	2010
60 (born 1934)	John Wimber	Anaheim Vineyard, Anaheim, CA	17	1	1994	0	Carl Tuttle	41	1997
60 (born 1952)	Mike Ernst	Hales Corners Lutheran Church, Hales Corners, WI	19	9	2012	0	Keith Speaks	50	Still there
60 (born 1949)	Gilbert Thompson	Jubilee Christian Church, Mattapan, MA	31	1	2009	0	Matt Thompson	37	Still there
59 (born 1940)	Charles Keen	First Baptist Church, Milford, OH	35	2	1999	14	William Duttry	39	Still there
59 (born 1937)	Benjamin Reid	First Church of God, Inglewood, CA	25	1*	1996	0	Gregory Dixon	39	2012
58 (born 1949)	Darryl DelHousaye	Scottsdale Bible Church, Scottsdale, AZ	25	4	2006	19	Jamie Rasmussen	43	Still there
58 (born 1908)	Ralph Grant	First Baptist Church, Lubbock, TX	20	13	1966	7	David Ray	33	1971
58 (born 1953)	Larry Stockstill	Bethany World Prayer Center, Baker, LA	28	2	2011	0	Jonathan Stockstill	30	Still there
58 (born 1944)	Ted Roberts	East Hill Foursquare Church, Gresham, OR	22	2	2007	0	Jason Albelo	33	Still there

Pastor's Age at Transition	Outgoing Pastor	Church Name, City, State	Number of Years There as Sr. Pastor	This Person Was Pastor #	Year This Pastor Left	Months Until Successor Began	Successor's Name	Successor's Age at Transition	Successor Stayed Until
57 (born 1918)	Harold Lord Fickett	First Baptist Church, Van Nuys, CA	16	?	1975	?	Jess Moody	47	1987
57 (born 1957)	Frank Anthony Thomas	Mississippi Blvd Christian Church, Memphis, TN	13	4	2012	3	Jason Lawrence Turner	32	Still there
57 (born 1949)	Robert Lewis	Fellowship Bible Church, Little Rock, AR	26	2	2006	0	Tim Lundy	37	2011
56 (born 1935)	Jimmy Draper	First Baptist Church, Euless, TX	16	?	1991	?	Claude Thomas	48	2004
56 (born 1939)	Dale Galloway	New Hope Community Church, Portland, OR	22	1	1995	1	Ray Cotton	43	2012
56 (born 1923)	Ray Ortlund	Lake Avenue Church, Pasadena, CA	20	6	1979	15	Paul Cedar	42	1990
55 (born 1956)	Keith Butler	Word of Faith International Christian Center, Southfield, MI	32	1	2011	0	Andre Butler	34	Still there
53 (born 1946)	Wayne Benson Sr.	First Assembly of God, Grand Rapids, MI	25	11	2000	9	Scott Hagan	39	2005
49 (born 1914)	William Dowell	High Street Baptist Church, Springfield, MO	22	?	1963	?	David Cavin	46	1986
48 (born 1947)	John Maxwell	Skyline Church, La Mesa, CA	14	2	1995	4	Jim Garlow	48	Still there
48 (born 1953)	Charles Lowery	Hoffmantown Church, Albuquerque, NM	10	5	2001	8	Wayne Barber	58	2011
47 (born 1950)	Alvin Jackson	Mississippi Blvd Christian Church, Memphis, TN	18	3	1997	18	Frank Anthony Thomas	44	2012
46 (born 1951)	Randal Ross	Trinity Church, Lubbock, TX	12	5	1997	9	Gary Kirksey	56	2000
46 (born 1956)	Dan Southerland	Potential Church, Cooper City, FL (formerly Flamingo Road Baptist)	13	3	2002	0	Troy Gramling	35	Still there
46 (born 1953)	Jim Tomberlin	Woodmen Valley Chapel, Colorado Springs, CO	9	3	2000	13	Matt Heard	43	2014

Pastor's Age at Transition	Outgoing Pastor	Church Name, City, State	Number of Years There as Sr. Pastor	This Person Was Pastor #	Year This Pastor Left	Months Until Successor Began	Successor's Name	Successor's Age at Transition	Successor Stayed Until
44 (born 1951)	Doug Murren	Eastside Foursquare Church, Kirkland, WA	17	1	1996	3	Jim Hayford	55	2011
43 (born 1967)	Francis Chan	Cornerstone Church, Simi Valley, CA	16	1	2009	0	Todd Nighswonger	38	Still there
41 (born 1970)	Rob Bell	Mars Hill Bible Church, Grandville, MI	12	1	2011	0	Shane Hipps	55	2012
Averages Age of Pastor at Transition			Years as Sr. Pastor	This Person was Pastor #	Year This Pastor Left	Months Until Successor Began**		Age of Successor at Transition	Years Successor Stayed
65			30	6	1997	13		43	10***

Research by Leadership Network. Data taken from public records and personal communication with the churches. This list includes only pastors who intentionally and voluntarily passed leadership to a new pastor. It excludes those who vacated their role due to sudden death or moral failures.

Every effort has been made to verify this information. Please send corrections to research@leadnet.org. Suggestions of additional prominent pastors and their successors are most welcome as well for future expanded editions of this list.

*First Church of God, Inglewood, CA, was formed by the merger of two older churches. Benjamin Reid was the first pastor after the merger.

**The column that lists months between pastors indicates 0 both for immediate successions and also for overlap when the successor is on staff prior to the succession. This group represents almost two-thirds of the pastors listed. The average in the tally line at the bottom includes only those whose transition period was one or more months long.

***Average includes those still serving. Excluding that group, average is 11 years.

Appendix 2

Current Pastor Ages in Large US Churches

It's time for many large US churches to talk about succession. Fifty-five is the average pastor age in the 100 largest US churches. The list is in order from oldest pastor to youngest pastor, with tallies at the bottom.

Pastor	Pastor's Age in 2014	Years as Pastor Here	Church Name, City, State	Website	Denomination	Church's Age in 2014	2013 Atten-dance	F= Founder S= Successor
Ed Young Sr.	78	36	Second Baptist Church, Houston, TX	second.org	Southern Baptist	87	20,656	S
Dan Betzer	77	27	First Assembly of God, Fort Myers, FL	famfm.com	Assemblies of God	68	7,462	S
Charles Blake	75	45	West Angeles Cathedral, Los Angeles, CA	westa.org	Church of God in Christ	71	8,000	S
David Jeremiah	73	33	Shadow Mountain Community Church, El Cajon, CA	shadowmountain.org	Southern Baptist	41	7,513	S
David Demola	71	34	Faith Fellowship Ministries, Sayreville, NJ	ffmwoc.org	Non-denominational charismatic	34	10,100	F

Pastor	Pastor's Age in 2014	Years as Pastor Here	Church Name, City, State	Website	Denomination	Church's Age in 2014	2013 Atten-dance	F= Founder S= Successor
Floyd Flake	69	38	The Greater Allen Cathedral of New York, Jamaica, NY	allencathedral.org	African Methodist Episcopal	180	6,150	S
Steve Mays	68	34	Calvary Chapel South Bay, Gardena, CA	ccsouthbay.org	Calvary Chapel	34	9,000	F
Charles Nieman	66	37	Abundant Living Faith Center, El Paso, TX	alfc.com	Non-denominational	37	12,400	F
Don Wilson	65	32	Christ's Church of the Valley, Peoria, AZ	ccvonline.com	Non-denominational	32	22,199	F
Lon Solomon	65	34	McLean Bible Church, Vienna, VA	mcleanbible.org	Non-denominational	53	16,500	S
Douglas Schmidt	61	23	Woodside Bible Church, Troy, MI	woodsidebible.org	Non-denominational	59	7,174	S
Jack Graham	64	25	Prestonwood Baptist Church, Plano, TX	prestonwood.org	Baptist	37	15,815	S
Lee P. Washington	64	32	Reid Temple AME Church, Glenn Dale, MD	reidtemple.org	African Methodist Episcopal	198	7,450	S
Ron Vietti	63	39	Valley Bible Fellowship, Bakersfield, CA	vbf.org	Non-denominational	39	10,300	F
Glen Berteau	62	00	The House Modesto, Modesto, CA	thehousemodesto.com	Assemblies of God	82	10,441	S
Bill Hybels	62	39	Willow Creek Community Church, South Barrington, IL	willowcreek.org	Non-denominational	39	25,743	F
Ira V. Hilliard	62	30	New Light Christian Center Church, Houston, TX	newlight3.org	Non-denominational	30	6,000	F
Wayne Cordeiro	62	19	New Hope Oahu, Honolulu, HI	enewhope.org	Evangelical Pentecostal Christian	19	5,300	F

Pastor	Pastor's Age in 2014	Years as Pastor Here	Church Name, City, State	Website	Denomination	Church's Age in 2014	2013 Atten- dance	F= Founder S= Successor
Larry Osborne & Chris Brown	62 & 43	34	North Coast Church, Vista, CA	northcoastchurch.com	Evangelical Free Church	36	9,000	S
Johnny Hunt	62	28	First Baptist Church of Woodstock, Woodstock, GA	fbcw.org	Southern Baptist	177	6,115	S
Steve Munsey	61	29	Family Christian Center, Munster, IN	familychristiancenter.org	Non- denominational	60	15,540	S
Charles B. Jackson Sr.	61	43	Brookland Baptist Church, West Columbia, SC	brooklandbaptist.org	Baptist	12	8,075	S
Ken Foreman	61	?	Cathedral of Faith, San Jose, CA	cathedraloffaith.org	Non- denominational	55	7,800	S
Danny Carroll	61	24	Water of Life Community Church, Fon- tana, CA	wateroflifecc.org	Non- denominational	24	6,371	F
Rick Warren	60	34	Saddleback Church, Lake Forest, CA	saddleback.com	Southern Baptist	34	22,055	F
Steve Stroope	60	34	Lake Pointe Church, Rockwall, TX	lakepointe.org	Southern Baptist	35	11,225	F
Kenton Beshore	60	30	Mariners Church, Ir- vine, CA	marinerschurch.org	Non- denominational	51	13,567	S
Rufus Smith	55	1	Hope Pres- byterian Church, Cor- dova, TN	hopepres.com	Evangelical Presbyterian	26	6,978	S
Tom Mercer	60	30	High Desert Church, Vic- torville, CA	highdesertchurch.com	Transformation Ministries	60	6,313	S
Randy Frazee & Max Lucado	53 & 59	6 & 26	Oak Hills Church, San Antonio, TX	oakhillschurch.com	Non- denominational	56	8,663	S
Skip Heitzig	59	33	Calvary of Albuquerque, Albuquerque, NM	calvaryabq.org	Calvary Chapel	33	16,830	F
Ronnie Floyd	58	28	Cross Church— Northeast Arkansas, Springdale, AR	crosschurch.com	Southern Baptist	144	8,756	S

Pastor	Pastor's Age in 2014	Years as Pastor Here	Church Name, City, State	Website	Denomination	Church's Age in 2014	2013 Atten-dance	F= Founder S= Successor
Rick Blackwood	57	18	Christ Fellowship, Miami, FL	cfmiami.org	Southern Baptist	97	8,098	S
Rich Nathan	59	27	Vineyard Columbus, Columbus, OH	vineyardcolumbus.org	Vineyard	40	7,827	S
Mike Meeks	59	17	EastLake Church, Chula Vista, CA	eastlakechurch.com	Non-denominational	23	6,280	S
Bob Coy	58	29	Calvary Chapel Fort Lauderdale, Fort Lauderdale, FL	calvaryftl.org	Calvary Chapel	29	18,521	F
David Ashcraft	57	23	LCBC Church, Manheim, PA	LCBCchurch.com	Non-denominational	27	13,854	S
Cal Jernigan	58	15	Central Christian Church of Arizona, Mesa, AZ	centralaz.com	Christian Church movement	55	9,092	S
Dudley Rutherford	58	22	Shepherd of the Hills Church, Porter Ranch, CA	theshepherd.org	Christian Church Movement	102	8,675	S
Cam Huxford	58	30	Savannah Christian Church, Savannah, GA	savannahchristian.com	Independent Christian	50	7,474	S
Bob Merritt	57	23	Eagle Brook Church, Centerville, MN	eaglebrookchurch.com	Baptist General Conference	66	17,091	S
Ray Johnston	62	19	Bayside Covenant Church, Granite Bay, CA	baysideonline.com	Evangelical Covenant Church	19	11,327	F
Robert Emmitt	57	24	Community Bible Church, San Antonio, TX	communitybible.com	Non-denominational	24	14,031	F
T. D. Jakes	57	18	The Potter's House of Dallas, Inc., Dallas, TX	thepottershouse.org	Non-denominational	18	16,140	F
Chuck Booher	57	7	Crossroads Christian Church, Corona, CA	crossroadschurch.com	Christian Church movement	122	7,000	S

Pastor	Pastor's Age in 2014	Years as Pastor Here	Church Name, City, State	Website	Denomination	Church's Age in 2014	2013 Atten-dance	F= Founder S= Successor
Mike Lee	57	21	Hope Community Church, Raleigh, NC	gethope.net	Non-denominational	20	7,854	F
Steve Gaines	57	9	Bellevue Baptist Church, Cordova, TN	bellevue.org	Southern Baptist	111	6,806	S
Steve Poe	57	15	Northview Church, Carmel, IN	northviewchurch.us	Non-denominational	34	6,595	S
Craig Altman	57	20	Grace Family Church, Lutz, FL	GFConline.com	Non-denominational	20	6,187	F
Andy Stanley	56	19	North Point Community Church (North Point Ministries), Alpharetta, GA	northpoint.org	Non-denominational	19	30,629	F
Brad Powell	56	24	NorthRidge Church, Plymouth, MI	northpointministries.org	Baptist heritage, non-denominational	86	9,655	S
Kevin Cosby	56	35	St. Stephen Church, Louisville, KY	SSCLive.org	Non-denominational	88	10,714	S
Lee Powell	56	19	Cedar Creek Church, Perrysburg, OH	cedarcreek.tv	Non-denominational	19	9,155	F
G. Allen Jackson	55	26	World Outreach Church, Murfreesboro, TN	wochurch.org	Inter-denominational	34	7,926	S
Ralph Douglas West	55	27	The Church Without Walls, Houston, TX	churchwithoutwalls.org	Southern Baptist	27	6,411	F
Miles McPherson	54	14	The Rock Church, San Diego, CA	sdrock.com	Non-denominational	14	12,864	F
John McKellar	54	22	White's Chapel United Methodist Church, Southlake, TX	whiteschapelumc.com	United Methodist	143	6,149	S

Pastor	Pastor's Age in 2014	Years as Pastor Here	Church Name, City, State	Website	Denomination	Church's Age in 2014	2013 Atten-dance	F= Founder S= Successor
Dave Stone	53	8	Southeast Christian Church, Louisville, KY	southeastchristian.org	Christian Church Movement	52	21,764	S
Ed Young	53	25	Fellowship Church, Grapevine, TX	fellowshipchurch.com	Southern Baptist	24	19,913	F
Jentezen Franklin	53	25	Free Chapel Worship Center, Gainesville, GA	freechapel.org	Non-denominational	57	11,500	S
Robert Morris	52	14	Gateway Church, Southlake, TX	gatewaypeople.com	Non-denominational	14	26,500	F
Creflo Dollar Jr.	53	28	World Changers Church International, College Park, GA	worldchangers.org	Non-denominational	28	10,000	F
Kevin Myers	53	27	12Stone Church, Lawrenceville, GA	12Stone.com	Wesleyan	27	13,563	F
Steve Smothermon	53	12	Legacy Church, Albuquerque, NM	LegacyChurch.com	Non-denominational	34	10,100	S
Rick Bezet	53	13	New Life Church of Arkansas, Conway, AR	newlifechurch.tv	Non-denominational	13	10,500	F
Jim Burgen	51	9	Flatirons Community Church, Lafayette, CO	flatironschurch.com	Non-denominational	31	15,495	S
Jeff Manion	52	31	Ada Bible Church, Ada, MI	adabible.org	Non-denominational	36	7,636	S
Tim Harlow	53	24	Parkview Christian Church, Orland Park, IL	parkviewchurch.com	Christian Church movement	63	7,093	S
Gary Hawkins Sr.	53	20	Voices of Faith Ministries, Stone Mountain, GA	voicesfaith.org	Southern Baptist	20	6,900	F

Pastor	Pastor's Age in 2014	Years as Pastor Here	Church Name, City, State	Website	Denomination	Church's Age in 2014	2013 Attendance	F= Founder S= Successor
Kerry Shook	52	21	Woodlands Church, The Woodlands, TX	woodlandschurch.tv	Non-denominational	21	18,385	F
John Lindell	52	23	James River Church, Ozark, MO	jamesriver.org	Assemblies of God	23	8,500	F
Dale Bronner	51	23	Word of Faith Family Worship Cathedral, Austell, GA	WOFfamily.org	Inter-denominational	23	8,300	F
Chris Hodges	51	13	Church of the Highlands, Birmingham, AL	churchofthehighlands.com	Non-denominational	13	22,184	F
Joel Osteen	51	15	Lakewood Church, Houston, TX	lakewood.cc	Non-denominational	55	43,500	S
Todd Wagner	51	15	Watermark Community Church, Dallas, TX	watermark.org	Non-denominational	15	8,876	F
David Landrith	51	17	Long Hollow Baptist Church, Hendersonville, TN	longhollow.com	Southern Baptist	37	7,154	S
David Hughes	51	16	Church by the Glades, Coral Springs, FL	cbglades.com	Southern Baptist	32	6,457	S
Mike Housholder	50	20	Lutheran Church of Hope, West Des Moines, IA	lutheranchurchofhope.org	Evangelical Lutheran Church in America	20	10,578	F
Jamie Rasmussen	50	7	Scottsdale Bible Church, Scottsdale, AZ	scottsdalebible.com	Non-denominational	52	6,234	F
Bruce Frank	50	6	Biltmore Baptist Church, Arden, NC	biltmorebaptist.org	Southern Baptist	125	6,021	S
Scott Chapman	50	20	The Chapel, Libertyville, IL	chapel.org	Non-denominational	20	6,010	F
Brian Tome	48	19	Crossroads Church, Cincinnati, OH	crossroads.net	Non-denominational	19	16,792	F

Pastor	Pastor's Age in 2014	Years as Pastor Here	Church Name, City, State	Website	Denomination	Church's Age in 2014	2013 Atten-dance	F= Founder S= Successor
Guillermo Maldonado	49	18	King Jesus/ El Rey Jesus, Miami, FL	elreyjesus.org	Non-denominational	18	12,540	F
Adam Hamilton	49	24	The United Methodist Church of the Resurrection, Leawood, KS	cor.org	United Methodist	24	10,137	F
Jim Putman	48	16	Real Life Ministries, Post Falls, ID	RealLifeMinistries.com	Non-denominational	16	7,001	F
Jonathan Falwell	48	7	Thomas Road Baptist Church, Lynchburg, VA	trbc.org	Southern Baptist	58	8,350	S
Sergio De La Mora	48	16	Cornerstone Church of San Diego, National City, CA	turningthehearts.com	Non-denominational	16	6,300	F
Chip Henderson	47	15	Pinelake Church, Bran-don, MS	pinelake.org	Southern Baptist	43	9,091	S
Andy Thompson	47	11	World Over-comers Chris-tian Church, Durham, NC	WOCConline.org	Non-denominational	11	10,000	F
Brady Boyd	47	7	New Life Church, Colorado Springs, CO	newlifechurch.org	Non-denominational	29	12,000	S
Craig Groeschel	47	18	LifeChurch. tv, Edmond, OK	lifechurch.tv	Evangelical Covenant	18	50,000	F
Todd Mullins	47	3	Christ Fel-lowship, Palm Beach Gar-dens, FL	gochristfellowship.com	Non-denominational	30	20,000	S
Troy Gramling	47	12	Potential Church, Coo-per City, FL	potentialchurch.com	Southern Baptist	33	12,103	S
Mark Driscoll	44	18	Mars Hill Church, Se-attle, WA	marshill.com	Non-denominational	18	12,329	F
Gregg Matte	44	10	Houston's First Baptist Church, Houston, TX	houstonsfirst.org	Southern Baptist	173	6,458	S

Pastor	Pastor's Age in 2014	Years as Pastor Here	Church Name, City, State	Website	Denomination	Church's Age in 2014	2013 Atten-dance	F= Founder S= Successor
Luke Barnett	44	2	Phoenix First Assembly, Phoenix, AZ	phoenixfirst.org	Assemblies of God	90	21,000	S
Stovall Weems	45	16	Celebration Church, Jacksonville, FL	celebration.org	Protestant— unspecified	16	11,096	F
Jud Wilhite	43	11	Central Christian Church, Las Vegas, NV	centralonline.tv	Christian Church movement	52	21,055	S
Perry Noble	43	14	New Spring Church, Anderson, SC	newspring.cc	Southern Baptist	14	27,358	F
Solomon Kinloch Jr.	41		Triumph Church, Detroit, MI	triumphch.org	Non-denominational	94	11,600	S
Jon Weece	41	11	Southland Christian Church, Nicholasville, KY	southlandchristian.org	Christian Church movement	58	12,524	S
Matt Carter	41	12	The Austin Stone Community Church, Austin, TX	austinstone.org	Southern Baptist	12	7,428	F
Bil Cornelius	41	16	Bay Area Fellowship, Corpus Christi, TX	bayareafellowship.com	Southern Baptist	16	6,957	F
Craig L. Oliver Sr.	41	19	Elizabeth Baptist Church, Atlanta, GA	elizabethbaptist.org	Southern Baptist	86	6,733	S
J. D. Greear	41	12	The Summit Church, Durham, NC	summitrdu.com	Southern Baptist	52	17,467	S
Matt Chandler	40	11	The Village Church, Flower Mound, TX	thevillagechurch.net	Southern Baptist	36	10,577	S
Steven Furtick	34	8	Elevation Church, Matthews, NC	elevationchurch.org	Southern Baptist	8	13,232	F
(between pastors)	00	00	Elmbrook Church, Brookfield, WI	elmbrook.org	Non-denominational	56	6,100	S

Pastor	Pastor's Age in 2014	Years as Pastor Here	Church Name, City, State	Website	Denomination	Church's Age in 2014	2013 Atten-dance	F= Founder S= Successor
(between pastors)	00	00	Mission Community Church, Gilbert, AZ	mission68.org	Non-denominational	19	6,195	S
Averages	55	21				48	11,829	Founder is 44%, Successor 56%

Church rankings supplied from 2013 "Top 100" issue of *Outreach* magazine. All other details from Leadership Network, the church's website, or public records. Please send corrections or comments to research@leadnet.org.

Appendix 3

A Successful Pastorate Doesn't Always Guarantee Good Pastoral Succession

This table looks at what happened to America's sixteen largest churches from 1967, asking if too many aging pastors tend to stay too long. To decide, see the tallies at bottom.

Attendance 1967	Attendance 2013	Church, City, State	Year Church Founded	Pastor in 1967	Pastor Led How Many Total Years	Pastor's Age in Final Year Here	Date of Pastor's Final Year Here	Year of Peak Attendance under This Pastor	How Many Pastors Since	Average Tenure of Successor Pastors
5,762	1,100	Akron Baptist Temple, Akron, OH	1934	Dallas R. Billington	38	69	1972 (died in office)	mid 1960s	3	14
4,821	400	Highland Park Baptist, Chattanooga, TN	1890	Lee Roberson	40	73	1983	mid 1960s	4	8
4,371	3,000	First Southern Baptist Church, Dallas, TX (now First Baptist Church Dallas)	1868	W. A. Criswell	50	92	1990	1970s	4	5
3,978	7,500	First Baptist Church, Hammond, IN	1887	Jack Hyles	42	85	2001	1980s	2	6

Attendance 1967	Attendance 2013	Church, City, State	Year Church Founded	Pastor in 1967	Pastor Led How Many Total Years	Pastor's Age in Final Year Here	Date of Pastor's Final Year Here	Year of Peak Attendance under This Pastor	How Many Pastors Since	Average Tenure of Successor Pastors
3,581	1,300	Canton Baptist Temple, Canton, OH	1937	Harold Henniger	40	65	1989	1971	3	7
3,540	800	Landmark Baptist Temple, Cincinnati, OH	1798	John Rawlings	43	80	1994	1973	2	10
3,400	9,800	Temple Baptist Church, Detroit, MI (merged with NorthRidge Church, Plymouth, MI)	1929	Beauchamp Vick	25	74	1975 (died in office)	1954	3	12
2,847	7,280	First Baptist Church, Van Nuys, CA (now Shepherd of the Hills Church, Porter Ranch, CA—merge in 1995)	1912	Harold Lord Fickett	16	57	1975	1960s	2	18
2,640	13,500	Thomas Road Baptist Church, Lynchburg, VA	1956	Jerry Falwell	51	74	2007	2007	1	7
2,444	700	Calvary Temple, Denver, CO	1945	Charles Blair	51	77	1998	1977	3	5
2,243	750	First Presbyterian Church, Hollywood, CA	1903	Raymond Lindquist	19	65	1972	1960s	3	15
2,189	2,050	First Baptist Church, Amarillo, TX	1889	Winfred Moore	30	70	1989	1960s	2	7
2,130	1,335	First Baptist Church, Lubbock, TX	1891	William David Ray	5	38	1972	1968	6	6
2,039	125	Central Baptist Church, Orange, CA (now Victory Baptist Church, Anaheim, CA)	1956	Bob Wells	30	71	1986	1960	2	14
2,035	1,500	Madison Church of Christ, Madison, TN	1934	Ira North	31	61	1984	mid 1970s	5	6

Attendance 1967	Attendance 2013	Church, City, State	Year Church Founded	Pastor in 1967	Pastor Led How Many Total Years	Pastor's Age in Final Year Here	Date of Pastor's Final Year Here	Year of Peak Attendance under This Pastor	How Many Pastors Since	Average Tenure of Successor Pastors
2,014	135	Emmanuel Baptist Church, Pontiac, MI In 2011, Emmanuel Baptist and Silvercrest Baptist (Malone started both) merged to form the current New Beginning Baptist in Waterford Township	1942	Tom Malone	43	70	1985	late 1960s	2	6

Average Attendance 1967	Average Attendance 2013		Average Year Church Founded		Average Total Years Pastor Served	Average Age in Final Year of Service	Average Date of Final Year		Average # of Successors	Average Tenure of Successors
3,127	3,205		1911		35	70	1971		3	9

Church list comes from the earliest known contemporary list of largest-attendance churches in America, compiled by Elmer Towns and published in *Christian Life* magazine. All other details from Leadership Network, the church's website, or public records. Please send corrections or comments to research@leadnet.org.

Appendix 4

Research for This Book

Both the authors and their respective organizations have spent years gathering the interviews, research, statistics, trends, and principles unfolded in this book.

William Vanderbloemen and his team at Vanderbloemen Search Group have processed more than 450 pastoral successions since 2008, covering the vast majority of the United States and some international work as well. In any given year, William and his team interface with tens of thousands of potential candidates and conduct in-depth conversations with over five thousand pastoral candidates who are considering a transition into a new role or ministry. They also work with boards to develop succession plans. Nearly 20 percent of the transitions they managed in 2013 were on the heels of a crisis within the church. In addition to his search work, William served for over a decade as a senior pastor in churches ranging in attendance from three hundred to five thousand.

Beyond his work in the search and church trenches, William has spent a considerable amount of time studying succession outside of the church. He has interviewed Fortune 500 CEOs, talked in depth with leading search consultants in the corporate world, and read extensively on topics of succession planning in the business world. The marketplace bibliography in "For Further Reading" (page 207) lists the titles he recommends most from his reading.

Warren Bird conducted a significant number of in-depth pastoral succession interviews for this book: sixty-four in person, forty-three by phone or video, six by substantial email exchange, and dozens by other methods, such as reading succession books, magazine articles, or writings on specific church transitions. Many of these contacts were made possible through Leadership Network, which broadcast some of them through a still accessible 2013 video conference on pastoral succession.[1]

In addition, with significant support from Leadership Network, Warren has devoted several years to compiling the statistics reflected in this book's various figures, tables, and in-text statements. He has read numerous doctoral dissertations and academic articles on pastoral succession as well as every academic- and popular-level book he can find. The "church books" section of "For Further Reading" (page 207) lists the titles he recommends most from that reading.

The acknowledgments page also names many individuals and organizations that significantly helped with the research in this book.

For Further Reading

Boldface = especially recommended

Books for Pastors

Chand, Samuel R., and Dale C. Bronner. *Planning Your Succession: Preparing for Your Future.* Highland Park, IL: Mall Publishing, 2008.

> *Explains the necessities and the advantages of preparing any organization, large or small, for its future regardless of the age of the leader at the helm or where you are in your leadership journey. Makes many references to pastors and churches.*

Oswald, Roy M., James M. Heath, and Ann W. Heath. *Beginning Ministry Together: The Alban Handbook for Clergy Transitions.* Hendon, VA: Alban Institute, 2003.

> *Describes how clergy and congregations can better end and begin pastorates. Shows them how to say good-bye and discern their needs for the future and how to use the open space between pastorates for evaluation and preparation for a new day.*

Russell, Bob, and Bryan Bucher. *Transition Plan: Seven Secrets Every Leader Needs to Know.* Louisville, KY: Ministers Label, 2010.

> *In telling the story of Southeast Christian Church, this book deals with the reality of failed transitions and gives insights not only to avoid dropping the baton but also to strengthen your organization by preparing for upcoming transitions.*

Books for Church Boards or Search Teams

Achtemeier, Elizabeth. *So You're Looking for a New Preacher.* Grand Rapids: Eerdmans, 1991.

> *Emphasizes the importance of preaching in the life of the church, especially as a church is searching for a new pastor. Filled with pertinent suggestions, this book offers guidance on what marks quality preachers and quality preaching.*

Gripe, Alan. *The Interim Pastor's Manual,* rev. ed. Louisville, KY: Geneva Press, 1997.

> *Explains what an interim role is and how it's different from a stated supply or a temporary supply. Identifies five tasks of the interim pastor. Especially written for those in the Presbyterian Church (USA).*

Mead, Loren B. *A Change of Pastors: And How It Affects Change in the Congregation.* Hendon, VA: Alban Institute, 2005.

> *Leads readers through the time between one pastor's leaving and another's arrival, dealing with the challenges of forming committees, negotiating denominational relations, and managing the search process.*

Tyree, Gregory. *Helping Your Church Discover Its Next Pastor: A Manual for Pastoral Search Committees.* Madison Heights, VA: NorthPoint Life Coaching, 2013.

> *Explores the pastoral discovery process and helps churches understand the vital questions that must be answered if you are to successfully discover the pastor who "fits" your church.*

Umidi, Joseph L. *Confirming the Pastoral Call: A Guide to Matching Candidates and Congregations.* Grand Rapids: Kregel, 2000.

> *Guides search committees and candidates alike through both sides of the candidate process. Valuable appendixes help with selection of the search committee and offer self-evaluations for congregations and candidates.*

Vonhof, John. *Pastoral Search: The Alban Guide to Managing the Pastoral Search Process.* Hendon, VA: Alban Institute, 1999.

> *Detailed guide of the search process, including forming the search team, keeping the congregation informed, communicating with candidates, developing selection criteria, conducting interviews, managing the call process, and arranging for a smooth transition.*

Watkins, Ralph C. *Leading Your African American Church through Pastoral Transition.* Valley Forge, PA: Judson Press, 2010.

> *Provides insights, practical strategies, and biblical principles to help clergy, their families, and congregations negotiate the change in leadership. Features ministry profiles based on interviews with pastors and churches that have navigated a significant pastoral change of their own.*

Weese, Carolyn, and J. Russell Crabtree. *The Elephant in the Boardroom: Speaking the Unspoken about Pastoral Transitions.* San Francisco: Jossey-Bass, 2004.

> *Nuts-and-bolts guide to developing a succession plan for smoothing pastoral transitions. Filled with strategies and solid advice, this handy resource is based on solid research and the authors' many years of experience working with churches in a wide variety of denominations.*

White, Edward A. *Saying Goodbye: A Time of Growth for Congregations and Pastors.* Hendon, VA: Alban Institute, 1990.

> *Explains how to make pastoral transition a growth experience for all. Weaves accounts from clergy, laity, and educators of seven denominations with White's own insight as a former general presbyter to create a resource for meaningful and healthy partings.*

Marketplace Books

Adams, Thomas H. *The Nonprofit Leadership Transition and Development Guide: Proven Paths for Leaders and Organizations.* San Francisco: Jossey-Bass, 2010.

> *Shows how intentional leadership development and properly managed transitions provide nonprofits with the rare opportunity to change direction, maintain momentum, and strengthen their capacity. Includes illustrative stories, instructive lessons, and best practices.*

Carey, Dennis C. *CEO Succession*. Oxford, UK: Oxford University Press, 2000.

Articulates field-tested strategies and techniques boards need to create a systematic and transparent planning process that promotes a seamless transition of leadership at every level in the organization. Includes four key elements essential to the succession planning process.

Goldsmith, Marshall. *Succession: How to Prepare Yourself, and Your Successor, for the Transition*. Boston: Harvard Business School Press, 2009.

Offers candid advice on succession from the outgoing executive's perspective. From choosing and grooming a successor while sidestepping political minefields, to finally handing over responsibility, this book walks you through each step in the succession process.

Rothwell, William J. *Effective Succession Planning: Ensuring Leadership Continuity and Building Talent from Within*. New York: AMACOM, American Management Association, 2005.

Presents strategies for creating a complete, systematic succession planning program. Updated to reflect the latest trends and best practices in succession management, the book speaks on recruitment and retention as part of succession planning, with updated references and research.

Saporito, Thomas J. *Inside CEO Succession: The Essential Guide to Leadership Transition*. San Francisco: Jossey-Bass, 2012.

Presents strategies to enable boards to understand their role in succession planning and how to source leadership that best fits their organization's culture and requirements. Brings together business acumen and psychological insight to help better prepare for more effective succession.

Wiersema, Margarethe, Jay W. Lorsch, Rakesh Khurana, Michael E. Porter, Nitin Nohria, Dan Ciampa, Kevin P. Coyne, Edward J. Coyne Sr., Ram Charan, and Joseph L. Bower. *Harvard Business Review on CEO Succession*. Boston: Harvard Business School Publishing Corporation, 2009.

Compilation of articles, including: "The CEO's Real Legacy," "Holes at the Top," "Why CEO Firings Backfire," "Changing Leaders: The Board's Role in CEO Succession," "Surprises for New CEOs," "Almost Ready: How Leaders Move Up," "Surviving Your New CEO," "Ending the CEO Succession Crisis," and "Solve the Succession Crisis by Growing Inside-Outside Leaders."

Notes

Preface

1. Personal communication between Warren Bird and Kerwin Santiago.

2. Ruth Moon, "Quitting Time: The Pope Retired. Should Your Pastor?" *Christianity Today*, March 12, 2013, http://www.christianitytoday.com/ct/2013/april/quitting-time.html.

3. "Clergy and Retirement: An Exploratory Study on Housing and Financial Preparedness," question 24, *The Association of Religious Data Archives*, http://www.thearda.com/Archive/Files/Codebooks/RETIRE_CB.asp. See also "Pulpit and Pew National Survey of Pastoral Leaders, 2001," question 212, *The Association of Religious Data Archives*, http://www.thearda.com/Archive/Files/Codebooks/CLERGY01_CB.asp, which says the mean anticipated retirement age for clergy is 63.

4. Ibid., question 11.

5. Mark Driscoll and Brian Orme, "Church Leaders Live 2013," online video interview, http://www.churchleaders.com/churchleaders-live-mark-driscoll.html, accessed January 7, 2014. Quoted comments begin 6:30.

Chapter 1 Why Every Pastor Needs This Book

1. Lillian Kwon, "Pastors Challenged to Be Under-Rowers, Never Retire," *The Christian Post*, May 19, 2010, http://www.christianpost.com/news/pastors-challenged-to-be-under-rowers-never-retire-45224/.

2. Personal communication between Warren Bird and Pat Mazoral, head elder and search team chair. A lengthy video excerpt of their interview is available at

Leadership Network's online conference, "Succession: Essential Learnings on Healthy Leadership Transitions," www.churchleadersuccession.com.

3. Rose French, "New Pastor at Wooddale Church Hopes to Grow the Eden Prairie Megachurch," *Minneapolis Star Tribune*, August 17, 2013, http://www.startribune.com/lifestyle/220008271.html.

4. Personal communication with Warren Bird.

5. Grey Matter Research and Consulting, "Study Shows Why Protestant Clergy Change Jobs—Promotions Are a More Common Cause than God's Call," September 7, 2005, http://www.greymatterresearch.com/index_files/Job_Changes.htm. See also "2006–2007 National Congregations Study led by Duke Sociologist Mark Chaves," *National Congregations Study*, accessed May 7, 2013, http://www.soc.duke.edu/natcong/index.html. Other studies indicate a shorter pastoral tenure, such as this smaller study that reported a four years per pastorate on average: Thom S. Rainer, *Surprising Insights from the Unchurched and Proven Ways to Reach Them* (Grand Rapids: Zondervan, 2008). Of the 101 pastors interviewed, denominational composition included the following: 27% non-denominational, 22% Southern Baptist, 12% Wesleyan, 11% Presbyterian Church of America, 11% Evangelical Free Church, 9% other Baptist, 4% Nazarene, and 4% United Methodist. See also Andy Rowell, "Jim Belcher, Francis Chan, N. T. Wright, and Others Leave the Pastorate to Write and Speak," *Christianity Today*, May 6, 2010, http://www.christianitytoday.com/ct/2010/mayweb-only/28-41.0.html. Also an unpublished study by Clay Price using 2012 data concludes that "the typical senior pastor in a church affiliated with the Baptist General Convention of Texas has served 6.5 years, up from 2.4 years in 1972. The statistic is based on the median and

not the average, because the average is skewed upward by long-tenured pastors and larger churches. The larger the church, the longer the tenure. Median tenure (2012 data) for BGCT pastors in churches with 500 or more in worship attendance (N=247 churches) is 11 years.

6. Grey Matter Research and Consulting, "Study Shows Why Protestant Clergy Change Jobs," 2005.

7. Ibid.

8. Jackson W. Carroll, "First- and Second-Career Clergy: Some Comparisons and Questions," http://pulpitandpew.org/first-and-second-career-clergy-some-comparisons-and-questions, accessed June 20, 2013. The original sample consisted of over eight hundred clergy (the vast majority surveyed were senior or solo clergy/pastors) of Catholic, Mainline Protestant, Conservative Protestant, and historic Black churches. See also the book that came out of that study: Jackson W. Carroll, *God's Potters: Pastoral Leadership and the Shaping of Congregations* (Grand Rapids: Eerdmans, 2006).

9. All quotes based on personal communication with Warren Bird.

10. Robert E. Coleman, *The Master Plan of Evangelism* (Grand Rapids: Revell, 1993).

11. Gary E. Brandenburg, "The First Year: Developing a Preaching Plan to Accelerate the Successful Transition of a Pastor in His First Year of Succession," doctoral thesis, Gordon-Conwell Theological Seminary, 2010.

12. Carolyn Weese and J. Russell Crabtree, *The Elephant in the Boardroom: Speaking the Unspoken about Pastoral Transitions, How to Think about and Create a Strategic Succession Plan for Your Church* (San Francisco: Jossey-Bass, 2004), 14–15.

13. Ibid.

Chapter 2 The "Ten Commandments" of Succession Planning

1. See Warren Bird and Martin Sanders, "What Pastors Should Know *Before* Their Sabbatical," Church Leaders.com, http://www.churchleaders.com/pastors/pastor-articles/152163-martin_sanders_and_warren_bird_what_pastors_wish_they_knew_before_their_sabbatical.html, accessed January 7, 2014.

2. Larry Osborne, *Sticky Teams: Keeping Your Leadership Team and Staff on the Same Page* (Grand Rapids: Zondervan, 2010).

3. Ibid., 88.

4. Ibid., 23–24.

5. Besides *Sticky Teams*, see Larry Osborne, *Sticky Church* (Grand Rapids: Zondervan, 2008) and Larry Osborne, *The Unity Factor: Developing a Healthy Church*

Leadership Team, 4th ed. (Parkersburg, WV: Owl's Nest, 2006).

6. Osborne, *Sticky Teams*, 62.

7. Ibid., 111.

8. Ibid., 110.

9. Ibid.

10. All unattributed quotes are from personal communication with Warren Bird.

Chapter 3 Three Essential Questions

1. This article is a great assessment to help leaders evaluate their capability to navigate transitions: Christine M. Riordan, "Navigating through Leadership Transitions: Making It Past the Twists and Turns," *Ivey Business Journal*, May/June 2008.

2. Personal conversation between Warren Bird, Dennis Gingerich, Linda Gingerich, and Wes Furlong.

3. Frank Thomas, *The Choice: Living Your Passion from the Inside Out* (Chicago: MMGI Books, 2013), 161–62.

4. Portions of this story come from Paris Achen, "Longtime Crossroads Pastor Begins Handing Leadership to Younger Colleague," *The Columbian*, April 16, 2012, http://www.columbian.com/news/2012/apr/16/at-the-crossroads-longtime-pastor-begins-handing-l/.

5. Amy Hanson, *Baby Boomers and Beyond: Tapping the Ministry Talents and Passions of Adults over Fifty* (San Francisco: Jossey-Bass, 2010).

6. Personal communication between Warren Bird and Amy Hanson.

7. Two excellent resources for church salaries are Richard R. Hammar, *Compensation Guide for Church Staff* (Carol Stream, IL: Christianity Today), published every two years; and Leadership Network's various salary reports and customized compensation studies, available at www.leadnet.org/salary. The former covers small churches through 1,000-plus in attendance, and the latter begins at 1,000 and covers all megachurch size ranges.

8. Thom Rainer, "Five Things You Should Know about Pastors' Salaries," *ThomRainer*, December 17, 2012, http://thomrainer.com/2012/12/17/five-things-you-should-know-about-pastors-salaries/.

9. Peter Drucker, foreword to *Stuck in Halftime: Reinvesting Your One and Only Life* by Bob Buford (Grand Rapids: Zondervan, 2001), 9. Emphasis in the original.

Chapter 4 Deciding When It's Time to Leave

1. The usual retirement of Church of England bishops is at age seventy.

2. Robert W. Maggs, Francis E. Maloney, Patricia M. Haines, Edward F. Driscoll, *2010–2011 Board of*

Pensions Demographic Study, Figure 28, "Average Age at Retirement" (Louisville, KY: Board of Pensions of the Presbyterian Church USA, 2011), 35, http://www.pensions.org/AvailableResources/BookletsandPublications/Documents/DemographicStudy_2010-2011.pdf.

3. Linda Bloom and Linda Green, "Clergy Retirement Case Shows Nominee's View," *United Methodist Reporter,* June 9, 2009, http://www.umportal.org/article.asp?id=5443.

4. A fascinating article giving ages of all Roman Catholic popes at election and death or resignation for the last five hundred years can be found at http://en.wikipedia.org/wiki/List_of_ages_of_popes.

5. "2012 CEO Transitions," *Spencer Stuart,* February 2013, http://www.spencerstuart.com/research/articles/1637/?utm_source=Hootsuite&utm_medium=twitter&utm_campaign=2012CEOTransitions.

6. Emily Brandon, "Average Retirement Age Grows," *Money,* August 17, 2011, http://money.usnews.com/money/blogs/planning-to-retire/2011/08/17/average-retirement-age-grows.

7. "2012 CEO Transitions," *Spencer Stuart.*

8. All quotes by Mike LaMonica come from personal communication with Warren Bird. A lengthy video excerpt of their interview is available at Leadership Network's online conference, "Succession: Essential Learnings on Healthy Leadership Transitions," www.churchleadersuccession.com.

9. "Succession Planning. Your Church's Hope for the Future—Bill Hybels," YouTube video, 5:07, posted by wcavideo on September 25, 2012, http://www.youtube.com/watch?v=CukvjJ9N3Gk&list=PLFHN-xjWgPHumNQ4ooOE2-o7hm2N01wwT&index=8.

10. All quotes in this section about Leith Anderson and "parish poker" come from Leith Anderson, "How to Win at Parish Poker," *Leadership Journal,* January 1, 1986, http://www.christianitytoday.com/le/1986/winter/86l1044.html or http://www.ctlibrary.com/le/1986/winter/86l1044.html.

11. Lyle E. Schaller, *The Small Church Is Different* (Nashville: Abingdon, 1982).

Chapter 5 Resigning "Young" to Start Another Ministry Chapter

1. "Francis Chan interviewed by Mark Driscoll and Joshua Harris," YouTube video, 15:27, posted by ihatechurchcom on September 7, 2010, http://www.youtube.com/watch?v=3p-SYMis0-w.

2. Personal communication between Warren Bird and Todd Nighswonger.

3. Francis Chan and Brian Orme, "A Few Words with Francis Chan, *Outreach,* November/December 2012, 66.

4. Brian Orme, "The Simple Things That Make Francis Chan Cry," ChurchLeaders.com, http://www.churchleaders.com/outreach-missions/outreach-missions-articles/169235-brian-orme-making-culture-and-the-thing-that-makes-francis-chan-cry.html?p=1, accessed January 7, 2014.

5. Bob P. Buford, *Halftime: Changing Your Game Plan from Success to Significance* (Grand Rapids: Zondervan, 1998). See also Leadership Network's sister organization, www.halftime.org.

6. Pastors seeking help to find their "encore" might want to review Marc Freedman's material on Encore careers at www.encore.org. See also Anne Tergesen, "For Second Careers, a Leap of Faith," *Wall Street Journal,* May 19, 2013, http://online.wsj.com/news/articles/SB10001424127887323741004578416882961364450#mod=todays_us.

7. See "Number of Jobs Held, Labor Market Activity, and Earnings Growth Among the Youngest Baby Boomers: Results From a Longitudinal Survey," *Bureau of Labor Statistics,* July 2012, http://www.bls.gov/news.release/pdf/nlsoy.pdf; Steve Fenton and Esther Dermott, "Fragmented Careers?: Winners and Losers in Young Adult Labour Markets," *Work Employment Society* (2006), http://www.uk.sagepub.com/fineman/Reading%20On/Chapter%2020b%20-%20Fenton%20and%20Dermott.pdf; and Henry S. Farber, "Is the Company Man an Anachronism? Trends in Long Term Employment in the U.S., 1973–2006," *Princeton University,* June 2007, http://harris.princeton.edu/pubs/pdfs/518.pdf.

8. Grey Matter Research and Consulting, "Study Shows Why Protestant Clergy Change Jobs—Promotions Are a More Common Cause than God's Call."

9. The original wording and source of the Peter Principle is this: "In a hierarchy every employee tends to rise to his level of incompetence." Lawrence J. Peter and Raymond Hull, *The Peter Principle* (New York: Bantam Books, 1969), 7.

10. For example, see "Separation Ethics/Former Pastor Policy—With Boundaries Covenant," *The Presbytery of Los Ranchos,* March 2007, http://oga.pcusa.org/media/uploads/oga/pdf/midcouncil-resources/formerpastorpolicy.pdf.

11. Mark Conner, *Pass the Baton: Successful Leadership Transition,* 2nd ed., (Rowville, Australia: Conner Ministries Inc., 2010).

12. Ibid., 31.

13. Ibid., 18.

14. Emmitt Cornelius Jr., "Anatomy of a Church Split," *Leadership Journal,* December 10, 2012, http://www.christianitytoday.com/le/2012/december

-online-only/anatomy-of-church-split.html?utm
_source=leadership-html&utm_medium=Newsletter
&utm_term=96958&utm_content=146307721&utm
_campaign=2012.

Chapter 6 Four Church Cultures, Four Succession Styles

1. Jim Henry, "Pastoral Reflections on Baptist Polity in the Local Church," *Journal for Baptist Theology and Ministry* 3:1 (Spring 2005), 107. Available online at http://baptistcenter.com/06%20HenryRevised.pdf.
2. Ibid.
3. Ibid, 108.
4. "Dr. David Uth: Senior Pastor," *First Baptist Orlando*, http://www.firstorlando.com/About/Meet_Our_Leadership/Pastors_and_Ministry_Leaders_Bios/itemid/33/Dr_David_Uth_Senior_Pastor.aspx, accessed January 7, 2014.
5. Personal correspondence between Warren Bird and Sharon Daugherty.
6. Personal correspondence between Warren Bird and Andre Butler.
7. Personal correspondence between Warren Bird and Ben Dailey.
8. Samuel R. Chand, *Cracking Your Church's Culture Code: Seven Keys to Unleashing Vision and Inspiration.* (San Francisco: John Wiley & Sons, 2010).
9. Weese and Crabtree, *Elephant in the Boardroom*, 57–126.

Chapter 7 Founder's Syndrome

1. Arthur T. Vanderbilt II, *Fortune's Children: The Fall of the House of Vanderbilt* (New York: William Morrow, 2012), ix.
2. Ibid.
3. Personal communication between Warren Bird and Dale Burke.
4. Lyle E. Schaller, *Assimilating New Members* (Nashville: Abingdon, 1978), 127.
5. Lyle E. Schaller, *Survival Tactics in the Parish* (Nashville: Abingdon, 1977), 25, 27.
6. For additional biblical foundation, see Douglas L. Watson, "Planning for a Minister's Retirement," Orthodox Presbyterian Church, September 2012, http://www.opc.org/nh.html?article_id=763.
7. All quotes from here to the end of the chapter are from personal conversation between Warren Bird and Phil Cooke. See also "Church Succession—Phil Cooke," YouTube video, 5:01, posted by Todd Rhoades on March 22, 2013, http://www.youtube.com/watch?v=-QcR6JuXjdQ&feature=youtu.be.

8. For a biblically rich discussion of successors who lack the founder's fire, see Dallas Willard's "Living the Vision of God," accessed January 27, 2014, http://www.dwillard.org/articles/artview.asp?artID=96.

Chapter 8 Wisdom from Unlikely Sources

1. Warren Bird, "Biggest Megachurch Sanctuaries," *Leadership Network*, May 15, 2012, http://leadnet.org/blog/post/biggest_megachurch_sanctuaries.
2. "Joel Osteen: The Man Behind the Ministry," *ABC News Nightline*, June 16, 2006, www.abcnews.go.com/Nightline/story?id=2086670.
3. See this fascinating 2013 interview with TV producer Phil Cooke, "Joel Osteen: Gospel Communicator," *Ministry Today*, http://ministrytodaymag.com/index.php/features/20065-gospel-communicator#sthash.Dqp93ikf.dpuf.
4. Joel Osteen with Rachel Richardson, "How to Own the Room," *Esquire*, May 2013, http://www.esquire.com/features/own-the-room-0513.
5. NPR Staff, "Pastor Joel Osteen: An Everyday Message, Magnified," National Public Radio, April 28, 2012, http://www.npr.org/2012/04/28/151573487/pastor-joel-osteen-an-everyday-message-magnified.
6. Unless otherwise noted, all quotes are from personal conversation between Warren Bird and Charles Jenkins.
7. Charles Jenkins, *Thriving in Change: Ten Principles to Help Leaders Navigate the Opportunities They Face* (Friendswood, TX: Baxter Press, 2010), 19.
8. Ibid.
9. Ibid., 20.
10. Ibid., 21.
11. Ibid., 69.
12. Ibid.
13. See the update on the church by Warren Bird, "Building a Church for the Community," *Leadership Network Advance*, January 15, 2013, http://leadnet.org/resources/advance/building_a_church_for_the_community.
14. Story adapted from Jim Tomberlin and Warren Bird, *Better Together: Making Church Mergers Work* (San Francisco: Jossey-Bass, 2012), 187–88; also Greg Garrison, "Dwindling Pelham Congregation Rebounds After Merger with Megachurch," *The Birmingham News*, September 3, 2011, http://blog.al.com/living-news/2011/09/dwindling_pelham_congregation.html.

Chapter 9 What Happened at the Crystal Cathedral and First Baptist Dallas

1. Schuller, *A Place of Beauty*, 48.
2. Many of the details of the Schuller family story are found in the delightful coffee table book by Robert

H. Schuller, compiled by James Coleman, *A Place of Beauty, A Joy Forever* (Garden Grove, CA: Crystal Cathedral Ministries, 2005).

3. Robert H. Schuller, *Your Church Has Real Possibilities!* (Ventura, CA: Regal, 1974), 112–15, 119, 144–45, 160, quoted in Anne Loveland and Otis Wheeler, *From Meetinghouse to Megachurch* (Columbia, MO: University of Missouri Press, 2003), 119.

4. Kevin Miller and Dave Goetz, "How Schuller Shaped Your Ministry: A Conversation with Robert H. Schuller," *Leadership Journal* (Spring 1997), http://www.christianitytoday.com/le/1997/spring/7l2114.html.

5. Ibid.

6. Personal communication between Warren Bird and Robert A. Schuller. A lengthy video excerpt of their interview is available at Leadership Network's online conference, "Succession: Essential Learnings on Healthy Leadership Transitions," www.church leadersuccession.com.

7. William Lobdell and Dan Weikel, "Schuller Hands His Son Keys to Crystal Cathedral," *Los Angeles Times*, January 2, 2006, http://articles.latimes.com/2006/jan/02/local/me-schuller2.

8. Deepa Bharath, "Family Dynamics at Heart of Schuller Resignation," *Orange County Register*, December 16, 2008, http://www.ocregister.com/articles/schuller-126551-robert-penner.html.

9. Adelle M. Banks, "Son Says Sibling Rivalry Fueled Crystal Cathedral Downfall," *The Washington Post*, March 20, 2012, http://www.washingtonpost.com/national/on-faith/son-says-sibling-rivalry-fueled-crystal-cathedral-downfall/2012/03/20/gIQAD cy2PS_story.html.

10. Ron Keener, "Crystal Cathedral in Turmoil, Offers Properties for Debt Reduction," *Church Executive* (2009): 10. A shortened version of this article is available online: Ron Keener, "Crystal Cathedral: The Son Had It Right, but Siblings and Others Worked Against Him, Says Source," *Christian Newswire*, February 6, 2009, http://www.christiannewswire.com/news/504909401.html. See also Ron Keener, "Jim Poit, Executive Pastor, Crystal Cathedral, Garden Grove, CA," *Church Executive*, August 1, 2008, http://churchexecutive.com/archives/jim-poit-executive-pastor-crystal-cathedral-garden-grove-ca.

11. Keener, "Jim Poit, Executive Pastor, Crystal Cathedral, Garden Grove, CA."

12. Dana Parsons, "Robert Schuller Taps His Daughter to Lead Ministry's Grand Comeback," *Los Angeles Times*, June 23, 2009, http://articles.latimes.com/2009/jun/23/local/me-schuller-comeback23. See also Anna Gorman, "Famed Evangelist Robert H. Schuller Is Not Stepping Down, Daughter Says," *Los Angeles Times*, July 11, 2010, http://latimesblogs.latimes.com/lanow/2010/07/famed-evangelist-robert-h-schuller-is-not-stepping-down-his-daughter-said.html.

13. Deepa Bharath, "Lawsuit: Schullers Gained as Crystal Cathedral Lost," *Orange County Register*, October 3, 2011, http://www.ocregister.com/articles/schuller-320176-church-milner.html.

14. Ken Walker, "Church Drops Mortgage for Expansion," *Christianity Today*, September 27, 2011, http://www.christianitytoday.com/ct/2011/october/church-drops-mortgage-payments.html.

15. Mitchell Landsberg and Nicole Santa Cruz, "Crystal Cathedral's Tale of Two Ministries," *Los Angeles Times*, September 19, 2011, http://articles.latimes.com/2011/jun/19/local/la-me-Crystal-Cathedral-20110619.

16. Luiza Oleszczuk, "Crystal Cathedral Worship Goes on Despite Shake-Ups, Schuller Departure," *The Christian Post*, March 14, 2012, http://m.christianpost.com/news/crystal-cathedral-worship-goes-on-despite-shake-ups-schuller-departure-71397/.

17. Landsberg and Cruz, "Crystal Cathedral's Tale of Two Ministries."

18. Jennifer LeClaire, "Schuller Discusses What Went Wrong at Crystal Cathedral," *Charisma News*, April 2, 2012, http://charismanews.com/us/33122-schuller-discusses-what-went-wrong-at-crystal-cathedral.

19. Nicole Santa Cruz, "Crystal Cathedral's Senior Pastor Says She's Leaving to Start New Church," *Los Angeles Times*, March 12, 2012, http://articles.latimes.com/2012/mar/12/local/la-me-schuller-reax-20120312.

20. Roxana Kopetman, "Rev. Schuller: My Financial Future Is at Risk," *Orange County Register*, March 13, 2012, http://www.ocregister.com/articles/schuller-344482-cathedral-ministry.html.

21. Roxana Kopetman, "Crystal Cathedral: Schullers Lose in Court," *Orange County Register*, November 26, 2012, http://www.ocregister.com/news/creditors-378830-cathedral-claims.html.

22. Marshall Goldsmith, *Succession: Are You Ready?* (Cambridge, MA: Harvard Business Press, 2009), 7.

23. The speaker is Joseph L. Bower, author of "Succession Planning," *Harvard Business Review Online*, November 28, 2006.

24. James W. Powhatan, *George W. Truett: A Biography* (New York: MacMillan, 2011), 291.

25. Ibid., 301.

26. Joel Gregory, *Too Great a Temptation: The Seductive Power of America's Superchurch* (Fort Worth: The Summit Group, 1994), 49.

27. Ibid., 4–6.

28. Personal communication between Warren Bird and O. S. Hawkins.

Chapter 10 The Term Limit Factor

1. Val Toms, *First Presbyterian Church of Hollywood 1903–1978: A Seventy-Five Year Photographic Retrospective* (Hollywood: First Presbyterian Church, 1978), iv.

2. Ibid., 102.

3. Ibid., 101.

4. "Our History," First Presbyterian Church of Hollywood, accessed January 7, 2014, http://www.fpch.org/about-us/our-history.

5. "Our History," Plymouth Church, accessed January 7, 2014, http://www.plymouthchurch.org/our_history.php.

6. Debby Applegate, *The Most Famous Man in America: The Biography of Henry Ward Beecher* (New York: Image Books, 2007).

7. David R. Stokes, *The Shooting Salvationist: J. Frank Norris and the Murder Trial that Captivated America* (Hanover, NH: Steerforth Press, 2011), 48, 155, 160, 169.

8. Homer G. Ritchie, *The Life and Legend of J. Frank Norris: The Fighting Parson* (Fort Worth: Homer Ritchie, 1991).

9. History of the church taken from the church's website, http://www.abt316.com/?page_id=70, and also from Dallas F. Billington, *God Is Real: A Testament in the Form of an Autobiography* (Philadelphia: David McKay Company, 1965).

10. Personal communication between Warren Bird and Ed Holland.

11. Ichak Adizes, *Managing Corporate Lifecycles* (Santa Barbara, CA: Adizes Institute Publishing, 2004), 10.

12. George W. Bullard Jr., *Pursuing the Full Kingdom Potential of Your Congregation* (Lake Hickory, NC: Lake Hickory Resources, 2005), 79. See also Robert D. Dale, *To Dream Again* (Nashville: Broadman, 1981); Martin Saarinen, *The Life Cycle of a Congregation* (Herndon, VA: Alban Institute, 1986).

13. Bullard, *Pursuing the Full Kingdom Potential*, 79.

14. Jim Tomberlin and Warren Bird, *Better Together: Making Church Mergers Work* (San Francisco: Jossey-Bass, 2012).

15. "History of the Moody Church," The Moody Church, accessed January 7, 2014, http://www.moodychurch.org/get-to-know-us/history-moody-church/.

16. "Moody Church," *Wikipedia*, accessed January 7, 2014, http://en.wikipedia.org/wiki/Moody_Church.

17. Edmund Chan, *A Certain Kind: Intentional Disciplemaking That Re-Defines Success in Ministry* (Singapore: Covenant Evangelical Free Church, 2013).

18. This quote and all subsequent quotes from Edmund Chan are from personal communication with Warren Bird.

Chapter 11 Messy and Unexpected Endings

1. See the fascinating narrative of the pastoral transition in the chapter by Jack Schaap in *The Old Church Downtown: An Incomplete History of the First Baptist Church of Hammond, Indiana*, by Keith McKinney and Gail McKinney Merhalski (Hammond, IN: Hyles Publications, 2002), 359–60.

2. This account is taken from a compilation of public resources, including: Teresa Auch Schultz, "Preacher: Sex with 17-Year-Old Was Lord's Work," *Chicago Post-Tribune*, March 13, 2013, http://posttrib.suntimes.com/18835553-537/preacher-sex-with-17-year-old-was-lords-work.html; Chelsea Schneider Kirk, "Layoffs Hit First Baptist Church of Hammond," *NWI Times*, October 9, 2012, http://www.nwitimes.com/news/local/lake/hammond/layoffs-hit-first-baptist-church-of-hammond/article_96da89d3-6c86-57db-8d70-d0fbcf5e6d80.html; Staff Report, "Former Indiana Pastor Charged, Signs Federal Plea Deal in Relationship with Teen," *Chicago Tribune*, September 18, 2012, http://articles.chicagotribune.com/2012-09-18/news/chi-former-indiana-pastor-jack-schaap-indicted-signs-federal-plea-deal-in-relationship-with-teen-20120918_1_schaap-plea-agreement-indiana-pastor; and No author, "Hammond Pastor Dismissed for 'Improper Relationship with Young Woman,'" *CBS2 Chicago*, July 31, 2012, http://chicago.cbslocal.com/2012/07/31/hammond-pastor-dismissed-for-improper-relationship-with-young-woman/.

3. This account is based on personal communication between Warren Bird and New Destiny Christian Center's Marguerite Esannason and Doug Shackelford. See also Jeff Kunerth, "Zachery Tims Died of Heroin, Cocaine," *Orlando Sentinel*, December 19, 2013, http://www.orlandosentinel.com/news/local/breakingnews/os-zachary-tims-cause-of-death-20131219,0,4808202.story; "New Destiny Christian Center Announces the Rev. Paula White as New Senior Pastor and Successor," *Christian Newswire*, December 29, 2011, http://www.christiannewswire.com/news/6828718544.html.

4. This account is taken from a compilation of public resources, including: No author, "Jericho City of Praise Court Battle: Ruling Requires Defendants to Comply with Dispositions," *WUSA9*, December 13, 2013,

http://archive.wusa9.com/rss/article/285945/158/ Bishop-and-pastor-statement-on-City-of-Praise-rul ing; Michele Boorstein and Hamil Harris, "Ousted Megachurch Pastor Proclaims the Launch of a New Church and Ministries," *Washington Post*, August 3, 2012, http://www.washingtonpost.com/local/ ousted-megachurch-pastor-proclaims-the-launch-of-a -new-church-and-ministries/2012/08/03/329610e2 -dda6-11e1-af1d-753c613ff6d8_story.html; and Hamil R. Harris, "Jericho City of Praise Leaders File Dueling Lawsuits over Control of Md. Megachurch," *Washington Post*, July 9, 2011, http://www.washing tonpost.com/local/jericho-city-of-praise-leaders-file -dueling-lawsuits-over-control-of-md-megachurch /2011/07/07/gIQAQtt65H_story.html.

5. Personal correspondence between Warren Bird and Scott Thumma.

6. This account is taken from a compilation of public resources, including: Mark Galli, "Rob Bell's Bridge too Far," *Christianity Today*, March 14, 2011, http:// www.christianitytoday.com/ct/2011/april/lovewins. html; Lillian Kwon, "Teaching Pastor to Leave Mars Hill Bible Church," *Christian Post*, June 6, 2012, http:// global.christianpost.com/news/teaching-pastor-to -leave-mars-hill-bible-church-76202/; Sarah Pulliam Bailey, "Update: Rob Bell to Move to L.A. and Launch a Tour," *Christianity Today*, September 22, 2011, http:// www.christianitytoday.com/ct/2011/septemberweb -only/rob-bell-leaves-mars-hill.html?paging=off; and Heidi Fenton, "Months After Rob Bell Left, Mars Hill Bible Church Names Another Well-Known Religious Leader as Lead Pastor," *MLive*, August 22, 2012, http:// www.mlive.com/news/grand-rapids/index.ssf/2012 /08/months_after_rob_bell_leaves_g.html.

7. Charley Honey, "Rob Bell Talks about Why He Really Left Mars Hill," *The Grand Rapids Press*, March 8, 2013, http://www.mlive.com/living/grand-rapids /index.ssf/2013/03/rob_bell_talks_about_why_he _re.html.

8. This account is taken from a compilation of public resources, including: Anita Bates, "Tammy Faye Bakker, 65, Emotive Evangelist, Dies," *New York Times*, July 22, 2007, http://www.nytimes.com/2007/07/22/ us/22bakker.html?_r=0; No author, "Where Are They Now? Jim Bakker," *Charlotte Magazine*, August 2010, http://www.charlottemagazine.com/Charlotte -Magazine/August-2010/Where-are-They-Now/Jim -Bakker/; "Jim Bakker," Wikipedia entry, accessed January 26, 2014, http://en.wikipedia.org/wiki/Jim _Bakker; and "About Us," *Jim Bakker Show*, accessed January 26, 2014, https://jimbakkershow.com/about-us /about-jim/.

9. Quotes from personal communication between Warren Bird and Gary Lamb.

10. Quotes from personal communication between Warren Bird and Jason Gerdes.

11. Personal communication between Warren Bird and Brian Bloye.

12. Story adapted from personal communication between Warren Bird and Scott Hodge, and also from Scott Hodge, "The Orchard's Story," accessed January 7, 2014, http://www.theorchardcommunity.com/ whoweare/ourstory/.

Chapter 12 Unintentional Interim

1. "Frequently Asked Questions," *Max Lucado*, accessed May 15, 2013, http://maxlucado.com/about/ faq/; "Book List," *Max Lucado*, accessed May 15, 2013, http://maxlucado.com/about/book-list/.

2. "Best Preacher," *Reader's Digest*, May 2005, http://www.rd.com/advice/best-preacher/.

3. Lyle E. Schaller, *The Senior Minister* (Nashville: Abingdon, 1988), 39, quoted in Warren Bird, ed., *Wisdom from Lyle E. Schaller: The Elder Statesman of Church Leadership* (Nashville: Abingdon, 2012), 45.

4. Bob Russell and Bryan Bucher, *Transition Plan: Seven Secrets Every Leader Needs to Know* (Louisville: Ministers Label, 2010).

5. See for example, Dave Stone, Bob Russell, and Kyle Idleman, "When God Transitions a Church," A Changing Church: 2009 Leadership Conference, Session 4, October 24, 2009, Southeast Christian Church.

6. Bob Russell, "Top Ten Signs It's Time for You to Leave Your Church," *Church Leaders*, accessed January 28, 2014, http://www.churchleaders.com/pastors/ pastor-articles/170997-bob-russell-10-signs-time -for-you-to-leave-your-church.html?utm_source =newsletter&utm_medium=email&utm_campaign =clnewsletter&utm_content=CL+Daily+20131110. See also Bob Russell, "Pastoral and Church Transitions," *Ministry Grid*, accessed January 28, 2014, http:// www.ministrygrid.com/web/guest/training-viewer /-/training/pastoral-church-transitions.

7. Story adapted mostly from personal communication between Warren Bird and J. Don George and Ben Dailey.

8. Ben Dailey, *Collide: When Your Desires Meet God's Heart* (Springfield, MO: Influence Resources, 2012).

9. Personal communication between Warren Bird and Anthony Michael Chandler.

10. Anthony Chandler, *Blessed with a Burden* (First Edition Design Publishing, 2012), Kindle edition (Kindle locations 927–33).

11. Alan Gripe, *The Interim Pastor's Manual*, rev. ed. (Louisville: Geneva Press, 1997), 1. This is an excellent resource for intentional interim pastors.

12. "What Is Intentional Interim Ministry?," Baptist General Convention of Texas, accessed June 20, 2013, http://texasbaptists.org/education-discipleship/pastorless-churches/what-is-intentional-interim-ministry/.

13. Adapted from Scott K. Delashaw, *How to Search for a Pastor in Today's Church* (Maitland, FL: Xulon Press, 2010), 31–32.

14. PDI Ninth House, "Getting Succession Right: Six Essential Elements of Effective Succession Plans," http://www.pdinh.com/sites/default/files/Getting SuccessionRight_WP_Oct2011.pdf, accessed January 7, 2014. See also David Clutterbuck, *The Talent Wave: Why Succession Planning Fails and What to Do about It* (Philadelphia, Kogan Page, 2012), 8.

15. John Buekema, "Ask the Expert Discussion: John Buekema," *Building Church Leaders*, May 20, 2008, http://www.buildingchurchleaders.com/help/asktheexperts/johnbeukema/q1.html.

16. Lyle E. Schaller, *Growing Plans: Strategies to Increase Your Church's Membership* (Nashville: Abingdon, 1983), 24, quoted in Bird, *Wisdom from Lyle E. Schaller*, 42.

17. Ibid., 42–43.

18. For examples of both problems and remedies see G. Lloyd Rediger, *Clergy Killers: Guidance for Pastors and Congregations under Attack* (Philadelphia: Westminster John Knox, 1997).

19. Personal communication between Warren Bird and Randy Frazee.

20. Abe Levy, "Leader of the Future Already in Position at Oak Hills Church," *My San Antonio*, September 8, 2012, http://www.mysanantonio.com/news/local_news/article/2-sets-of-hands-on-reins-385 0612.php#photo-3426579.

Chapter 13 Forced Farewell

1. Marcus M. Tanner, Anisa N. Zvonkovic, and Charlie Adams, "Forced Termination of American Clergy: Its Effects and Connection to Negative Well-Being," *Review of Religious Research*, vol. 54 (March 2012): 1–17.

Chapter 14 Where to Find a Successor

1. Story based on personal communication between William Vanderbloemen and Tom Pace.

2. The quotes from Jim Tomberlin as well as the Jay Passavant story are from Jim's blog "Pastor Succession, Multisite & Mergers," *MultiSite Solutions*, August 1, 2013, http://multisitesolutions.com/blog/pastor-succession-multisite-mergers.

3. "Planning for Transition: An Interview with Robert J. Stevens, Chairman and Chief Executive Officer, the Lockheed Martin Corporation," *Korn/Ferry Briefings* (Winter 2013): 16–24, http://www.kornferry institute.com/briefings-magazine/winter-2013/planning-transition.

4. Personal conversation between Warren Bird and Laurie Beshore.

5. Jim Tomberlin and Warren Bird, *Better Together: Making Healthy Church Mergers Work* (San Francisco: Jossey-Bass, 2012).

6. Todd Rhoades, "Bill Hybels on Church Planting," January 22, 2013, http://toddrhoades.com/bill-hybels-on-church-planting/.

Chapter 15 The Money Question

1. See the calculator that adds up all the costs of a bad hire at www.epsenfuller.com/bad-hire-calculator.xlsx.

2. Personal correspondence between William Vanderbloemen and Rich Kannwischer.

3. Donald Scott, *From Office to Profession: A Social History of the New England Ministry, 1750–1850*, cited in Jackson Carroll, ed., *Small Churches Are Beautiful* (New York: Harper & Row, 1977), 7.

4. Two excellent resources for church salaries are Richard R. Hammar, *Compensation Guide for Church Staff* (Carol Stream, IL: Christianity Today), published every two years; and Leadership Network's various salary reports and customized compensation studies, available at www.leadnet.org/salary. The former covers small churches through 1,000-plus in attendance, and the latter begins at 1,000 and covers all megachurch size ranges.

5. Church Law Group, www.churchlawgroup.com, is sponsored by Anthony & Middlebrook, P.C., 4501 Merlot Ave., Grapevine, Texas 76051, (972) 444–8777. See also D. Albert Brannen, "10 Tips for Reducing the Risk of Employment-Related Litigation," *MultiBriefs*, http://www.multibriefs.com/briefs/exclusive/10_tips_for_reducing_employment_litigation.html#.UgUc_tId5Kg, accessed January 7, 2014.

6. Weese and Crabtree, *Elephant in the Boardroom*, 31.

7. Personal communication between Warren Bird and DJ Vick.

8. www.generis.com.

Chapter 16 Preparing for the Next Pastor

1. PDI Ninth House, "Getting Succession Right: Six Essential Elements of Effective Succession Plans."

2. Ibid.

3. "Planning for Transition," *Briefings*.

4. "ECFA Governance Survey 2012," http://www.ecfa.org/Content/GovernanceSurvey, 43, accessed January 7, 2014.

5. Personal communication between Warren Bird and Tom Pfotenhauer.

6. Eric Swanson, "A Day with Jim Collins," *Learnings*, July 24, 2013, http://leadnet.org/blog/post/a_day_with_jim_collins.

7. Jim Collins and Jerry I. Porras, *Built to Last: Successful Habits of Visionary Companies* (New York: Harper Collins, 1997); Jim Collins, *Good to Great: Why Some Companies Make the Leap . . . and Others Don't* (New York: Harper Collins, 2001); Jim Collins, *How the Mighty Fall: And Why Some Companies Never Give In* (New York: Harper Collins, 2009).

8. William Bridges, *Managing Transitions: Making the Most of Change*, 3rd ed. (Philadelphia: Perseus Books, 2009), 3.

9. Ibid.

10. Elisabeth Kübler-Ross, *On Death and Dying: What the Dying Have to Teach Doctors, Nurses, Clergy and Their Own Families* (repr., New York: Routledge, 2009).

11. Elisabeth Kübler-Ross and David Kessler, *On Grief and Grieving: Finding the Meaning of Grief through the Five Stages of Loss* (New York: Simon & Schuster, 2005), 24–25.

12. John W. James and Russell Friedman, *The Grief Recovery Handbook: The Action Program for Moving Beyond Death, Divorce, and Other Losses*, 20th anniversary exp. ed. (New York: Harper Collins, 2009), 11–12.

13. Nancy R. Hooyman and Betty J. Kramer, *Living Through Loss: Interventions Across the Life Span* (New York: Columbia University Press, 2006), 40.

14. Ralph C. Watkins, *Leading Your African American Church through Pastoral Transition* (Valley Forge, PA: Judson Press, 2010), 1.

15. Pete Scazzero and Warren Bird, *The Emotionally Healthy Church: A Strategy for Discipleship That Actually Changes Lives*, rev. ed. (Grand Rapids: Zondervan, 2009).

16. All material thus far in this church profile comes from Laura Poe, ed., *Peachtree Presbyterian Church 100 Years Centennial History* (Atlanta: Peachtree Presbyterian Church, 2010), 23, 40, 44, 48, 51–53, 64, 86, 104, 113, 148–50, 154, 170, 191, 219, 230, 232, 239.

17. John Dart, "Wanted—Megapastors: Can Successors Find Success?" *Christian Century*, 119:8 (April 2002), 22.

18. All quotes from Vic Pentz to this point are from personal communication with Warren Bird.

19. Jason Kovacs, "Atlanta Pastor: 'We Will Care for Any Newborn,'" *The ABBA Fund Blog*, August 17, 2009, http://abbafund.wordpress.com/2009/08/17/atlanta-pastor-we-will-care-for-any-newborn/.

20. Adelle M. Banks, "For Aging Religious Leaders, Is It 'Til Death Do Us Part'?" *Church Executive*, February 25, 2013, http://churchexecutive.com/archives/for-aging-religious-leaders-is-it-still-%E2%80%98till-death-us-do-part%E2%80%99.

Chapter 17 Thinking Long Term

1. John C. Maxwell, *The 21 Irrefutable Laws of Leadership: Follow Them and People Will Follow You*, 10th anniversary ed. (Nashville: Thomas Nelson, 2007), 257.

2. Geoff Surratt, *Measuring the Orchard: Changing the Scorecard on Church Growth* (Exponential Resources, 2012), 11–13.

3. Personal communication between Warren Bird and Lee Powell.

4. Entire story based on personal communication between Warren Bird and Matthew Thompson.

5. John Meyer, untitled talk at Leadership Network's video conference, "Succession: Essential Learnings on Healthy Church Leadership Transitions," http://churchleadersuccession.com/. See also "Piper and Meyer Talk Succession for the First Time," *Gospel Coalition Voices*, May 29, 2012, http://thegospelcoalition.org/blogs/tgc/2012/05/29/piper-and-meyer-talk-succession-for-the-first-time/.

Appendix 4 Research for This Book

1. Leadership Network's video conference, "Succession: Essential Learnings on Healthy Church Leadership Transitions," is archived for public access at http://churchleadersuccession.com/.

Index